Dabbling in Diplomacy

Authorised & Otherwise

RECOLLECTIONS OF A NON-CAREER DIPLOMAT

S.D. MUNI

UNN NEWS · KONARK

Konark Publishers Pvt. Ltd
206, First Floor,
Peacock Lane, Shahpur Jat,
New Delhi - 110 049
+91-11-4105 5065
india@konarkpublishers.com, us@konarkpublishers.com
www.konarkpublishers.com

TheUNN Corporation
One Boca Place, 2255 Glades Road,
Suite 324A, Boca Raton, FL 33431, USA
editor@theunn.com
+1 (203) 583-6750
https://theunn.com/

ISBN: 979-83-277058-1-4

Edited by Ranjana Narayan
Jacket design by Syed Dilshad Ali
Cover Image © S.D. Muni
Typeset by Saanvi Graphics, Noida

ADVANCE PRAISE FOR DABBLING IN DIPLOMACY

In the widest sense, a diplomat is described as a tactful person. Time and experience have added to the term a professional calling, of a person assigned to undertake specific or general tasks for a principal be it a government or an organisation. In this sense, the calling has persisted throughout human history whenever the need arose to communicate and reconcile different viewpoints on matters considered significant enough to seek a solution short of a resort to force.

Hence the need for emissaries who are loyal, knowledgeable, observant, faithful and precise in communications. Accounts of their encounters therefore tell much about the times. Professor S. D. Muni has given us a volume that adheres to these requirements.

Interstate relations are at all times a tally of assets and liabilities. It is of greater relevance with neighbours with whom every act of commission and omission assumes significance across the boundary line. Hence the relevance of these accounts. For the same reason, every action or utterance of the emissary is also, as a medieval manual on statecraft put it, 'a guide to the conduct, wisdom, judgment and greatness' of his master.

Ambassador Muni represented India in Laos and acquired academic knowledge in other capacities about South Asia and Southeast Asia. He was selected for these assignments by Prime Ministers whose style of thought and action was somewhat at variance with the Indian mainstream. For this reason, his perceptions are invaluable.

This collection of his writings will be read with interest by both academics and regional experts.

Mohammad Hamid Ansari
Former Vice President of India

S.D. Muni has written a unique diplomatic memoir which combines the human aspects of diplomacy with the knowledge and analysis of a scholar. This insider's account of our relationships with Nepal, the author's forte, Sri Lanka, Laos, and other Southeast Asian countries is a description of developments at crucial moments of political transition in the countries and the region as a whole. His multiple vantage points and experiences make this a valuable book not just for the scholar but also for those interested in the working of diplomacy, and Indian diplomacy in particular, and in the evolution of our neighbourhood.

Shivshankar Menon
Former National Security Adviser of India

The present book encapsulates the political dynamics, foreign and security policies of the three major countries of South Asia—India, Nepal and Sri Lanka—and subsequently extends the academic domain to Laos and Cambodia. Professor Muni's tenure as ambassador to Laos and as Special Envoy to both Laos and Cambodia, has added a diplomatic dimension to his academic enterprise.

The author's personal rapport with the leaders of India, Nepal and Sri Lanka and his knack of handling diplomacy and academic pursuits has made him the most discussed scholar of the region. Making a debut in Nepal's foreign policy in the early 1970s and extending his scope of studies to other countries, this book would be immensely useful in the field of political studies.

Lok Raj Baral
Professor & Former Ambassador of Nepal to India

Dedicated To

My Grandparents: Late Su-Kavi Roop Ram Kalla & Smt. Brij Kaur

My Parents: Late Sh. Radhey Shyam Purohit & Smt. Kishan Kaur

and

My Mentors: Late Professor S.P. Varma of Rajasthan University, Jaipur;

Late Professor Aloo J. Dastur, University of Bombay, Bombay and

Late Prime Minister Inder Kumar Gujral

Their nurturing, guidance, and support made me what I am today.

Contents

Preface

THE CREDIT FOR writing this book must go to my students, friends and well-wishers. In my casual conversations, I used to narrate anecdotes of my experiences in diplomacy, some of which I indulged in as a part of my academic contacts and queries, and some that came out of my responsibilities as Ambassador to Lao PDR during 1997-99, and also as Special Envoy of the Government of India for Southeast Asian countries (Laos and Cambodia) during 2005-06.

I was a non-career diplomat, and my appointment covered two different regimes, first during the Prime Ministership of Shri I.K. Gujral and the second time during the United Progressive Alliance (UPA) government, led by Dr Manmohan Singh. In-between, I also served under the National Democratic Alliance government headed by Shri Atal Bihari Vajpayee. My friends, students and well-wishers found these anecdotes interesting and suggested that I must pen them down and publish them.

I have been avoiding writing about them for publication for two specific reasons. One was that I never kept regular diaries so any writing will have to be based entirely on my memory which may not recapture all the relevant details, insights and nuances. Secondly, publication of one's experiences always involved others with whom we interacted and one's version of those events may have consequences, both pleasant and otherwise for them. In some cases, it involves violating the confidentiality and informality under which events in our life take place. However, having entered the last leg of my lifespan and in view of the repeated affectionate persuasion by friends and well-wishers, I have decided to pen them down. The narration is as true and honest as I could memorise. In the process, there may be slips of dates, days and details for which I submit my sincere apology in advance.

These recollections deal with my acquaintance and involvement in some of the critical political developments in Nepal and Sri Lanka. They also deal with my official diplomatic assignments in Laos and Cambodia, as well as casual encounters with some Heads of State and/or Governments. I have reflected on insights and understandings gained out of this involvement, which enriched me both personally and professionally. My teaching and research would have been much poorer without them. They taught me that governance and politics are not always what appears on surface. Textbooks and official documents do not always tell us the complete or even the correct story. The human factor which is at the core of every development, with all its prejudices and preferences, egos and attitudes, aspirations and desperations, make them far more complex and fascinating. It is indeed thrilling and challenging to see how events that create history unfold themselves.

This writing would not have been possible without encroaching on my family and social obligations. My wife, Anuradha was kind to read the first draft and point out slips in memory and language.

I am thankful to Shri K.P.R. Nair for readily agreeing to undertake its publication. The competent team of Konark editors, Miss Jiza Joy and Ranjana Narayan, improved and polished the manuscript and facilitated its publication.

I hope my effort will be found of some use by the students of diplomacy and area studies working on the countries covered. The journalists, policymakers and common readers interested in India's regional engagements may also find it worthy of browsing.

S.D. Muni

1

Introduction
School Teacher to Special Envoy

DIPLOMACY AS A career for me was nowhere on our antenna, either mine or of my parents. Born in a poor Brahmin family in Jodhpur, I was the first formally educated person in my family. I was brought up and educated by my maternal grandparents. This was because my father as a railway employee, got postings to small stations where there were no proper school facilities. My mother was educated in Hindi and father knew a smattering of English for reading and writing, relevant for his job in those colonial days. My maternal grandmother was illiterate and my maternal grandfather had no formal education, though he established himself as an efficient manager of estates. He served the princely state of Bundi and was later manager of a big temple in Jodhpur princely state. He had his contacts with members of the extended Jodhpur royal family. He was a poet who informally earned the title of *Su-Kavi* (Good Poet) from his peer group. He would often take me along to recite his poems on various social occasions and gatherings.

After India's independence there were two principal career streams for the middle-class families, namely, medical and engineering education, which could ensure permanent, reasonably well paid and secure government jobs. Medical education being considered more expensive, I was encouraged to study for the engineering stream. For this, I moved through all the stages of education – starting to learn Hindi alphabets and counting arithmetic tables in a *pathshala*, under a tree in a temple compound with a single *guru* for about 40 students. Next stage was to study in primary, middle and higher secondary government schools. During school years, I was also made to learn Sanskrit under private free voluntary coaching by a distant relation of my maternal grandfather.

Financial conditions of my family did not allow me to join an engineering college. Instead, I graduated with Science and Mathematics as optional subjects in government colleges of Jodhpur and Bikaner, affiliated to the University of Rajasthan, Jaipur. We were the inaugural batch of the Three-year Degree Course (TDC), which featured a distinct and more extensive curriculum compared to the regular stream of 10+2+2 graduation in science subjects. Due to it being a new stream with a rigorous course structure, the results of the first batch of TDC graduates were very poor. Many of my colleagues could not clear the exam. I managed to pass with a moderate second division.

I secured admission for a Master's course in Chemistry at the University of Rajasthan, but family finances did not permit me to continue my studies. Even as a school goer, I had to do extra work to supplement the family income. I cannot forget those days when I worked during my summer vacations as a casual labourer, earning Rs.1.5 per day. The job was of digging earth and assisting technicians in laying electrical cables in the under-construction Railway Hospital in Jodhpur.

I become nostalgic whenever I visit Jodhpur and pass by the Railway Hospital building. My maternal grandmother also had to work in addition to fulfilling her role as a dedicated homemaker. She had to sell a part of her matrimonial traditional jewellery (*streedhan*) to supplement the household and my educational expenditure. I distinctly remember the moment she had to sell her earrings to pay for my graduation examination fee of Rs 250. My father, with meagre earnings, had to provide for his mother, his elder brother who was mentally not very alert, my mother and my two younger sisters. At the age of 75, my maternal grandfather faced a setback when he lost his temple job in 1960, prompting the relocation of all the three of us—himself, my maternal grandmother and me—from Jodhpur to Bikaner in search of livelihood. In Bikaner, I supplemented our income by tutoring school students after my college hours. Soon, it became impossible for my grandfather to work because of his advancing age and fragile health. Therefore, I had to look for work as soon as I completed my graduation in Science from Dungar College, Bikaner in 1961-62. I found a job very soon as a science teacher in secondary school for which there was a big demand and extensive recruitment.

My first posting was at a junior secondary school in the small district town of Sri Karanpur, situated in the canal loop area of western Rajasthan. Soon, I was transferred to Sardul Higher Secondary School in Bikaner. There, I had a colleague named Prithipal Singh Kalair. I addressed him by his family name, Pal. Our friendship grew rapidly, and Pal, hailing from Sri Ganganagar, suggested that we relocate to Sri Ganganagar, where opportunities for earning through tuition in Mathematics and Science after regular school hours were promising. He offered his efforts to manage the transfer by bribing lower officials in the Education Department. Both of us contributed Rs 300 each for this purpose, and soon we were both transferred to Sri Ganganagar. He was posted at the Government Boys' Higher Secondary School and I was assigned to the Government Girls' Secondary School. Just as I had been promised by Pal, I got tuitions.

Soon, my family finances got stabilised, though I had to work for extra four hours after my school teaching. My maternal grandmother, who joined me in Sri Ganganagar from Jodhpur, was content with our improved financial situation, as we now had a monthly income of around Rs 300, including Rs 125 from my school salary. I bought a new cycle to facilitate my running around on private tuitions. I had no complaints about my teaching job, where students liked and respected me, and colleagues were supportive and affectionate. However, I found my work not up to my expectations and aspirations. I aspired to pursue further studies and advance in my career, but as the sole breadwinner for my family, I couldn't afford to take a break from my job.

Some of my colleagues suggested that there would be a number of vacancies for Senior Teachers in Civics with the required qualification of a Master's in Political Science, a degree in arts (MA). My service conditions said that I could do my MA as a private candidate, without leaving the job or becoming a regular student, only after putting in two years of teaching service. I proceeded on that line and completed my MA in Political Science, without attending any classroom teaching in the subject and studying whatever books I could access in various school and college libraries of Sri Ganganagar. Frankly, I had no idea of the quality of textbooks for political science, but studied whatever I could lay my hands on, including some of the original texts of established political philosophers and thinkers.

Acquiring a Master's degree in Political Science in 1965 proved to be a turning point in my career. In the final examination, there was an Essay paper with an option for viva voce test. Private candidates usually opted for Essay because viva was to be conducted in Rajasthan University's Department of Political Science. For this, one had to travel to Jaipur and face questions from senior professors and an external examiner. Unlike most of my fellow teacher co-examinees, I opted for viva. The examiners included senior professors of the Department along with the external examiner, Professor Miss Aloo Dastur, Head of the Political Science Department of Bombay University. She was impressed by my reading of original Political Science texts like those by Plato, Hans Morgenthau, Andrew Hacker, etc. I was awarded the highest marks, 76 per cent, in the whole University among viva examinees that included regular students. The viva examiners had not expected a private teacher candidate to have access to and proficiency in original texts. Not only this, Professor Dastur strongly recommended to the Head of the Department of Political Science in Rajasthan University, Professor S.P. Varma, to get me to do research in Political Science.

On completion of my viva, I was asked to get in touch with the Department after the announcement of results. When I did so, I was asked by Professor Varma to join the Department as a research scholar. This was not possible for me. I explained that I could not leave my job to join as a regular research scholar. The Department had launched a new programme of South Asian Studies. It had no provision for scholarship grants yet. To find a way out for me, Professor Varma wrote a long letter to the then Director of School Education in Rajasthan Government, whom he knew personally, to get me transferred to Jaipur. This was to facilitate my joining research in the Department of Political Science, while teaching in a Secondary School in Jaipur. To my pleasant surprise and good luck, this was done. I shifted from Sri Ganganagar to Jaipur in July 1965.

In Jaipur, I started teaching in a Girls Secondary School in Choura Rasta; rented a modest one room accommodation near the university campus and started pursuing research after school hours.

I shall always remain highly indebted to both Professor Dastur and Professor Varma who brought this completely unexpected change in my career path. While teaching at the secondary school in Jaipur, I also got an invitation for interview for the post of Senior Teacher in Civics from the Rajasthan Public Service Commission. Fortunately, I topped the list of those selected and was posted in Poddar Government Higher Secondary School, Jaipur, which was located very close to the University Campus. This selection gave me a higher salary package; a jump from Rs 125 to Rs 375 per month.

I had hardly availed of this higher salary package for a couple of months when another offer of a scholarship of Rs 200 per month became available from the South Asia Study Centre (SASC) of Rajasthan University. On persuasion from Professor Varma and other teachers as well as scholars in the SASC, I decided to leave my teaching job and accept the scholarship offer at lower amount. This caused a great commotion in the family as I was opting for less money and an uncertain future against a permanent government job with, what was then considered as a reasonably handsome, emoluments. I had lost my maternal grandfather a year back in 1964, and my father did not question my decision to accept the scholarship. However, my mother and maternal grandmother expressed their dismay during this transition, questioning the necessity of pursuing studies beyond MA and scolding me for my decision. They had not heard of research degree and were not sure of the job that I may get after my PhD which would easily take at least three to four more years. Eventually, they got reconciled as I tried to explain and calm them down without changing my decision.

University of Rajasthan

Joining the University as a regular research scholar greatly thrilled me. I was re-entering my student life after a gap of three years and the Department of Political Science of Rajasthan University was considered one of the best in India during those days. The SASC was considered one of the pioneering institutions of its type. In the context of the Chinese attack on India in 1962 and the India-Pakistan war of 1965, there was considerable attention on South Asian studies. The US was particularly enthusiastic in encouraging South Asian studies in India, for which funds were being offered by institutions like The Asia Foundation. Subsequently, The Asia Foundation funding got much maligned due to the alleged CIA involvement with it. We in the Department were not much aware of these international dimensions but did see a number of well-known American scholars, like Hans Morgenthau, Lloyd and Susan Rudolf(s), Leo E. Rose, etc. visit our department for lectures and as guest scholars.

On joining the SASC as a research scholar, Professor Varma asked me to draft a couple of proposals for finalising my PhD theme. This was the beginning of my first formal education in Political Science. At that point, I had limited knowledge of the breadth of the discipline, and though my colleagues at SASC were willing to assist, they were unaware of the extent of my ignorance. In retrospect, I think it was almost a fluke that, through my viva examination for MA, I transitioned from being a secondary school teacher in Science and Mathematics to becoming a research scholar in Political Science. Thinking along highly parochial and narrow lines, I decided to focus on Rajasthan politics. Thank God, I soon left them far behind.

My hometown Jodhpur had produced a charismatic Chief Minister of Rajasthan named Jai Narayan Vyas soon after India's independence. He belonged to my community and therefore, after consulting books and other literature on Rajasthan politics available in the university library, I wrote a research proposal on 'Post-Independence Chief Ministers of Rajasthan'. I was instructed to present it to Dr C.P. Bhambhri, a Reader in the Department specialising in public administration and India's domestic politics. He identified seven or eight grammatical and spelling mistakes in my four-page proposal and threw the script at my face, asserting I was incapable of doing research.

With tears in my eyes, and nervousness in my thoughts, I went to Professor Varma and narrated my experience with Dr Bhambhri. I explained that all my formal education has been in Science/Maths and through Hindi medium, though I had written my MA Political Science examination and taken my viva in English. He was very understanding and patient with me and asked me to wait and work on another proposal. He suggested to think of 'India in South Asia', since I was a scholar in SASC. Fortunately, there was a new development in the Department at that time.

A well-known expert of India's Foreign Policy, Professor K.P. Karunakaran joined our Department as a Visiting Professor for six months. He was previously an Associate Professor at the prestigious Indian School of International Studies (ISIS), housed in New Delhi's Sapru House, with the Indian Council of World Affairs (ICWA). Just a couple of months back, he had been rejected for the post of Professor in South Asian Studies programme of the ISIS, against Professor Bimal Prasad, who came from Patna. Professor Prasad was a historian and had written his PhD dissertation on the 'Origins of India's Foreign Policy'. This study was based on the Indian National Congress Party's foreign policy resolutions during the struggle for India's independence. Karunakaran had displeased the establishment in New Delhi by his critical writings on India's foreign policy. His one article criticising Nehru's forward policy in the Himalayas (and this was much before Neville Maxwell's book on 'India's China War' had been published) in the aftermath of Chinese aggression in 1962 was subjected to much disapproval and criticism, including in the Indian Parliament. In inviting Karunakaran to Jaipur, Professor Varma wanted to show his respect for Karunakaran's expertise and help him manage his hurt feelings. I was asked to work under his guidance for developing my PhD theme.

I was fortunate to develop a good working rapport with Professor Karunakaran. I took my draft proposal on 'India in South Asia' to him. He was happy with it, though he underlined few grammar and spelling mistakes, and gave some suggestions. I revised the draft accordingly; it was finally approved and I started working on the subject. I also soon became friendly with Karunakaran's family; his wife Vijayam and twin sons, Gopal and Govind. Vijayam loved painting as her hobby. She, on a cloth canvass, painted a Kerala girl worshiping and watering the Tulsi plant, and presented it to me saying that I must marry a Kerala girl. Gopal and Govind were studying in primary classes. They occasionally sought my help in Mathematics for completing their school homework.

The collection of research material on 'India in South Asia' gradually made me realise that the subject was much too extensive for me to complete PhD on time. I also presented a paper on this subject at the Indian Political Science Association's Annual Conference in 1966, which was headed by Professor Dastur. We continued to remain in touch as she used to mentor me on my research work. She also suggested that the subject taken by me was good but somewhat unwieldy. When I discussed this aspect with Professor Karunakaran, he suggested that I change the subject and pick up 'Foreign Policy of Nepal' as there was no credible research work available on it, except studies on India-Nepal Relations. At SASC, one of my colleagues, R.S. Chauhan was working on 'Domestic Politics of Nepal'. Therefore, on Karunakaran's recommendation and with the approval of Professor Varma, I changed my subject.

Nearly six months of hard work on 'India in South Asia', proved to be of little use for the new PhD theme. It was, however, educating on South Asian affairs, and proved to be helpful in my future studies. This was the time for Professor Karunakaran to complete his term in Jaipur and return to ISIS, New Delhi. While leaving, he promised to see if I could be called to ISIS, as it would be easier to work in Delhi on my new subject. By then, I also discovered that Rajasthan University Library was not well equipped to carry on research work on 'Nepal's Foreign Policy'. Within weeks of Professor Karunakaran's return to Delhi, I received a telegram from the Registrar of ISIS, Mr T.V. Raghavan that I have been offered admission with a research fellowship of Rs 250 per month at ISIS and should join soon. The news of joining ISIS on an enhanced fellowship (Rajasthan University offered Rs 200 per month) was indeed exciting.

When I took the proposal to Professor Varma, he was not very happy. He agreed that the library resources were good in Sapru House and fellowship enhancement will ease my financial condition, but he did not want me to leave Jaipur. The SASC was still coming up gradually and he was keen that more scholars joined it rather than leave it. Professor Varma had been so kind and helpful to me that I had no heart to defy him. He assured me that I will soon be sent to New Delhi to collect research material at ISIS/Sapru House (ICWA) Library, but I will remain affiliated to Rajasthan University and will work under his own supervision, since Professor Karunakaran had gone back.

Sapru House/ICWA Library

Joining ICWA, Sapru House Library was an exceptional experience for me. I had never lived in a hostel. I came armed with a seat in ISIS hostel attached to Sapru House and a letter of introduction from Professor Varma for Dr (Mrs) Urmila Phadnis, an Associate Professor in ISIS with expertise on Sri Lanka and Indian Politics. She was a very gentle, friendly and popular person, and most of her students addressed her as Urmila *ji*. Sapru House Library was an impressive building with a beautiful lawn and a small canteen attached. Mr Girija Kumar, the librarian, was devoted to the upkeep of the library, ensuring it remained clean and quiet.

The library was the best resource centre on India's foreign affairs. It housed full newspaper files, subject-wise clippings, microfilms, the latest and rare books, authentic documents and unpublished PhD dissertations. ISIS was located within Sapru House, where regular discussions on diverse foreign affairs themes were held, which we could freely attend. The library was thronged by research scholars and teachers from other universities, Union Public Service Commission competitors (for IAS/IFS, etc.), journalists, political and social activists and senior bureaucrats from all over India. It could easily be called the intellectual hub of New Delhi, particularly on foreign affairs. Sapru House, which also housed the ICWA, was the venue for addresses by visiting world leaders, cultural programmes (dance, drama and musical concerts) and film shows, which we scholars residing in the adjacent hostel could sneak in and enjoy for free.

ISIS's Sapru House Hostel was also a unique institution. It was the first mixed hostel of young boys and girls, divided in two wings. Although primarily meant for ISIS students, it was open to scholars and academics from other universities, depending on room availability. Non-ISIS residents had to pay more for rooms and mess as they did not pay establishment charges. This taught me to live on a very tight budget, as I also had to send money to my maternal grandmother. An ISIS faculty member worked as a warden, and there was an elected body of residents responsible for managing its day-to-day affairs.

Being in the midst of a locality inhabited by civil servants and businessmen of well-to-do middle class families, it had an easy access to the famous snack joint of Bengali Market. Although the families living around the hostel occasionally seemed uncomfortable with a mixed hostel, there were never any untoward incidents. The hostel residents were young and mature, and the surrounding atmosphere encouraged healthy relationships. The hostel must have played a role in bringing together more than a dozen happy couples who led responsible married lives after leaving the hostel. On the other side of the hostel was the Mandi House area, where institutions like the Federation of Indian Chambers of Commerce and Industry, Triveni Kala Sangam, National School of Drama and others were situated. This constituted the cultural centre of New Delhi. The famous shopping centre of New Delhi, Connaught Place, was also within walking distance from Sapru House hostel.

Studying in the library, attending lectures at ICWA and ISIS, engaging in discussions with colleagues and benefitting from mentors like Urmila *ji* significantly expanded my intellectual horizons. I started understanding the complexities of world affairs, foreign policy and diplomacy. I had access to literature, research journals and media writings covering various aspects of international relations. This deepened my commitment to crafting my PhD dissertation. I would gather research materials at Sapru House and work on drafting my chapters, subsequently travelling to Jaipur to get guidance and instructions from my supervisor, Professor Varma.

After completing the drafts of the first three chapters and exhausting material collection for the remaining chapters at Sapru House Library, I was ready to go to Nepal for fieldwork in 1968. It was during this fieldwork that I had my first brush with unauthorised diplomacy, as we shall discuss in subsequent chapters. The fieldwork also brought me into contact with Nepal's political elite representing various parties and different levels of official decision-making in both India and Nepal. My data collection work in Kathmandu was greatly aided by Dr Mahesh Regmi's extremely useful compilation of Nepali newspapers called 'Nepal Press Digest'. Besides writing my chapters, I also did other research writings.

In 1967, before going to Nepal, I was roped in the Department's research on India's fourth general elections and was sent to Jhunjhunu in Rajasthan to study the election. Two local industrialists, R.R. Morarka and R.K. Birla, were contesting against each other. On the basis of my study, I published an article on 'Politics of the Symbol' in the Journal of our Department. In 1968, I presented a seminar paper at the Department's international conference on South Asian Foreign Policies. Gradually, I also started writing for newspapers and weekly magazines.

After my fieldwork in Nepal and through regular shuttling between Rajasthan University and Sapru House, I managed to complete the writing of my PhD dissertation in 1971. After results from the external examiners, I completed my viva examination and was awarded PhD in February 1972. Professor Leo E. Rose of the University of California, Berkeley, USA, was one of my external examiners. He appreciated my work in his evaluation report. He was a well-known Nepal and South Asia expert who subsequently became editor of *Asian Survey*, a popular journal of Asian Studies.

There were two other important developments that helped broaden my perspective on foreign policy and diplomacy that occurred during the course of PhD work. One was my selection in 1969, for the Constitutional and Parliamentary Studies Fellowship. The fellowship offered an amount of Rs 500 per month which attracted me more than the subject of training. The duration of this fellowship was for six months. The fellowship was for a training programme initiated by a newly-established Institute of Constitutional and Parliamentary Studies, under the leadership of Dr L.M. Singhvi, an eminent jurist, and Dr Subhash Kashyap, who subsequently served as the Secretary General of the Seventh, Eighth and Ninth Lok Sabha (House of Representatives). Dr Singhvi also belonged to Jodhpur but I first met him only after joining as a Parliamentary Fellow.

Under this fellowship, we were lectured by various scholars, active politicians, Members of Parliament, senior journalists, etc. on different aspects of the working of the Constitution and Parliament. Useful insights in the evolution of foreign policy making and its implementation were also explained in the course of these lectures. The group of fellows also got a chance to meet and interact with Prime Minister Indira Gandhi and the then President V.V. Giri. During these lectures and interactions, I raised queries related to India's policy and relations with our immediate neighbours. The answers provided help in sharpening my perspective.

The second significant development in my life was related to an event that left a lasting impact on the way I thought about foreign policy matters. British Prime Minister Edward Heath visited India in January (8-11), 1971. Among the prominent issues that dominated this visit was the question of apartheid in South Africa. Public sentiment in India was against the British approach and there were strong demonstrations against Prime Minister Heath on this issue.

During his visit, Heath was scheduled to deliver a public lecture at ICWA/Sapru House. The students' union of Jawaharlal Nehru University (JNU), where ISIS had become an integral part since its establishment in 1969, decided to protest against Heath. Hostel residents joined the demonstration and I was one of them. Subsequently, the police detained most of the demonstrators and took us to the nearby police station. After spending several hours in detention, we were released when G. Parthasarathi, Vice-Chancellor of the University, and Professor Bimal Prasad, warden of Sapru House hostel, personally intervened. We were served with tea and *samosas* prior to our release. For me, this was an unusual experience. It deepened my dislike for colonialism, imperialism and racialism perpetrated and supported by the West. Moreover, it strengthened my appreciation for and commitment to India's policy of non-alignment which was clearly reflected in my subsequent writings, teaching and research endeavours.

Achieving a PhD degree may be considered as a significant milestone in my career graph. I felt quite satisfied and even surprised upon attaining the title of Doctor of Philosophy in Political Science, despite not participating in traditional classroom teachings, aside from attending about half a dozen lectures by Professor Varma on political theory. In 1972, after obtaining my PhD, my financial situation improved as I was awarded a Senior Fellowship of SASC, providing a monthly stipend of Rs 500. Shortly thereafter, I also secured a position as Research Associate the SASC, holding a grade equivalent to that of a lecturer/assistant professor in the University's regular departments.

In May 1972, I married Anuradha, who was one of my hostel mates at Sapru House. I first met her with Urmila ji in the Sapru House canteen. Anuradha was pursuing her PhD in Sri Lanka's (then called Ceylon) foreign policy under Urmila ji's guidance. She was also the president of the students' association of ISIS, and had a talent for singing. She was teaching at Daulat Ram College of Delhi University. After our marriage, she secured a position as a Research Associate in SASC, Department of Political Science at the University of Rajasthan, Jaipur, in 1972. We lived in a one-bedroom apartment in the Teachers' Hostel of Rajasthan University. While life was comfortable, we weren't satisfied professionally. Eventually, we realised that it was not ideal for both of us to work in the same institution. Anuradha found it more convenient to return to Delhi University. Therefore, after a year at SASC, she moved back to Daulat Ram College, where she had her lien on her previous job. I then started searching for a job in Delhi, much to the displeasure of Professor Varma.

Between September and November of 1973, I took three interviews in three institutions for jobs in Delhi. These were: (i) Himachal University, Shimla (interviews were held in New Delhi), (ii) Institute for Defence Studies and Analyses (IDSA), also housed in Sapru House as ISIS had become a part of JNU and moved to a new building on Ferozeshah Road, just a walkable distance from Sapru House, and lastly, (iii) the JNU, located on New Mehrauli

Road, on the campus originally built for the Administrative Academy for training of selected civil servants. I was selected by all the three institutions, but I opted for JNU. IDSA Director K. Subrahmanyam called me and offered 50 per cent more salary, but I preferred JNU because a university job gave greater freedom. Subrahmanyam was highly respected by all of us for his intellectual prowess and strategic thinking and I promised him to work at IDSA, under his guidance. I did that later during 1983-84, on lien from JNU.

JNU and New Delhi Location

Besides the freedom offered by a university as compared to the one by a government-run institution like IDSA, JNU had other attractions as well for me. It was a new, research-centric, postgraduate elite university established with a political bang on India's academic terrain. I also had a personal sense of achievement in my selection at JNU for two reasons. One was that I had been rejected earlier, in 1969, for the same post in the Division of Diplomatic Studies. That division had been established as a new discipline of studies in JNU under the headship of Professor Shishir Gupta, well known for his expertise on India's Foreign Policy. Earlier, he was associated with ISIS. He was also known for his contribution on India's strategy for Bangladesh, in 1971. Secondly, I got selected for the post over a candidate who was rumoured to have been preferred by the JNU establishment.

I was in Kathmandu on a study visit when my wife Anuradha informed me about the possibility of interviews for this post in the coming days. I had not received any interview call and when I informed her accordingly, she did some leg work in the JNU academic branch of administration and found out that there was an acknowledgement of the receipt of my application form but it was not being traced back and so I was not invited. With her continued efforts for days together, my application was traced and I was invited through a telegram in Kathmandu, just three days before the interview date. I packed up my study visit in Nepal fast and reached Delhi by air to face the interview. The so-called preferred candidate was rumoured to have had the support of the Dean of the School of International Studies (SIS, the changed name of ISIS after merger in JNU) and the Vice-Chancellor, and also perhaps a large number of Sapru House hostel residents. However, the rest of the faculty members of the Diplomatic Studies Division, like Professor Satish Kumar and Professor R.P. Anand, stayed fair and objective in the selection process.

To my good luck and surprise, Professor Dastur was also a member of the selection committee in her capacity as the Visitor's Nominee for the SIS selections. Other outside experts were from the Ministry of External Affairs, where Vice-Chancellor G. Parthasarathi had his old association and clout. I was grilled for more than 45 minutes by the selection committee and was happy to become a 'surprised' selected candidate.

Becoming a part of the JNU faculty in international affairs, and being based in New Delhi, opened up several avenues and opportunities for me personally and professionally. I joined JNU on 1, January, 1974, as Assistant Professor, in the Division of Diplomatic Studies, of the Centre for Studies in International Law, Economics and Diplomacy. By 1978, after one rejection, I shifted, through open selection process, to South Asian Studies, of the Centre for South, Southeast and Central Asian Studies, as Associate Professor.

After completing the required eight years of service as Associate Professor, I was promoted as Professor in South Asian Studies in 1987, under the scheme of personal promotion. In 1993, through open selection process, I was also selected for the prestigious 'Appadorai Chair' in International Politics and Area Studies, attached to the Centre for International Politics, Organisation and

Disarmament (CIPOD) studies. Engaging in reading, writing, teaching and research, with easy access to various libraries in Delhi, as well as active participation in national and international conferences, seminars and discussions, helped me build on my skills and capabilities in the chosen academic fields. My faculty status at JNU also facilitated my access to the national media, the corridors of power in Delhi, exclusive clubs like the India International Centre (IIC), and numerous foreign visits, mostly for academic purposes. I also participated in many official and unofficial conferences of Track 1.5 (having both official and unofficial participants) and Track 2.0 (having only non-official participants).

I had started writing for newspapers even while working at Jaipur. Soon after joining JNU, I met a number of media stalwarts, like the editors of national dailies and weeklies; Girilal Jain, Nikhil Chakravarty, Dilip Mukherjee, Pran Chopra, B.G. Verghese, Inder Malhotra, H.K. Dua, S.Nihal Singh, K.K. Katyal, etc. With help and encouragement from them, I started writing edit page and magazine (weeklies) articles frequently. This helped me develop an academic identity beyond JNU. I was invited by the Ministry of External Affairs and the Joint Intelligence Committee (which later became the National Security Council (NSC) Secretariat) to do research reports for them on specific subjects of their interests. In all, I did two reports each for the MEA and the NSC Secretariat throughout my academic career. With these contacts, I also started getting invited for official consultations on specific subjects and formal lunches and dinners for visiting dignitaries by the Ministry of External Affairs. This was a great learning process through a tiny but close window on the actual functioning of India's foreign policy and diplomacy.

JNU's School of International Studies (SIS) used to host Indian Foreign Service probationers for six weeks every year as a part of their training process. The probationers' groups were lectured on different themes of international relations, foreign policy and diplomacy. They were also asked to write papers on chosen subjects under the guidance of faculty members. This practice continued until the establishment of a separate Foreign Service Institute (FSI) by the MEA in 1986. Some of the faculty members of SIS, including me, however, continued to be invited by the FSI periodically for regular lectures to the probationers and foreign diplomats under training programmes. Thus, we had direct personal contacts with the generations of future diplomats. JNU/SIS also had a practice of recruiting serving and retired senior diplomates for shorter durations as Visiting Professors. I.J. Bahadur Singh, T.N. Kaul, M.K. Rasgotra, A.K. Damodaran, Hamid Ansari, and many others have been associated with JNU at one time or other. Muchkund Dubey joined us as a Professor in South Asian Studies in 1992, through open selection after he completed his term as Foreign Secretary. He remained on the faculty for seven subsequent years. Students enjoyed his teaching and as a professor, he also published a couple of useful books on South Asian affairs. Informal interactions with all these stalwarts about their experiences and contributions also greatly enriched my understanding of India's foreign policy and diplomacy.

Within a couple of years of my joining JNU, I became a member of India International Centre (IIC), New Delhi's elite club for academics, journalists, civil servants, politicians and social activists. Three of its Directors, K.S. Bajpai, Eric Gonsalves and N.N. Vohra have been very supportive and affectionate to me. They enabled me to participate in many seminars, conferences and discussions organised by the IIC. I was also invited to be part of Track 2.0 delegations of IIC to countries like China and the US. The delegation to China was led by Eric Gonsalves in 1989, soon after the Tiananmen Square uprising. This was also the time when India-China relations had started warming up following then Prime Minister Rajiv Gandhi's visit to China in 1988 and promise by the two countries to normalise their relations pending resolution of the border dispute.

This was my first and unique exposure to China as we were treated with considerable respect and generous hospitality because of Eric's friendship with his host who held an influential position in the Chinese official hierarchy. Obviously, the Chinese side also wanted to use this visit to tell India and the world that things were normal and stable in China after the Tiananmen incident. India had not criticised China for the Tiananmen atrocities. Eric Gonsalves also led a delegation of IIC for a Track 2.0 conference to the US in 1991. That was the time when India was looking forward to a new beginning in its relations with the US after the end of the Cold War.

The IIC membership also brought me in contact with two other very important persons who immensely helped me enrich my understanding of international affairs, including India's foreign policy. They were Shri P.N. Haksar, former Principal Secretary to Prime Minister Mrs Indira Gandhi, and Shri Brajesh Mishra, who later became Principal Secretary and National Security Adviser to Prime Minister Shri Atal Bihari Vajpayee. There was a whispering criticism of Brajesh Mishra holding two very critical positions in the Vajpayee government. After his retirement, Haksar had suffered serious degeneration of his eyesight, but he would come to IIC and share his experiences with close friends and admirers. I was privileged to be part of some of his gossip sessions.

Anecdotes of Haksar's several visits to Pakistan and meetings with Prime Minister Zulfikar Ali Bhutto for implementing the Simla Agreement of 1972, underlined that Pakistan was acutely conscious of its identity vis-à-vis India and that Bhutto was serious about implementing the Simla Agreement. On sensitive matters, Bhutto would talk to Haksar outside his office, on the lawns attached to it, perhaps to avoid being eavesdropped by the suspected intelligence cameras fixed by the army in his office. When Bhutto proudly displayed relics of the Mohenjo-Daro and Indus Valley civilisations in his office, Haksar questioned him, asking to why he was war mongering against India, which also shared the same ancient civilisation. In response, Bhutto promised not to repeat his rhetorical '1,000 years' war with India' slogan. Haksar narrated this incident to Nikhil Chakravarty and others in the 'gossip group' and asked them to write to Benazir Bhutto, who had also started repeating her father's slogan when in power, to desist from such slogans. Haksar used to counter allegations of India's periodic interference in the internal affairs of smaller neighbours by saying that 'India and its neighbours are lodged in each other's intestines'. Accordingly, interference in each other's affairs was an organic part of their existential reality and comes naturally from both the sides.

Brajesh Mishra, after retirement from Foreign Service, had joined the Bharatiya Janata Party (BJP) and become the convener of its foreign policy cell. He, knowing that I was close to I.K. Gujral, used to tease me by criticising the 'Gujral Doctrine' on neighbourhood and questioning Gujral's weakness on the question of India's nuclear status. On the Gujral Doctrine, I told Brajesh that it did not include Pakistan and China and there was no question of 'non-reciprocity in relations', which was the key component of this Doctrine, applying to these two adversarial neighbours. On the nuclear question, I asked Gujral if the criticism had any relevance. He responded, stating, 'Yes, the scientists were ready to work on explosion, but we could not give the political "go ahead" because the CPI-M (Communist Party of India-Marxist), a strong partner in the United Front coalition government, was dead set against India's nuclear advancement. They had taken a clear position that if the government moved in this direction, they would withdraw support.' Defending the 'Gujral Doctrine', he added: 'There are deliberate attempts to criticise the 'Doctrine' by labelling it as a compromise on India's security. This is not true. India's security interests are insulated from the promise of non-reciprocity in bilateral relations. I rejected a draft of the revised 1950 treaty by Nepal because it ignored India's security concerns.'

When Brajesh joined Shri Vajpayee's PMO, I would retaliate and tease him saying that his government and prime minister were implementing the 'Gujral Doctrine' quite seriously, in view of Vajpayee's Lahore bus journey (19 February 1999) and his subsequent invitation to then Pakistan Chief Executive General Pervez Musharraf in 2001 to visit India for the two-day Agra Summit. Brajesh was very accommodative of my access to his office in the PMO on Nepal and Sri Lanka as we shall discuss later. During 2006-08, Brajesh joined the Observer Research Foundation (ORF), as a Member of the Governing Board, when I was serving there as its Research Director. He offered very valuable insights on dealing with China in a conference organised by ORF in Kolkata in 2007 on 'India and China: The Next Decade'.[1]

The IIC has yet another elite club within itself. This is called the Saturday Discussion Group (SDG). It was initiated as an informal arrangement by the Centre for Policy Research in the aftermath of the National Emergency of 1975. Its membership is by co-option by the organisers of the group and the objective is to discuss current and controversial national and international issues over lunch. Members pay for their lunch which is arranged by the IIC at discounted price. The meetings are held in the private dining hall of IIC. The idea is to understand these issues in all their complexities with the help of speakers who have practical experiences and expertise that go beyond available published and available sources.

Discussions are held following the Chatham House Rules, which prohibit the public attribution of any views expressed within the group. I felt privileged to be coopted to become its member, courtesy

---

1. The conference was inaugurated by then Foreign Minister, Pranab Mukherjee. The proceedings of this seminar were edited by Suranjan Das (Vice-Chancellor, University of Calcutta) and me. Please see S.D. Muni and Suranjan Das (Eds), *India and China: The Next Decade* (New Delhi: Rupa & Co., 2009).

the initiative taken by Mohammad Ayoob, who was my colleague in JNU, South Asian Studies. We were earlier co-residents in the Sapru House hostel. The SDG has had members coming from different walks of national life like former ministers, former Governors, eminent politicians, Members of Parliament, celebrity journalists, social activists and academics. Some of the members rose to acquire high national positions, like I.K. Gujral became Prime Minister in 1997 and Ambassador Hamid Ansari Vice-President in 2007.

Networking in the SDG has been greatly helpful to me in my professional career. Two of my SDG contacts deserve special mention in this respect; they were Dr K.B. Lall and Gujral. Dr Lall was an ICS officer (pre-independence civil servant). He played a significant diplomatic role in trade and economic matters. He was also for some time a Visiting Professor in JNU. I wrote a research paper in collaboration with him for a seminar on non-alignment organised by Vice-Chancellor K.R. Narayanan and Professor K.P. Misra of SIS/JNU. He introduced me to Shri Dinesh Singh, who had served as India's Foreign Minister under the governments headed by Mrs Indira Gandhi, Rajiv Gandhi and P.V. Narasimha Rao. Gujral was a close associate of Dinesh Singh. Both of them had worked with Mrs Gandhi as her Ministers. Dinesh Singh and Gujral launched the Indian Council for South Asian Cooperation (ICSAC) in 1985 with the view to promote regional cooperation between India and its South Asian neighbours. I was actively involved in its founding and functioning and was assigned the task of organising its conferences/ seminars. I was also the founding editor of its quarterly journal, called *South Asia Journal*, published by Sage India Publications. I left its editorship in 1992 and the journal, after some hibernation period, was relaunched as *South Asian Survey*. The journal, ICSAC Conferences, as also other activities of ICSAC helped me considerably in building my knowledge on and contacts in South Asia, at both political and academic levels.

Periodically, I was also called upon by Dinesh Singh to draft speeches and 'notes' for him on specific subjects. My work was appreciated by him. Dinesh Singh enquired about my aspirations if given an opportunity to join the government. I had always been fascinated by the concept of 'policy planning' in the MEA; having got to know and work with some of those who worked there like G. Parthasarathi, A.K. Damodaran and Jagat Mehta. When I told him so, Dinesh Singh chuckled and remarked, 'The "policy planning" Division in the MEA doesn't really plan policies and is not being given the importance that its name suggests.' So he suggested I consider alternative options. Unfortunately, before he could explore the possibility of inducting me in the government, he suffered a severe stroke that partially paralysed him and eventually led to his passing. Gujral, during his different tenures as Minister of External Affairs and Prime Minister, included me in delegations led by him to foreign countries and appointed me as a Ambassador.

I was included in three Indian delegations headed by Gujral as Foreign Minister: for Nepal in March 1990, for Sri Lanka in January 1997 and for the Indian Ocean Rim ministerial meeting in Mauritius in March 1997. The Nepal and Sri Lanka visits were for the bilateral Joint Commission meetings. We shall discuss them in detail later. In Mauritius, the first meeting of the Council of Ministers (COM) was held to institutionalise the Indian Ocean Rim-Association for Regional Cooperation (IOR-ARC). The idea of such cooperation had been initiated by India and South Africa in 1995. I did a research report on 'The Prospects of the Emergence of Indian Ocean Economic Community: The Security Dimension' for India's Joint Intelligence Committee in April 1996. At the Mauritius meeting, a Charter for IOR-ARC was drawn and the structure of COM meetings was finalised. In his address at the meeting, Gujral underlined the gradual economic rise of the Indian Ocean Rim countries and India's emergence as a big and fastest growing market in the region. He called for enhanced participation of business and academic communities in the collective regional efforts and proposed setting up of Indian Ocean Chairs and Associate Fellowships. It was an enriching experience for me to be present in the meeting as a part of the media section of the Indian delegation.

JNU also opened up for me the opportunities of foreign travel. I travelled extensively visiting all of India's immediate neighbours, most of the countries in Southeast Asia and Europe, some countries in Africa, West Asia, Persian Gulf, and North America. Most of these visits were for academic purposes, on scholarships, working on specific research projects, for conferences and lectures, as part of Track 1.5 and Track 2.0 conferences, on invitation from host countries under their visitors' programmes and also as member of official delegations led by ministers. These visits greatly helped me understand the dynamics of international politics and India's foreign policy. They also made me an object of envy and criticism (for frequent absence from the University) from my colleagues, but the accumulated experience was extremely useful in my teaching and research. Its impact shaped my career and personality in many intangible ways.

After retiring from JNU in 2003, I received three years extension of service under the University's established norms. After complete retirement from JNU in 2006, I served in three different think tanks: the Observer Research Foundation (ORF), New Delhi (informally since 2002, but formally for two years from 2006 to 2007); The Institute of South Asian Studies (ISAS) of the National University of Singapore, Singapore (for six years from 2008 till the end of 2013); and the Institute for Defence Studies and Analyses (IDSA), New Delhi (In 1983-84; and from 2007 till 2021, in different capacities, including as an elected member of its Executive Council).

This did not bring about any change in the nature of my professional work. I continued to do research, writing and attending conferences. My foreign travels also continued as usual. I published two books during my association with the ORF, six books with IDSA and three books with the ISAS. The IDSA kept my association intact even when I had joined ISAS, as I was not taking any money and was designated as a Distinguished Fellow. I was however, paid an honorarium for editing IDSA's *Asian Strategic Review* between 2007 and 2018, with some gaps during my absence to the ISAS. While in association with the ORF, I received a pleasant and surprise offer from the MEA to be appointed as India's Special Envoy to Southeast Asian Countries on India's issue of UN Security Council Reforms. Not knowing the significance of this offer, I sought Shri M.K. Rasgotra's advice. Rasgotra was my senior colleague in ORF, as a member of the Governing Board. He encouraged me to promptly accept the offer as the status of Special Envoy is usually equivalent to that of a Minister of State for a specific diplomatic assignment. I shall come to my experience as the Special Envoy again later, but this was yet another opportunity for me to dabble in diplomacy in an authorised capacity. My association with think tanks even after retirement from the University gave me opportunities to dabble in diplomacy in an unauthorised manner.

2

Nepal: Struggle for Democracy

IT IS SAID that your first love never leaves you. Nepal has been my first academic love and it refuses to go completely out of my personal and professional space. Usually, once a scholar completes their PhD the tendency is to shift to another theme if you want to continue with the academic career. I also widened my academic interest and switched to other subjects for research, writing and teaching, but Nepal never left me, nor did I ever become disinterested in Nepal.

My engagement with Nepali politics and the dabbling in diplomacy related to Nepal began in 1968, when I first visited it for fieldwork to collect material in pursuance of my PhD research on 'Foreign Policy of Nepal'. Financial support for my fieldwork was limited to my Rs 200 per month scholarship. The fieldwork was for a period of six months and the Department of Political Science which administered SASC of the University of Rajasthan, Jaipur, used to send me my scholarship in cash through registered post every month. There was no other grant or financial support to enable me to take a flight to Kathmandu from New Delhi.

I took a train to Muzaffarpur (in Bihar) and changed there for the border town of Raxaul. From there, one had to cross the land border through the checkpost in Birganj to Nepal to take a bus to Kathmandu. By the time I reached the bus station, the last bus for Kathmandu had left. People at the bus station suggested that I could either wait for the next day or take a private truck going to Kathmandu, as the drivers sometimes took passengers to make little extra money. I decided on the latter option, went to the point where truck drivers pick passengers and after waiting for about an hour, got picked up for Kathmandu for a fare less than what I would otherwise be charged on a regular bus. It was a truck loaded with consumer goods without much space to spread out.

The journey took nearly 16-17 hours. The truck stopped in-between at four to five places for rest and refreshment. It was a difficult and tiring journey passing through sharp mountainous curves, which would shake all your body. I had to keep awake and sitting through the night. In early morning of the next day, we stopped in Hetauda, a major junction and the last stop before Kathmandu. It was a scenic place bustling with activity for being a junction for going to different parts of Nepal from Kathmandu. Almost every bus, car or truck stops in Hetauda in their journey to and from Kathmandu.

Research Fieldwork and B.P. Koirala's Release

The truck dropped me in Kathmandu at a place where I could hire a cycle rikshaw for my next destination of *Marwari Sewa Samiti* (Marwari Service Centre). This was a visitors' place established by the business community of Indian origin in Nepal to cater to the needs of those who came from India or other Nepali towns for business or visits of short duration. It provided one room accommodation with a restaurant for vegetarian meals attached. The accommodation provided to me at the Marwari Sewa Samiti was only for a week and I had to look for alternate accommodation within this period. I succeeded in getting one room accommodation in a sprawling 'Pande Niwas' in Dhoka Tole area within Kathmandu city.

I soon made friends with one of the younger sons of the landlord, Vinay Pande, who also on weekends took me out for cricket and football games. I had never played cricket but he pushed me in his team for a friendly match only to realise his mistake. I continued to take my meals in the Marwari Sewa Samiti restaurant as it catered to my taste and vegetarian requirement at affordable price. Having sorted out the existential issues of accommodation, etc., I launched my work for the collection of research material.

Before leaving for Nepal, I had obtained a letter of introduction and reference for the newly-appointed Indian Ambassador, Raj Bahadur. He was earlier a minister in Mrs Gandhi's cabinet but lost the 1967 elections. He belonged to Bharatpur in Rajasthan. Mrs Gandhi appointed him as ambassador in Nepal in January 1968, after his electoral defeat. The Introduction letter for him was given to me by Ram Niwas Mirdha, another minister in Mrs Gandhi's government from Nagaur, Rajasthan. I had known Mirdha through one of my distant maternal uncles, Rama Krishan Kalla, who was a prominent lawyer in Nagaur and a strong supporter of Mirdha and the Congress party.

Thanks to this letter, Ambassador Raj Bahadur received me very kindly and promised to help me in whatever way possible in facilitating my work in Kathmandu. I got contacts of and appointments with key Nepali leaders and senior bureaucrats for my interviews with the help of embassy staff. My discussions with the ambassador and other diplomats in the Indian mission were also very useful in understanding the then prevailing political situation in Nepal.

Relations between India and Nepal, which had been severely strained following King Mahendra's coup in December 1960 and the Nepali Congress agitation against the King from their bases in India, were gradually getting back to normal. Chinese aggression on India in 1962 radically changed the situation. India asked the Nepali Congress to stop its agitation. The King also was apprehensive of the Chinese intentions, though just before the aggression was launched, the King had welcomed Chinese support for Nepal's independence and sovereignty from the Chinese Defence Minister, Chen Yi, to counter pressure from India against his coup. No one knew the consequences, if the Chinese would have opened their Nepal front to put additional pressure on India. After then Prime Minister Jawaharlal Nehru's death, the Indian ambassador was asked to keep the King in good humour. The beginning of the process of normalisation was made by India's new ambassador in Nepal, Shriman Narayan, who assumed his duties after Nehru's death in November 1964. He started welcoming the King with *aarti*, a mode of auspicious welcome. India and Nepal had also revised one of the provisions of the 1950 Treaty regarding procurement of arms by Nepal. A new Exchange of Letters took place between the two countries in 1965, under which India agreed that Nepal could buy arms from the US and UK if and when India was unable to meet Nepal's needs. Shriman Narayan's book *India and Nepal: An Exercise in Open Diplomacy*, published after his term in 1968, details the process of normalisation in bilateral relations.

Besides normalisation of relations with China, the King was active on two other fronts to deal with the developing situation in the Himalayas. He quietly allowed the US to train and arm Khampa tribals in Nepal's villages bordering Tibet, to fight the Chinese. This had started in 1960 after the Dalai Lama's flight to India and the Chinese moves to control the Tibetans. On the other front, King Mahendra started relaxing curbs on the Nepali Congress, the only democratic force in Nepal, to counter the possibility of growing Chinese influence. There were political speculations that soon after the 1962 Chinese aggression, the King wanted even to release B.P. Koirala, the deposed Prime Minister, (popularly called BP) but was dissuaded by two of the Koirala baiters, Dr Tulsi Giri and Dr Bishwa Bandhu Thapa. They were with the Nepali Congress and were BP's close former associates, but they left the Nepali Congress and joined the King's cabinet after the coup. Many of the Nepali Congress detainees were being gradually released. By 1967, pressure started building on the King for the release of BP for two reasons: the spill over of the Chinese Cultural Revolution had intervened in Nepali domestic politics, and BP's health in prison was deteriorating to the point where urgent and extensive medical attention was required.

The repercussions of the Chinese Cultural Revolution became evident through a political incident that occurred in Kathmandu in May 1967. A national exhibition took place at Tundi Khel, Kathmandu's football and sports stadium. There was a Chinese stall in this exhibition, where Mao-tse-Tung's photograph was prominently displayed, even more so than that of King Mahendra. This caught the attention of some Nepali youths, who voiced their objections to the Chinese stall. When the Chinese stall ignored their objections, the youth resorted to vandalising it, alleging that the Chinese were insulting Nepal's King and Nepali nationalism. This incident was played up in Nepali media and was strongly supported by Nepali leaders.

During my fieldwork in Nepal, in my interviews with Nepali leaders, journalists and diplomats in the Indian Embassy, I learned that Indian diplomats had quietly supported this incident and encouraged the Nepali youth who actively participated in raising objections to the Chinese and vandalising the Chinese stall in *Ramailo Mela* (fun exhibition). Indian diplomacy was maintaining a file on the increasing Chinese activities in Nepal. In the course of my discussions in the Indian Embassy, I was given a file on the Communist activities in Nepal supported by China. It was somewhat amusing to see many printed newspaper clips in this confidential file, otherwise marked as 'strictly confidential' with three red lines in one of the corners. The *Ramailo Mela* incident proved to be helpful in nudging the King towards releasing BP. A strong argument was made to the King and his associates that only by strengthening democratic forces in Nepal led by Nepali Congress, can the Chinese influence be curbed. BP's deteriorating health was another strong reason in asking for his release.

Through my discussions with Ambassador Raj Bahadur and other Indian diplomates, I got a good idea of the nature of the then prevailing Nepal's relations with India, China, Pakistan and the US. I also got a good diplomatic briefing on Nepal's internal politics and learnt that the issue of BP's release was under active consideration. Raj Bahadur had succeeded Shriman Narayan and was pursuing some of his initiatives. The King had agreed in principle to release BP, and the logistics and timetable of the release were being worked out. The ambassador also involved me in this process, which was otherwise being pursued at different diplomatic levels.

I had established contacts with BP's younger brother Girija Prasad Koirala (known popularly as GP or *Sanoba* i.e.; younger brother) with the help of Indian Embassy staff. I was asked to carry messages between Ambassador Raj Bahadur and GP towards working out the logistics of BP's release. The issues were related to his role after the release. The King did not want BP to issue any political statements after his release and not to start any violent activities against the state. BP was expected to go into exile to India where his family lived in Banaras. I carried such messages faithfully, without sharing them with anyone. I had no definite idea but I had an uncanny feeling that the Indian Embassy was in close touch with the Palace, through Prime Minister Surya Bahadur Thapa, and Rishikesh

Shah (senior Nepali politician), in working out the logistics of the release. I felt privileged to have been a part, howsoever insignificant, of the preparations for BP's release. This participation opened many doors for my involvement in promoting the cause of democracy. It also opened opportunities for me to have friendly relations with the Koirala family and other important players in Nepali politics.

I left Nepal after completing my research work by August end, 1968, and BP was eventually released on 10 October, 1968. He had probably agreed to the Nepali Congress ending its violent activities against the King's 'Panchayat Democracy' system, but not the peaceful agitation for the restoration of parliamentary democracy. After release, BP came to Banaras to be with his family and then also to New Delhi, for treatment of his disease, which turned out to be throat cancer.

In the process of carrying messages back and forth, I developed very good personal understanding and friendship with GP. I started addressing him as 'Girija Babu'. I also developed amicable personal relations with Surya Bahadur Thapa and Rishikesh Shah. Both of them were close to the Palace at that time, but with a liberal approach and in support of BP's release. Rishikesh Shah was also an eminent diplomat with a scholarly bent of mind. He published nearly six books on various aspects of Nepal's history, diplomacy, politics and his own biography.

I remained in continuous touch with both Thapa and Rishikesh Shah. Surya Bahadur Thapa was trusted by the Royal Palace and was appointed Prime Minister many times during the Panchayat System. I met him every time I went to Nepal. In one of the meetings after the end of the panchayat system, he said he was thankful to the Government of India, especially Mrs Indira Gandhi, in 'helping us manage the referendum of 1980'. This indicated that Mrs Gandhi favoured a stable monarchy in Nepal. I had developed friendship with two other persons who were also helpful in getting my credentials as a genuine scholar established with Girija Babu. They were Naresh Koirala and Daman Nath Dhungana. Naresh was a member of the extended Koirala family, a nephew of BP and GP. Daman Nath Dhungana was a budding lawyer and a prominent Nepali Congress activist. We three would meet for tea/coffee at Indra Restaurant in Kathmandu's popular commercial area, the New Road, almost every day. On our way back from the New Road, we would sit down in Ratna Park, a small garden attached to the Tundi Khel, on a bench and discuss for long hours, the future of democracy in Nepal. These discussions made me a strong supporter of Nepali Congress and democracy in Nepal and consolidated my dislike for the autocratic monarchy. Both these friends also greatly helped me to establish contacts with all important leaders of Nepali Congress.

We, all the three, still remain good friends, periodically exchanging our notes on Nepali politics. Frequent meetings with Girija Babu also made my association long lasting with him. I had to go to Biratnagar to interview Shri Matrika Prasad Koirala, the first Nepali Congress Prime Minister of Nepal, for my PhD work. I arranged my interview with the help of Naresh and Matrika Koirala's daughter, Kabita Koirala. Matrika Koirala gave me a slightly different perspective on India-Nepal relations as well as on Nepal's domestic politics, from that of GP and B.P. Koirala. He also drove me to Kosi barrage and explained how Bihari engineers working on the construction of the Kosi dam initially were indifferent towards Nepal's genuine concerns.

Girija Babu also was to travel to Biratnagar, to their ancestral house called 'Koirala Niwas', to brief the rest of the Koirala family about the developments regarding BP's release. When he came to know about my planned visit to Biratnagar, he asked me to coordinate my travel with his and offered to host me in Koirala Niwas. We met at the check-in counter at Kathmandu airport; he managed to get our seats together. In the flight, he ordered beer for himself and me, and got irritated to know that I don't take beer and don't drink any alcohol at all. On his insistence, I took a sip, but could not bear its bitter taste. I then told him that I will drink beer the day Nepali Congress and he come to power. He completely forgot this promise and never offered me beer when in power, after the end of the Panchayat System in 1990.

I enjoyed very affectionate and generous hospitality at the Koirala Niwas; was introduced to all the members of the family, except BP's family, as they were in Banaras. I also met Shailaja Acharya, niece of the Koirala brothers, and an active Nepali Congress leader. She had been jailed for opposing King Mahendra's coup. Besides meeting other important leaders for my research, I had long sittings in Biratnagar with Matrika Prasad Koirala. The relationship developed in Koirala Niwas with the Koirala family members became lasting. GP and Keshav Prasad Koirala also kept coming to New Delhi and met me several times in Sapru House Hostel. I remember taking Girija Babu to Bengali Market many times where he used to buy cigarettes 'India Kings', a substitute for his favourite '555'. Once, he also asked me to accept the responsibility of being his daughter Sujata Koirala's local guardian. Sujata was studying in a New Delhi school. One of the Indian socialist leaders, Surendra Mohan, was her local guardian. I happily accepted the responsibility during Surendra Mohan's absence from Delhi for a few months.

After I joined JNU faculty, we (I and Professor Bimal Prasad) also admitted BP's son, Prakash Koirala, in South Asian Studies as a research scholar, but he eventually did not join. We (I and my wife Anuradha) remained in touch with Sushma Koirala (Nanu), Prakash's wife, when she lived in the Bengali Market area. Manisha Koirala, daughter of Prakash and Sushma, became a renowned Bollywood actress later. I remember her playing as a growing up girl, with her grandmother and BP's wife, Sushila Koirala, in their Varanasi house during 1985-86. Prakash Koirala was elected as

Member of Parliament in 1999, but he joined hands with King Gyanendra later and became one of the Ministers in his cabinet in 2005. This led to his dismissal from the Nepali Congress. But he along with his wife and daughter, remained the King's supporters. I had a chance meeting with Sushma and Manisha at a Kathmandu hotel where I was attending a conference in 2007. When I questioned her support for the King, she justified it by referring to BP's call for national reconciliation that resulted in referendum on the Panchayat System in 1980. She did not care about the continuous struggle for democracy by the rest of the Koirala family against the King.

During my stay in Sapru House Hostel, besides the Koirala family members, Yogendra Man Sherchan also used to visit us frequently. He was a staunch Nepali Congress activist and loyal supporter of BP and Girija Babu. Unfortunately, he was killed in an accident in 1972, which clearly looked like a case of political assassination. Once, Tarini Prasad Koirala, BP's younger brother, also came to meet us at Sapru House Hostel. He was an acknowledged author and a great media activist, actively involved in Nepali Congress' struggle for democracy with his brothers BP and G.P. Koirala.

JNU Strengthens Nepal Connection

As has been noted earlier, I joined JNU in January 1974. After residing outside the campus for about a year, I got a residence on the campus as warden of the newly-established Ganga Hostel. My meetings and interactions with the Nepali leaders and activists continued. I had the privilege of hosting B.P. Koirala, Rishikesh Shah and Pushpa Lal Shrestha in my Ganga Hostel residence. I also used to visit BP at his rented accommodation in South Extension to enquire about his health and have discussions on the status of the democratic struggle in Nepal. BP gradually appeared to be despondent about any success of the struggle in the near future, but he would never leave hope. BP had actively supported the Government of India during the war for Bangladesh and also in the process of democratisation and integration of Sikkim. Emergency in India imposed in 1975 was a serious setback to his hopes. All his socialist Indian friends and supporters, including Jayaprakash Narayan and George Fernandes, were fighting against the Emergency. This turned Mrs Gandhi unsympathetic to his struggle. I learnt through him the details of the hijacking of Royal Nepal Airlines flight from Biratnagar, with Rs 3 million in Indian currency in 1973 to fund the Nepali Congress' struggle against the Panchayat System. The Congress had run out of money to carry out its various activities. The hijacking was planned by Girija Babu and his close family associates namely; Shailaja Acharya, Sushil Koirala and Chakra Bastola. It was executed by Durga Subedi, Basanta Bhattarai and Nagendra Dhungel. No passengers were hurt in the hijacking. Within minutes of its take off from Biratnagar, the plane was forced to land in Forbesganj, Bihar, on grass fields. It took off again for its destination in Kathmandu after the currency boxes had been offloaded. I knew about the incident vaguely while I was still in Jaipur. Details were shared with me by Sushil Koirala and Chakra Bastola.

I kept my contacts with BP as much as I could. He returned to Nepal from India in 1976 and decided to cooperate with the King. He was kept under detention for two more years after his return but was released in 1978, cleared of all the charges of terrorism and subversion. In cooperation with King Birendra, he participated in a national referendum to choose between multi-party democracy and a liberalised Panchayat System. His case for multi-party democracy lost, though in a manipulated referendum process. Surya Bahadur Thapa's reference to 'managing the referendum' may be recalled here. BP was allowed by the King to travel to New York for cancer treatment. He later went to Thailand for check-up but the doctors had given up hope on him by 1982. He spent his last days in Kathmandu. I met him there and had long discussions on two occasions. He explained his frustrations with India's attitude towards his struggle, but was hopeful that eventually, democracy will win the day against monarchy. He was highly appreciative of Girija Babu's efforts to keep the movement alive. He described Girija Babu to me as Lord 'Hanuman' for the movement because he delivered on all the tasks assigned, no matter however challenging or intricate they were, though his methods were, at times crude and questionable.

Pushpa Lal Shrestha was the founder of the Communist Party of Nepal. He visited my Ganga Hostel residence for dinner with his wife Sahana Pradhan. Notwithstanding the ideological differences, he was working closely with BP and the Nepali Congress against the King's Panchayat System. He died rather young in 1978, at the age of 54. His wife Sahana Pradhan was serving as a teacher in Kathmandu to look after the family during Pushpa Lal's struggle against the King from India. Sahana Pradhan joined the Communist Movement in 1986 and rose to become Nepal's Foreign Minister in 2007. She very warmly welcomed me in her office when I visited Kathmandu, and explained to me Nepal's approach towards India under her leadership. In the course of conversation, she kept on assuring me that 'Indians should not react unduly to the rhetoric of Nepali Communist leaders. We all want and work for a very friendly and cooperative relationship with India.' I kept meeting her on my subsequent visits to Kathmandu, even when she was not a minister. She died in 2014.

My association with Rishikesh Shah was most valuable both for my research work as also continuing involvement in the affairs of Nepal. I first met him in Kathmandu in 1968 to interview him regarding my research. He was then also representing the 'Graduate Constituency' of the Panchayat System. His books, writings and experiences were an important source of research material for my PhD work. After that whenever he came to New Delhi or I went to Kathmandu, we met for long hours to discuss Nepal's affairs. He frequently visited me in JNU and also agreed on occasions to speak to my students on Nepali and world affairs.

During one of my visits to Kathmandu, accompanied by Anuradha, Rishikesh Shah graciously and generously hosted us as his house guests in his Lal Durbar residence. With a royal lineage, Rishikesh had easy access to the palace in Kathmandu but was deeply committed to liberal ideals. He stood for democratic values. He was even detained briefly for openly opposing the Panchayat System and calling for its liberalisation. He also actively mobilised support for the protection and promotion of human rights in Nepal. He sympathised with the Maoist movement in principle while disapproving the associated violence. Unfortunately, Rishikesh died of lung cancer in 2002. During one of Rishikesh's visits to JNU, a young couple working with him in Nepal's Human Rights Organisation came to meet him. Rishikesh introduced them to me. The couple, Baburam Bhattarai and Hisila Yami, were pursuing their PhD research in the School of Social Sciences. Later on, they became the famous couple that led the Maoist movement with Pushpa Kamal Dahal 'Prachanda'.

There is widespread misperception in Nepal that Baburam was my student. He was a student in my university but was not in my School of International Studies. I never taught him. He has been kind in speaking to me with respect and deference and that is because I am elder to him and I was introduced to him by Rishikesh Shah, his mentor in some respects. Of course, I have learnt a lot from Baburam on Nepali politics. Baburam and Hisila kept meeting me after being introduced by Rishikesh. They would tell me how they were organising Nepali menial workers in India (domestic helps, security guards, casual labourers, etc.) who were being treated shabbily by their Indian employers. They also shared with me their experiences on human rights in Nepal's remote and backward rural areas. Even after their completion of studies and leaving JNU, we have maintained close contact with each other. During the Maoist movement, Baburam asked me to be the local guardian of his college-going daughter Manushi for some time in Delhi. I happily accepted that.

Another very important friendship developed with a Nepali on the JNU campus was with Lok Raj Baral who was doing his PhD in South Asian Studies on Nepali Opposition parties. He was teaching at the Department of Political Science in Tribhuvan University, Kathmandu, and had come to India for higher studies under the Indian government's fellowship. We worked together in Sapru House Library and he got his PhD soon after I joined JNU in 1974. Baral has been a pillar of my academic contacts in Nepal. He prescribed my book on 'Foreign Policy of Nepal' as a reference reading in his Department of Political Science.

During one of my visits to Kathmandu, he invited me to lecture at the department, and one of the students in audience was Sher Bahadur Deuba, who was in active politics and rose to become Nepal's five-time prime minister. He is the President of Nepali Congress at present. I was appointed external examiner for some of Baral's PhD students, and was involved in the activities of the Centre for Nepal Studies established under his leadership. We also worked together on the Governing Board of the Regional Centre for Strategic Studies (RCSS), established in Colombo, Sri Lanka, in 1992 with the help of the US-based Ford Foundation. We together edited a book project for the RCSS entitled 'Refugees and Regional Security in South Asia'.

We consistently reunite during visits to each other's countries and keep close contact with each other when we are in our respective countries. Our shared commitment to championing the cause of democracy in Nepal will be seen in the subsequent pages. Baral has had the distinction of being appointed as Nepal's Ambassador to

India (March 1996–October 1997). I stay well-informed about Nepal affairs through some of my Nepali students. One of the very capable students, Yashoda Suval, unfortunately, succumbed to cancer in the early 1980s before completing her PhD. On a brighter side, two other students, Amresh Kumar Singh and Deepak Prakash Bhatt, have risen to become Members of Parliament and are in active politics.

It has been noted that as a JNU faculty member, I had access to the MEA. I was assigned to write two research reports on Nepal by the MEA, first on the dynamics of domestic politics when Shri N.N. Jha was the Joint Secretary in-charge dealing with Nepal, and the second one on the status of the India-Nepal Treaty of Peace and Friendship of 1950, when Mrs Shyamala Kaushik was the Joint Secretary in-charge. Both these reports were well received by the MEA officers. The MEA had paid an honorarium for writing these reports and that was accordingly mentioned in the Annual Report of MEA. This was used as evidence for attacking me as an agent of the Government of India, mostly by supporters of the Panchayat System during the monarchy's direct rule, to counteract my support for democracy.

While I was writing my first report, I received an invitation to a luncheon hosted by Prime Minister Mrs Indira Gandhi in 1976 for Royal Prince Gyanendra Shah. It was a small gathering not exceeding 8-10 persons. Conversations during the luncheon primarily revolved around pleasantries and discussions on bilateral trade. At the end of the lunch, Mrs Gandhi waited to see Gyanendra off. I was standing behind her at the pickup point of Hyderabad House talking to N.N. Jha. After bidding farewell to Gyanendra, Mrs Gandhi, while waiting for her own car, turned to me and said: 'Professor, closely observe the Nepali Prince in your studies.' Her words left me perplexed as I had not been tracking Prince Gyanendra's political activities in my research for the MEA, or even otherwise. Nevertheless, from that point forward, I started following him carefully and found that both he and Queen Aishwarya regularly opposed King Birendra's liberal initiatives. They took a keen interest in Nepal's business affairs, contributing to King Birendra's declining popularity and playing a role in the emergence of the Peoples' Movement (*Jan Andolan-I)* in the late eighties (1988-90) that dissolved the Panchayat System and restored multi-party democracy.

My second report on the treaty of 1950 was used as a briefing material for the newly-appointed ambassadors to Nepal. On directions from the MEA, I personally briefed Lt. Gen. S.K. Sinha over a lunch in the IIC before he left to assume his charge of the Indian Embassy in Kathmandu in 1990.

Struggle for the Restoration of Multi-Party Democracy

The dissolution of the Panchayat System after three decades, even with strong monarchical support was a major transformation in Nepal's contemporary history. The context of this transformation was prepared by two factors. One, there were serious difficulties in the India-Nepal relations and the other was persisting turbulence in Nepal's domestic politics arising out of conflict between the reigning feudal order and democratic aspirations.

India-Nepal relations had been seeing many ups and downs, particularly since King Birendra's assumption of power. King Birendra was upset and worried with the developments, like the hijacking of the RNAC plane with Indian currency of Rs 3 million by the Nepali Congress in 1973 and the integration of Sikkim into the Indian Union in 1975. These developments made him perceive India as a major challenge to his regime through the support of democratic forces led by Nepali Congress. To counter this challenge, he came up with the proposal of Nepal as a Zone of Peace in 1975. This was seen in New Delhi as a dubious move not only to keep

India out of Nepali politics but also to undermine the 1950 Treaty. Further, India's intervention in Sri Lanka and Maldives in 1987 and 1988 respectively were seen in Nepal as a possible military threat to its security and territorial integrity by Nepal's royal regime. To guard against that imaginary threat, King Birendra sought arms from China, particularly anti-aircraft guns which could be mounted on the hill tops to protect Kathmandu Valley from any air intrusion and attack. King Birendra also took the initiative to propose that China be made a member of SAARC (South Asian Association for Regional Cooperation) and in this, Pakistan stood as a strong supporter of Nepal. This seriously offended New Delhi because it was in violation of the 1950 Treaty and an indication that Nepal will use China to counterbalance India.

The other major issue of irritation between the two countries was related to Trade and Transit. The Treaties of Trade and Transit concluded in 1978 expired in March 1988. Negotiations for the renewal of the Treaties got stuck in the dispute between the two sides as India insisted on a single Treaty, both for trade and transit, to stop the misuse of transit provisions by the Nepali and Indian vested interests. Nepal, however, was insisting on having two treaties. Strong commercial interests were there in both the countries respectively behind these two positions.

In the absence of any meaningful efforts toward negotiations for treaty renewal, India blocked 15 of the 17 transit points of goods and services going to Nepal. Only two transit points were kept open in compliance of international obligations towards a landlocked neighbour. This created a situation of economic blockade for Nepal resulting in severe difficulties for ordinary Nepalese. King Birendra reacted through counter measures like introducing work permits for India's migrant workers in Nepal which only aggravated the tensions between the two countries. He also tried to secure petroleum, kerosene and other consumer items from third countries but did not succeed. He tried to mobilise the Nepalese against Indian pressures by raising nationalist sentiments but there too, he did not get his way.

Economic hardships resulting from the Indian action fuelled public resentment against the Panchayat System and the royal regime. The economy was already doing badly, growing around 1 per cent only. There were widespread rumours of corruption in the royal family, particularly involving the Queen, King's brother Prince Gyanendra Shah, and the royal administration. The banned political party, Nepali Congress, was preparing to launch an agitation for the restoration of the multi-party democratic political system. They organised a conference to take a decision in this respect. The United Left Front, which was a conglomeration of Left and Communist parties in Nepal, decided to join hands with the Nepali Congress in February 1990 to start Jan Andolan-I (Peoples' Movement), the Movement for the Restoration of Democracy (MRD). King Birendra tried to suppress this movement by arresting political leaders and unleashing state violence on protesters but without much success.

Finally, in April 1990, he conceded the principal demands of MRD by agreeing to dissolve the Panchayat System and allow political parties to function in a constitutional democratic system. For this, a new Constitution was to be framed by a Constitutional Commission. A new, multi-party government headed by Krishna Prasad Bhattarai of Nepali Congress was installed as an interim government to run the day-to-day affairs and oversee the work of the Constitution Commission. This Commission completed its task in November 1990 and restored the multi-party system. My friend Daman Nath Dhungana had played a significant role in the drafting of the Constitution of 1990, as a representative of the Nepali Congress in the Constitution Commission.

India made a significant contribution in the success of Nepal's MRD. Rajiv Gandhi's unhappiness at the bilateral relations with King Birendra's regime led him to lend active support to the popular agitation. He encouraged Nepal's political parties to come together. He was reported to have disapproved Mrs Indira Gandhi's earlier decision in 1976 that forced B.P. Koirala to return to Nepal and support King Birendra. One of the R&AW (Research and Analysis Wing) operatives claimed in his book that efforts were made even to bring Maoists/ extreme Left parties into the United Front and join hands with Nepali Congress in removing the Panchayat System.[1]

Imposition of blockade on the expiry of the Trade Treaties was seen in Nepal as a calculated move by the Rajiv government to pressurise the King and give a push to the public resentment and protests. Rajiv Gandhi lost the elections of November 1989 and the V.P. Singh government that succeeded took a relatively softer stand towards Nepal. It lifted the blockade, initiated negotiations with the King's regime on the Trade Treaty and proclaimed non-interference in the MRD. However, members of many political parties within and outside the Indian Parliament, including those from the ruling coalition, refused to toe the official line and went to participate in the conference of the Nepali Congress to support the MRD. Socialist leader Chandra Shekhar was one of the prominent leaders among them, who was also the strongest supporter of the Nepali Congress owing to his close personal relations with the Koirala family members. He came to Nepal to endorse Nepali Congress' resolution at this conference to launch Jan Andolan-I. There was also extensive support for Nepal's MRD in India at various levels, in Parliament, media and various social groups. During a discussion on the Nepal situation, Gujral told me that Chandra Shekhar and other political parties' representatives have gone to Nepal without the approval of the V.P. Singh government. Explaining the government's position,

---

1 Amar Bhushan's book, *Inside India,* is quoted in this respect in a *Times of India* 'Readers' Blog'. Rajeev Tiwari@*Shandilya Uvach,* July 16, 2020 www.timesofindia.indiatimes.com/readersblog/Shandilya-uvach/Nepal-succumb-to-dragon-23211.

he said: 'We are in favour of democracy in Nepal but without any direct involvement of India.'

When King Birendra conceded the demands of MRD, India's Parliament adopted a resolution proposed by Gujral as foreign minister, in support of democracy in Nepal. India subsequently tried to help in the framing of a new Constitution. By the time the Constitution was ready for adoption, there was another change of government in India where Chandra Shekhar became Prime Minister with the outside support of the Congress Party led by Rajiv Gandhi. That government openly supported the multi-party democratic system in Nepal.

Since the days of my first visit to Nepal in 1968, I have always been in support of democracy in Nepal. When the blockade was imposed in March 1989, I supported it in my opinion page writings in the Indian media. There were many stakeholders in India on Nepal policy who opposed the blockade. Those who pressurised Rajiv Gandhi against the blockade included the Bharatiya Janata Party, the Shankaracharyas of Puri and other Hindu religious establishments, like Gorakhnath temple in Uttar Pradesh's Gorakhpur, army, business lobbies who gained through misuse of the transit provisions under the expiring Treaties, and those who had married into Nepal's Shah and Rana families.

I supported the peoples' movement in many conferences and seminars. I met India's then army chief Vishwa Nath Sharma and questioned him on his meeting with Rajiv Gandhi to lift the blockade. He defended his action by saying that he could not let the families of his Gurkha soldiers suffer on account of difficulties in getting kerosene and other essential supplies. I explained the political situation in Nepal to him in detail and asked him to reconsider his position on the blockade. He promised he would no longer oppose the government's decision. The blockade had also created strong international resentment against India for 'harassing a small and poor neighbour'. Indian diplomacy was trying to counter it in its own way.

I was called by the then Foreign Secretary S.K. Singh to write a detailed article to explain India's position. I said, 'I will do that but who will publish a long paper.' He said: 'Leave that to me.' He got the paper published in the IDSA *Quarterly*. IDSA was headed at that time by Air Commodore Jasjit Singh who was also a close friend of mine. Additional off-prints of this paper were published for distribution in various Indian and foreign embassies to explain India's Nepal approach. I was told by S.K. Singh later that the paper was helpful in their efforts.

My support for MRD in Nepal continued even after the coming to power of the V.P. Singh government. At one level, the support was articulated in seminars and conferences as earlier. But due to the change of government in New Delhi, the Nepal Embassy had also become active in mobilising support for the royal regime; and some of my senior colleagues joined the Nepal Embassy to organise lectures and conferences where I countered them. My media writings and appearances in the television channels in favour of Nepal's MRD continued. I also succeeded in involving my Nepali friends like Professor Lok Raj Baral and Rishikesh Shah in such media writings and TV appearances. While nothing happened to Rishikesh Shah, Baral had to face problems. Due to one of his writings in the *Times of India* that had been arranged by me with the help of Dilip Mukherjee, Tribhuvan University suspended him and threatened to remove him from service. Eventually he survived in his job.

I also had to pay some price. My hobnobbing with the Nepali Congress leaders and my writings in favour of the MRD had been taken note of by the palace secretariat. They used some pliant media channels to label me as an R&AW agent to erode my credibility as an independent scholar. The Panchayat regime was dubbing the whole MRD movement as an Indian conspiracy to pressurise Nepal and its King. At the political level, I explained to about half a dozen non-BJP members of Parliament the case of the MRD in Nepal. In some cases, I had taken the support of another Member of Parliament, Digvijay Singh, who was a former student in SIS/JNU and politically associated with George Fernandes and Chandra Shekhar. BJP members were strongly in support of the King. Some of these members had supposedly been funded in their elections by the royal family.

I also talked to Gujral on Nepalese affairs as he was the Minister of External Affairs in the V.P. Singh government. He clarified to me that the government's stand of non-interference was formal. The government, he said, neither allowed nor stopped Chandra Shekhar from visiting Nepal and speaking at the Nepali Congress conference. The V.P. Singh government was also not restraining any support for the Nepali agitation in the Indian Parliament, media or at the social level. He added that while 'negotiations for the Trade and Transit Treaty had been initiated, we are slow in concluding them'.

Gujral also included me as a member of the official Indian delegation that visited Nepal under his leadership in August 1990. I was made a member of the media party and was assigned the task of interviewing Prime Minister K.P. Bhattarai for India's official TV channel, Doordarshan. Gujral had always been in favour of a softer approach towards the neighbours. While in Nepal, Gujral met all the sections of politics and realised that there were serious tensions between the King and the Nepali Congress as also between the Nepali Congress and the Left parties. He also addressed Nepal's business community and assured them that India will help them to contribute in the development of Nepal. On the sidelines of many of the official engagements, he also informed me that he was going to accept the Nepali demand for a transit corridor to Bangladesh through India to promote their third country trade on an experimental basis for six months to begin with. The Indian bureaucracy had not been sympathetic to this idea for years. In their assessment, the corridor could be misused for illegal purposes like smuggling, diversion of trade and even illegal flow of arms. It may be interesting to note that this corridor was not really used by the Nepali side for months after Gujral allowed its use. Nepal was raising this issue only for political purpose.

In drafting the Constitution, the Commission appointed by King Birendra was being guided more by Western experts. No consultation and advice were being sought from India. Gujral secured from the King the permission to send Indian constitutional experts to advise on the new Constitution. On his return from this visit, he sent Dr L.M. Singhvi and A.G. Noorani to advise on the Constitution making. Dr Singhvi, whom I had known since my Fellowship at the Institute of Constitutional and Parliamentary Studies, called me to brief him on the political situation in Nepal. I informed him that in the Constitution making, efforts are being made to reserve residual powers for the King and keep his position as strong as possible, specially his control on the Royal Nepal Army. Dr Singhvi pleaded with the Members of the Constitution Commission to make the parliamentary system strong under a constitutional monarchy because the King had accepted that sovereignty belonged to the people. But his advice was ignored.

These residual powers were in fact used by King Gyanendra in dissolving the Parliament in 2002 and assuming direct rule in 2005. During my visit to Kathmandu as part of the delegation led by Gujral in 1990, Baburam Bhattarai came quietly to see me in my hotel room from his underground location somewhere in rural Nepal. He appeared keen to understand the changed stance of the V.P. Singh government on the peoples' movement. Having exhausted his patience with the Human Rights Organisation, he had turned to radical politics.

Post-restoration Nepal

Hopes and expectations of a vibrant democratic governance under a multi-party system started fading away soon. The new Constitution adopted in November 1990 was presented as a grant from the King. His control of the army along with his hold over the residual powers continued to facilitate his efforts to break the MRD coalition. Political parties were also driven by their ambitions to have as larger a share in the new power structure as possible. This led to tensions between the Nepali Congress and the United Left Front, between the Nepali Congress and the King and also among the parties of the United Front, including within the Nepali Congress.

Elections for Parliament were held in 1991 where Nepali Congress gained absolute majority of 110 seats in a house of 205. The Communist Party of Nepal (Unified Marxist-Leninist) was left behind with 69 seats. The interim Prime Minister Krishna Prasad Bhattarai lost the election in one of the Kathmandu constituencies. This made room for G.P. Koirala to emerge as the leader of the party and its prime ministerial candidate. I was happy with this outcome because of my close relations with Girija Babu and the Nepali Congress. I visited Kathmandu and congratulated Girija Babu and other Nepali Congress friends. One of them, Daman Nath Dhungana, asked me to support his case with Girija Babu for the post of Speaker of the Parliament. This surprised me a bit as I thought that Daman should be looking for a good ministerial position, which he was likely to get because of his strong electoral performance in Kathmandu and his role in the making of the Constitution. It seemed that Daman was not very comfortable working directly under the strong leadership of Girija Babu. As Speaker of the House, he could have an independent and an influential position. I met Girija Babu to convey Daman's preference. I am sure Daman must have used other sources as well to reach out to Girija Babu, who in turn must have made his own political calculations. The Nepali Congress did put him up as a candidate for Speaker's post which he won comfortably.

After my return from Kathmandu, within about 10 days, I had a surprise visit from Ramesh Nath Pandey to my residence in JNU. He came with a small gift of two yak wool chair cushions and asked me to recommend him for a ministerial berth to Girija Babu. I thanked him for the beautiful gift and said I am in no position to interfere in Girija Babu's government formation. He kept on insisting on his demand. I had to concede saying to him that if and when I get a chance to meet Girija Babu, I shall forward his request. I explained to him that asking Girija Babu on telephone for appointing him was neither appropriate on my part nor practically possible. My efforts not to accept his gift did not succeed as he was very polite and insistent. Pandey has been an intelligent and dynamic politician. He was a minister under the Panchayat System and again became a minister after the King dissolved Parliament in 2002.

Pandey remained in contact with me, as we will explore in detail later, on various political matters. I have also known his son, Nishchal Nath, who has established himself as a promising scholar and commentator on contemporary foreign policy issues of Nepal. Daman and I have been friends since 1968, and we make it a point to meet whenever the opportunity arises. He graciously invited me to participate in a couple of seminars in Kathmandu organised by his think tank. In February 2023, in a tweet asking for non-partisan candidates to be considered for the post of Nepal's President, I mentioned his name as one of the four prospective candidates. This created a bit of a stir in the Nepali media.

Girija Babu's 1991 government did not last its full term. There were serious allegations of corruption and inefficiency from the

Opposition parties. There was also a formidable faction within his own party, periodically supported by two most senior leaders of Nepali Congress, Ganesh Man Singh and K.P. Bhattarai. During one of my Kathmandu visits, Sushil Koirala requested me to speak to Ganesh Man Singh and Bhattarai to discourage their supporters from opposing and criticising GP's government. I met both of these Nepali Congress stalwarts. Ganesh Man ji and his wife Mangala Devi warmly welcomed me and invited me to join them for lunch in their modest house. When I broached the topic of Girija Babu's government, Ganesh Man ji attributed its challenges to Girija Babu's impulsive and autocratic governing style. Prakash Man Singh, Ganesh Man ji's son, saw me off, and I urged him to ensure the completion of the Nepali Congress government's term.

Bhattarai, too, expressed his grievances, asserting that Girija Babu made crucial decisions without consulting other party leaders, relying solely on a close-knit group. Personally aggrieved, Bhattarai believed Girija Babu played a role in his electoral defeat. However, neither of the two leaders provided firm assurances that they would prevent the fall of Girija Babu's government.

In July 1994, the government fell to a no-confidence vote by the Opposition, supported by the dissenters of Nepali Congress. The King had to accept the prime minister's recommendation of dissolving the Parliament and ordering fresh elections as he failed to appoint a new government through Opposition coalitions. The elections were scheduled in November 1994.

In October, I received a call from the MEA asking me to visit Nepal for studying the upcoming elections. The MEA offered to cover the expenses for a two-week visit and expected me to submit my report at least a week before the election. Accepting the request, I travelled extensively throughout the Terai and mid hills, meeting a large number of party leaders, candidates, academics, journalists and influential voters. During this period, Professor Bimal Prasad, my former senior colleague at South Asian Studies SIS/JNU, was India's ambassador in Nepal. Having assumed office in 1991, he was in his second term—a rarity for political appointees. Appointed during Chandra Shekhar's government, his second term had been extended by Narasimha Rao's government. I had an extensive discussion with him to understand the then prevailing electoral dynamics in Nepal. He was very kind in explaining all the relevant aspects. His assessment, based on the embassy sources, that included the intelligence feedback, as well as his own personal calculations based on his travels and meetings with various sections of the political class, was that Nepali Congress would have a comfortable victory securing over 100 seats in a House of 205. He predicted that the Communists would emerge as a poor second, and the royalist Rastriya Prajatantra Party (National Democratic Party-NDP) would make gains but remain in the third position.

This did not conform to my assessment. I had been meeting with the Nepali Congress, the Communist UML and various other party leaders, including royalist Surya Bahadur Thapa and leftist Narayan Man Bijukchhe. Both the Congress and the Communist leaders appeared confident of victory. My discussions with independent academics and social activists, as also people in the streets of various towns, suggested that it was going to be a close contest.

After concluding my election study visit, I submitted the report to MEA, specifically to Shivshankar Menon, the joint secretary in-charge of the Northern Division dealing with Nepal. This was my first interaction with him, but that helped me to develop a good personal rapport and friendship with him subsequently. In my assessment, both the Nepali Congress and the Communists were running neck and neck, without any clear edge in favour of the former. My number for both was 80 seats, plus-minus five. I had not applied any known empirical methods in my study but relied on what I had learnt about election studies at Rajasthan University while undertaking a study of Jhunjhunu parliamentary constituency in the 1967 General Elections.

A few days after submitting the report, I got a call from Menon's office to meet him. In the meeting, he told me that my assessment was at variance with that of the Indian Embassy in Kathmandu and of R&AW, both of which had predicted a clear victory for the Nepali Congress. Despite this, I stood by my assessment. We engaged in a thorough, constituency-wise discussion where I explained the rationale behind my evaluation. The election results, declared three days after these discussions, closely aligned with my assessment. The Nepali Congress got 83 seats, the Communists 88, and the NDP improved its tally to 20 seats and was a poor third.

The day after the election results were announced, India's then Foreign Secretary Krishnan Srinivasan reached out to me early in the morning, inviting me to join him for breakfast. I requested to meet him later in the day, and when we met at his office in MEA, he appeared quite disturbed by the Communist victory in Nepal. He expressed his dissatisfaction with the prospect of the Communists forming the government in Kathmandu. I tried to assure him that there was nothing to be worried about that. After all, we had the CPI-M in power in Kerala, and the CPI (Communist Party of India) often formed alliances with the Indian National Congress. In my assessment, the Communist Party of Nepal (UML) were 'royal communists', supported and promoted by the monarchy in Nepal to contain and balance the Nepali Congress.

He wanted me to go to Nepal to gauge the perspectives of the new rulers when the Communists assume power. His specific concern was that during the election campaign, leaders like Man Mohan Adhikari and others from the Communist party had called for a revision of the 1950 Treaty. I agreed to undertake the trip to Kathmandu. The Constitution of 1990 permitted a coalition of smaller parties over the largest single party in government formation if the smaller parties could muster numbers more than that of the largest single party. Under this provision, the Nepali Congress initially tried to form the government with the support of the NDP, but they found it challenging to accept the conditions laid down by the NDP for extending their support. Eventually, with the backing of the NDP and the Terai-based Nepal Sadbhawana Party, the path was cleared for the installation of the Communist government led by Man Mohan Adhikari. In this case, the largest Communist Party collaborated with smaller parties to assume power.

I visited Kathmandu again in December 1994. I first met Sahana Pradhan, who graciously hosted me for lunch at her residence and assured me that Man Mohan Adhikari, as a seasoned and prudent leader, valued the friendship between India and Nepal and would not take any actions to damage this relationship. I met Adhikari at the official prime ministerial residence, and our discussion lasted for about an hour.

Adhikari was affable and reiterated that his government had no intentions of damaging India-Nepal relations. Specifically addressing the Treaty of 1950, he explained that the Royal Palace sought more autonomy in the matter of importing arms and therefore wanted that clause to be revised. I pointed out the provision made in a separate exchange of letters in 1965, allowing relaxation of conditions for Nepal's arms purchase from third countries. Adhikari responded that the Palace was dissatisfied with that arrangement. Under the 1990 Constitution, the army was directly under the King's control, and given the huge financial transactions involved in arms purchases, the King sought complete freedom in this matter. Adhikari assured me that on other issues related to the 1950 Treaty and overall India-Nepal relations, there were no major concerns. Any differences could be resolved through normal diplomatic discussions, according to him. In an interview to *India Today* (15 December 1994), Adhikari made it clear that 'One cannot survive with dogmatism. We have to be realistic.' Additionally, he suggested that I also meet Madhav Nepal, who served as both the Defence and Foreign Minister. Madhav Nepal echoed a similar perspective and assured me that Nepal's relations with India would not be compromised.

On my return to New Delhi, I briefed the Foreign Secretary accordingly. Adhikari undertook an official visit to India in April 1995, just a couple of months before his government was voted out of power as a result of the defection by NDP and Sadbhawana Party. In the perception of many Nepalis, the behaviour of Sadbhawana Party constitutes an indication of where India's support lies in Nepal's domestic power struggles.

Elections for a new Parliament in Nepal took place in 1995. By then, Nepal had also come in the grip of Maoist insurgency (Peoples' War). I shifted, for the next two years, to Vientiane, the capital of Lao Peoples' Democratic Republic, to serve as India's Ambassador. After returning from Vientiane, I spent six months in 2001 in Singapore on an academic fellowship. I continued to follow developments in Nepal but my active interest was revived only after 2002.

The author meeting
President V.V. Giri at
the Rashtrapati Bhavan,
New Delhi, in 1970.

With Uttar Pradesh Chief Minister N.D. Tiwari (wearing Nehru cap)
and Foreign Secretary Kewal Singh in New Delhi in 1976.

The author (extreme right) with Bollywood actress Shabana Azmi at a South Asia Conference in Melbourne, Australia, in 1986.

Being welcomed at the US Army War College, Washington, D.C., in 1986.

With Eelam People's Revolutionary Liberation Front leader Ketheeswaran Loganathan in New Delhi in 1987.

Bhutan King HM Jigme Singye Wangchuck with the author (second from right) and Centre for Policy Research (CPR) delegation in Thimphu 1988.

The author (behind PM Rajiv Gandhi) introducing him and Union Minister Dinesh Singh to the participants of the Indian Council for South Asian Cooperation (ICSAC) Conference in New Delhi in 1988.

The India International Centre (IIC) delegation during a visit to China in Beijing in September 1989. The author can be seen in the back row, extreme right.

The author (second from left) and a CPR delegation with Sri Lanka President Ranasinghe Premadasa (extreme left) in Colombo in 1990.

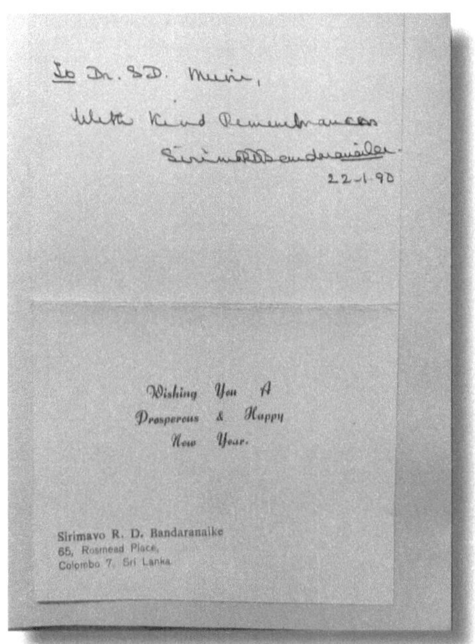

Season's greetings from former
Sri Lanka Prime Minister
Mrs Sirimavo Bandaranaike
in 1990.

Dinner with Chandrika Bandaranaike Kumaratunga at Sri Lankan
academic and activist Kumar Rupesinghe's residence in Oslo, Norway,
in 1991.

The IIC delegation for Indo-US Dialogue in California, US, in February 1991. The author can be seen in the second row, extreme left.

Explaining a point to Minister of External Affairs Dinesh Singh in the presence of Dr K.B. Lall in New Delhi in October 1994.

With Rajya Sabha MP I.K. Gujral (right) and former Foreign Secretary M.K. Rasgotra at the ICSAC Conference in New Delhi in 1994.

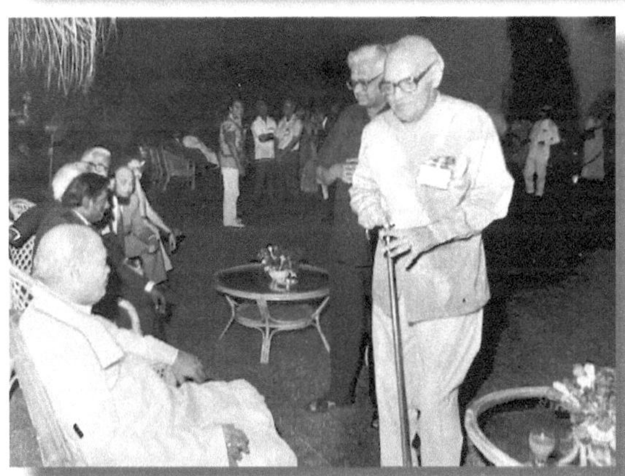

Prime Minister P.V. Narasimha Rao at a dinner during the 1994 ICSAC conference. Dr K.B. Lall and Amb. Eric Gonsalves are also seen.

The author (second from right) with External Affairs Minister I.K. Gujral at the Research and Information System (RIS) for Developing Countries in New Delhi in 1996.

Arriving at the President's House of Laos in Vientiane in December 1997 to present the credentials to the Head of State.

With Lao Ministers and Indian participants at the India-Lao Seminar in Vientiane in July 1998.

With the Indian Embassy staff in Vientiane in 1998.

Flag hoisting on 15 August 1998 at the Embassy residence with the Indian community in Vientiane.

With the Governor of Champasak Province, Lao PDR, in Pakse, Laos, in 1999.

Briefing Lao President Khamtai Siphandone on the Kargil War, in Vientiane in 1999.

Introducing Indian Minister of State Vasundhara Raje to Lao Agriculture Minister Dr Siene Saphangthong and Vice-Minister of Foreign Affairs Phongsavath Boupha (left to the author) at the Embassy House Dinner reception in Vientiane in 1999.

MoS Vasundhara Raje and her delegates with Lao President Khamtai Siphandone in Vientiane in 1999.

The author and his wife Anuradha receiving dinner guests at Embassy residence in Vientiane in 1999.

Dinner with Singapore President S. R. Nathan (wearing a blue shirt) at The Istana, Singapore, in 2001.

Third meeting with Bhutan King HM Jigme Singye Wangchuck in Thimphu in 2003.

With Bhutan's Prime Minister Jigme Y. Thinley (appointed by the king, not elected) in Thimphu in 2006.

Courtesy call on Cambodian Monarch HM Norodom Sihamoni at Phnom Penh in 2005.

Discussing ORF research projects in New Delhi in 2005. ORF President R.K. Mishra is also seen.

With Bhutan's second Queen HM Tshering Pem Wangchuk at the Royal residences in Thimphu in 2006.

In front of the Punakha Dzong (Monastery), Bhutan in 2006.

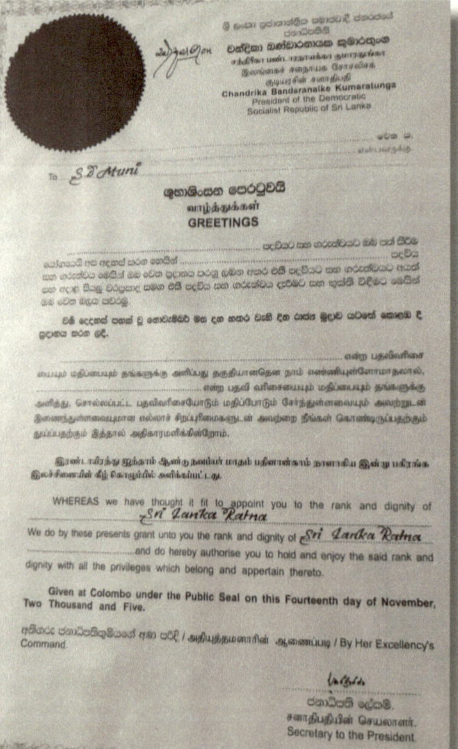

C.R. Jayasinghe, High Commissioner of Sri Lanka to India, presents the 'Sri Lanka Ratna', a national honour of Sri Lanka for foreigners or non-nationals, to the author at his JNU residence in New Delhi in 2006.

(Left): The 'Sri Lanka Ratna' Certificate.

3

Nepal: Mainstreaming of the Maoists

MY INFORMAL ASSOCIATION with the Observer Research Foundation (ORF) in late 2002 started with writing a paper on the Maoist insurgency in Nepal. Politics in Nepal had been going through radical developments since 1995. In June 2001, in the palace massacre, the entire family of King Birendra was eliminated. To fill up the vacant throne, Gyanendra was crowned as new King. No proper and credible investigations took place to find out the culprits of the massacre. The blame for killing the members of the royal family was put on Crown Prince Dipendra. The then Prime Minister G.P. Koirala called it an accident, but Maoist leaders like Baburam Bhattarai described it as a political conspiracy involving foreign intelligence agencies of India and the US. In subsequent Nepali writings on the subject, King Gyanendra and his son Prince Paras have also been suspected of being behind the tragic event.

Since 1995, the Maoist uprising had also been gaining momentum. King Birendra's efforts to find a negotiated solution to the insurgency did not succeed. After taking over, King Gyanendra initially tried to co-opt the Maoists but failing in this effort, wanted to deal with them strongly. He blamed the government headed then by Sher Bahadur Deuba, as incompetent in containing the insurgency and dismissed it. He also dissolved the Parliament and started governing through handpicked prime ministers. India was generally indifferent and/or adhocist in its responses to these developments. It was extending its support to the King to let him handle the situation in a manner he thought fit. Keeping these developments in mind, I wrote in my paper, published as a small booklet in 2003:[1]

> India needs to get engaged with the ongoing peace process and help Nepal take a direction towards reinforcing democratic forces and institutions reflecting aspirations of the ordinary Nepalese. India cannot meaningfully get engaged with the peace process unless it gets constructively engaged with the Maoists. India's image in Nepal today is that it is an ally and supporter of monarchy. India needs to bring the Maoists and the political parties together which in the process, will also moderate the Maoists' extremist stance and use of violent methods. It is this combination of the mainstream political parties and the Maoists which can contain the monarchy's powers, help India emerge as a people-friendly neighbour and reduce the excessive influence and strategic presence of the Western powers. (pp. 66-67 of the book)

I was, however, quite convinced that India will not take this line. India had officially, and repeatedly, stated its two-pillar theory, of supporting both the monarchy and the mainstream political parties. It was not realising the inherent contradiction and seriousness of conflict between these two pillars. How can the structure of a policy

---

1 The paper was published as a small booklet by Rupa & Co. in 2003, entitled 'Maoist Insurgency in Nepal: The Challenge and the Response'.

be sustained when its main pillars are at cross purposes with each other? I discussed this policy line with M.K. Rasgotra in the ORF but he took a position in favour of monarchy in the interest of stability in Nepal. He and Vice Admiral K.K. Nayyar, another member of the ORF Governing Board, had been to Nepal where they met the King. While my paper was being published as a book, I visited Nepal to participate in a conference. I took the opportunity to meet India's then ambassador in Kathmandu, Shyam Saran, and presented a copy of my unpublished paper. 'What is your recommendation?,' he asked. I stated the thrust of the above quoted para to him and requested him to ask the government in Delhi to consider this approach. His response was: 'No, no, I am not going to do anything like this. My brief is to extract as much concessions as possible from the King when he is under pressure. I have asked the King to let India open a consulate in Birganj and he is going to grant this to us.'

This disappointed me. I was hoping against hope that someone in the MEA will have a look at this paper when published, and consider this option for some action. This did not happen. The only acknowledgement that I got was from Nancy Powell, then National Intelligence Officer for South Asia in the National Intelligence Council of the United States of America. She was on a visit to India in 2006 and came to IDSA. There she asked me if I had written that policy option at the behest of MEA. She refused to accept my firm denial. Nancy Powell served as the US Ambassador to Nepal during 2007-2009 and also to India, during 2012-2014. I shall come back to her again later.

In late 2003, Bamdev Chhetri, a Nepali national working in JNU library and known to me, visited my home one day. He said Dr Baburam Bhattarai, who was then Maoist second in-command, was in town and wanted to meet me urgently. He said that Baburam would not be able to come to JNU, because he is operating underground, so I will be taken to him tomorrow, whenever it is convenient to me.

The next morning, he took me to a government employees' housing complex in Moti Bagh area of New Delhi. In a small two-room flat on the second floor, Baburam was staying as a guest of a Nepali citizen working in India. We met warmly after a long gap of more than a decade. After exchanging pleasantries, Baburam said that he had read my comments in the *Outlook* magazine, published a couple of weeks back, about Indo-US relations warming up, with continuing differences on the situation in Nepal. He was sent by his party to assess the situation in India because if India and the US narrow their differences on Nepal, 'both of them may agree to support the King in crushing our movement.' He asked for my help in exploring the possibility of contacting Indian policymakers so as to explain to them that the Maoists were not terrorists, as then External Affairs Minister Jaswant Singh had labelled them during his August 2001 visit to Nepal.

Baburam's explanation of Maoist activities indicated that they could lay down their arms and were willing to join hands with Nepal's mainstream parties to change the system in favour of democratic functioning. I did not know how to respond to him. There was nothing that I could offer instantaneously. Influencing the official policy in India was a herculean task for me. I said: 'Give me some time, I shall think about it.' With the promise to meet again, I left.

After coming home, I seriously thought over the meeting and came to the conclusion that if the Maoists sincerely want to join the mainstream national politics and lay down arms, they must be helped. That would be in the interests of both India and Nepal. I had argued on the same lines in my ORF book. However, I was not sure if the Maoists were really prepared to lay down arms and if anyone in the Indian establishment would be prepared to meet them and support their proposition.

Within a week of this meeting, Baburam suddenly came home one day unannounced. He wanted my help in meeting Sitaram

Yechury and D.P. Tripathi. Both were in active politics and had access to leaders in India's political establishment. Sitaram Yechury was second in-command in the CPI-M party and Tripathi was one of the secretaries in the Nationalist Congress Party headed by Sharad Pawar. Tripathi also had extensive links with his former party, the Indian National Congress. I said: 'Baburam, you have studied with them in the School of Social Sciences. They should meet you easily. I have had only a limited contact with them for being in the SIS.' Baburam said he had been trying but they are not meeting him. In his presence, I called both Yechury and Tripathi one by one, but both expressed their inability to meet Baburam as 'this was a sensitive matter'. I promised Baburam that I shall try and explore other possibilities, but for that he must have patience.

In the following days, I broached the matter with the ORF president R.K. Mishra. He sounded sympathetic to the proposal, and said he would consult Pranab Mukherjee, a senior Congress leader. After three to four days, Mishra conveyed to me that Pranab Mukherjee sought a written commitment from the Maoists, ensuring that their actions would not jeopardize India's core interests in Nepal. He referred particularly to the Maoists' campaign for revising the 1950 Treaty and the Gurkha recruitment agreement. Baburam's response was that these demands were not invented by the Maoists; they had been longstanding issues reiterated by various political forces in Nepal, including the King. After consulting with his leader, Pushpa Kamal Dahal, alias 'Prachanda', and other associates, Baburam provided the letter requested by Pranab Mukherjee. I passed on this letter to R.K. Mishra, but there was no response for weeks. When I enquired, Mishra mentioned the possibility of Pranab Mukherjee having second thoughts.

Then I requested former Prime Minister I.K. Gujral. He agreed to meet Baburam and Prachanda and also fixed a date and time for the meeting. But hours before the scheduled time of meeting,

Gujral's office called me to cancel the meeting. I suspected that he must have consulted persons like M.K. Rasgotra and K.V. Rajan (India's former ambassadors in Nepal), and they might have advised him not to meet the Maoists.

It was a very frustrating experience since nothing was working out. In desperation, I went to Brajesh Mishra in the PMO to request if the Maoists could be helped as they were willing to join the mainstream. He asked me, 'What do they really want?' I said, 'They want to remove monarchy, change the system and join the mainstream Nepal politics.' On the question of monarchy, Mishra reacted very sharply, got up from his seat and said, 'This is not possible. I have nothing more to talk on this issue.' I pleaded with him to calm down, sit down and answer my one question, after which, I said I would leave. My question was: 'What has the King done to promote India's national interests? Is he not inviting China, Pakistan and Western powers to counter India in Nepal?' In response, after a pause, he sat down and said, 'Will they put in writing that they will not do anything that harms India's interests in Nepal?' The same commitment had been asked for by Pranab Mukherjee, so I said, 'Yes they will do so.' I was then asked to bring such a letter. After a couple of days, I got such a letter and personally handed it over to Brajesh Mishra. He warned me not to talk about this to any one, and if I did, he would publicly deny this. I promised to respect his confidentiality as long as he was in power.

A few weeks later, during an official lunch for a foreign dignitary by the Prime Minister at Hyderabad House, I had the opportunity to meet Prime Minister Atal Bihari Vajpayee. On such occasions, guests are introduced to the visiting dignitary before settling down for lunch. As I was making my way to the main hall for lunch, Prime Minister Vajpayee gestured for me to come over. He said, 'Muni ji, we have got your message on Nepal. Will do something.' I did not hear from Mishra about the government's response to the Maoists' letter for a long time after that. A couple of months later, Baburam told me that the intelligence surveillance on Maoists in India had been relaxed and they could now move more freely than earlier. He speculated that this development might be attributed to the letter they provided to Mishra. After the National Democratic Alliance (NDA) led by Vajpayee lost power in the 2004 elections, Mishra also joined ORF. I collaborated with him on the India-China Conference organised by ORF in Kolkata and inaugurated by Minister of External Affairs Pranab Mukherjee. In 2007, I obtained Mishra's permission to reference our discussions on the Maoists' agenda from 2003 in my future research writings.

In May 2004, the NDA government changed and the United Progressive Alliance (UPA), led by the Congress Party's Dr Manmohan Singh assumed power. The Maoists' demand to establish contacts with India's political leaders and policymakers continued. I was attending a conference on SAARC in Chandigarh organised by Rashpal Malhotra of the Centre for Research in Rural and Industrial Development (CRRID). Prime Minister Manmohan Singh inaugurated this conference. After the inaugural function, at the tea break, when I met him, he said: 'Professor, I must sit with you to understand Nepal.' I said, 'Sir I am honoured, and am at your beck and call. Please let me know your convenience.' He said his office will get in touch with me in New Delhi. But I received no call from the PMO for months. It seems someone in the PMO advised the Prime Minister not to see me.

In my informal discussions with Ranjit Rae, then Joint Secretary in charge of Nepal, I requested him to organise a Maoists' meeting with Natwar Singh, the new External Affairs Minister. His answer was, 'This is impossible.' I also met Shyam Saran, then Foreign Secretary, and requested him to meet the Maoists and listen to them. The government could always refuse to accept anything that they ask for. He said: 'How is it possible for me to meet them?' I offered to organise such a meeting at my residence or some other place, if he approved. He said he will explore his own sources and mechanisms if he decides to meet the Maoists. Perhaps the contacts were established between Shyam Saran and the Maoists in some way later, but I am not sure about that. I then tried Prakash Karat, Secretary General of CPI-M. Karat was a former JNU student in my South Asia Centre. I explained to him that the Maoists were keen on entering the mainstream politics and laying down arms, but no politician in India was willing to listen to their side of the story. Karat agreed to meet them, and the meeting took place in his office. Karat's office was under constant watch by India's intelligence agencies.

Within a couple of days of the meeting between Maoist leaders and Prakash Karat, it was flashed in the media by a Dubai-based Indian journalist who, I learnt later, was close to M.K. Narayanan, Adviser to the Prime Minister on intelligence affairs. The idea in exposing this meeting was perhaps to discredit the CPI-M, an ally in the UPA government, by blaming them for their alleged links with Nepal's Left extremists like the Nepal Maoists. There were continuing tensions between the Congress and the CPI-M within the ruling alliance. Reacting to the press report on the meeting, Prakash Karat called me to say that he will deny it publicly. I told him to do whatever he thought appropriate.

My contacts with the Maoists continued. Baburam introduced me to Prachanda, and both of them used to come home for discussions. Prachanda also came with his wife, the late (Mrs) Sita Dahal, to our residence in JNU for dinner a couple of times. In my long discussions with the Maoist duo, it became clear that the Maoists had come to realise that there was no final military solution to their 'Peoples' War'. They were sure that even if they win against the Royal Nepal Army (RNA) at the national level and force the King to surrender, neither would the other political parties, nor the international community, including India and the US, allow them to retain power in Nepal for long. Therefore, they were looking for cooperation with the mainstream parties and joining the democratic stream of Nepali politics. Their minimum demands were: (i) removal of Monarchy, (ii) election of a Constituent Assembly and (iii) adoption of a new Constitution prepared by a freely elected Constituent Assembly (CA) for a new people-oriented polity. The other Maoist leaders whom I met in New Delhi periodically were Krishna Bahadur Mahara, Narayan Kaji Shrestha, Ram Karki and Suresh Ale Magar.

During these meetings with the Maoists, I received anonymous calls twice, asking me to keep away from Nepal Maoists otherwise I may be detained under India's draconian Prevention of Terrorism Act (POTA). I never knew who the callers were, but suspected them to be from India's Intelligence Bureau (IB). I ignored these calls in the belief that I was doing something in India's national interest. One of the influential Nepali Congress leaders and a friend, Sagar Shumsher Rana, who had close family links with the senior RNA officers, told me years later that in the RNA's intelligence assessment, a good deal of the Maoists' strategy was finalised in consultation with me.

Lack of intelligence of the official intelligence agencies, be it in India or Nepal, was indeed amazing. The information regarding my contacts with the Maoists had also reached Dr Karan Singh, who was the Chancellor of JNU. He called me one day to his residence and asked me over a cup of tea: 'Tell me Professor Muni, what is happening in my *sasural* (in-laws place).' I said: 'Sir, you would know better. I only want Nepal to be peaceful, stable and democratic.' He heard me very kindly on my assessment of the Maoists' efforts to join the mainstream and the evolving situation in Nepal where King Gyanendra was not prepared for any compromise with the political parties. He did not react to my views.

Jan Andolan II

After the dissolution of Parliament by the King in October 2002, the Nepali Congress faction led by Girija Babu established contacts with the Maoists. Girija Babu visited India frequently for this purpose. I was in contact with Girija Babu, who used to stay at the Hotel Ambassador, near New Delhi's popular Khan Market.

Efforts were to forge a United Front against the monarchy between the Maoists and the Nepali Congress. The CPN (UML) was still hesitating in its attitude towards the King, and one of its leaders, Madhav Kumar Nepal, even offered himself as a candidate for the prime minister's position when King Gyanendra invited applications for that position. But they soon got disillusioned with the King and joined the Nepali Congress in forging a United Front for the restoration of Parliament. Some of their leaders also started visiting India. Other smaller parties of Nepal also joined in these efforts of forging an anti-King United Front. All this underlined the desperate nature of these contacts and multi-level talks because the political situation in Nepal had turned frustrating due to the obstinacy and dictatorship of the King. Many of the political groups like the Nepali Congress faction led by Deuba and the UML, that were softer towards the King initially, started drifting away from him and moved towards the idea of a United Front with the Maoists.

The situation turned into a crisis when in February 2005, King Gyanendra staged a coup. He terminated even his pliant prime minister and took control of power himself directly. He detained all the political leaders and imposed emergency. He also doubled the strength of RNA and unleashed it against the Maoists as well as political parties. It may be recalled that King Birendra had not allowed the use of army against the Maoists. King Gyanendra's use of army against the Maoists, his public claim to finish the Maoist insurgency in six months and repression against the political parties facilitated the political parties getting together with the Maoists. It escalated violence in Nepal as a result of clashes between the Maoists and the RNA. The King's drastic moves also alienated him from the international community.

There were various points of contact between the mainstream political parties and the Maoists. All the major parties had come together in a new formation of Seven Party Alliance (SPA) for negotiating with the Maoists and fighting the King's autocracy. The principal negotiations for forging a United Front were carried out between the Nepali Congress (NC) of G.P. Koirala group and the Maoists. The SPA, including the CPM (UML), generally followed Girija Babu's lead. The negotiations between the NC-led SPA and the Maoists were protracted and difficult as there was strong lingering trust deficit between them

There were serious differences on some of the critical issues like the complete abolition of monarchy, accountability for the violence due to the Maoists' 'People's War' and the nature of systemic changes envisaged with the restoration of democracy. Eventually, the negotiations succeeded in November 2005 with the signing of a 12-Point Agreement between the Maoists and the SPA. This Agreement (Attached as Annexure) was considerably facilitated by India as we shall see later. In this agreement, there was a clear attempt on both the sides to accommodate core concerns of either side. They accepted that absolute monarchy that King Gyanendra wanted to re-establish must end. For this, they agreed to launch a joint peoples' movement (Jan Andolan II). They refused to participate in the local elections announced by the King.

The Maoists accepted multiparty system and its necessary values like civil liberties and human rights. However, on the post-absolute monarchy system, disagreement between the two sides continued. The SPA insisted on the restoration of the dissolved Parliament where the Nepali Congress had majority and G.P. Koirala was the

Prime Minister. The Maoists' preference was for a freely elected Constituent Assembly to frame a new Constitution under an independent interim government. They both stated their positions in the Agreement (para 2) and agreed to continue dialogue to resolve the differences.

In a small way, I was also active in the process of working out this 12-point mutual understanding between the Maoists and the SPA. Both Baburam and Prachanda were in regular touch with me, as they were with many other interlocutors. From the Nepali Congress side, Dr Shekhar Koirala and Krishna Prasad Sitaula were in regular contact. I met Bam Dev Gautam of the Communist Party of Nepal (UML) just once at my residence. I also occasionally met Girija Babu in conveying the Maoists' messages and bringing back his reactions to them to be worked upon.

There was a strong resistance from the SPA side in appearing in the company of Maoists publicly. Girija Babu refused to share any public platform with the Maoists, but the Maoists were keen to appear as equal partners of the SPA. A solution to this problem was found in the simultaneous announcement of mutually agreed decisions both by SPA and the Maoists. This gave at least a semblance of the two sides working together in public perception. The King refused to change his line even after announcement of the 12-Point Agreement. Maoists and the SPA did not participate in the local bodies' elections conducted under the King's command so as to delegitimise these elections. Their stand was for the restoration of the Parliament dissolved by the King. There were serious difficulties in launching the 'Peoples' Movement' to remove 'absolutist monarchy' as agreed under the 12 Points. The SPA leadership lacked confidence in mobilising people to protest against the King. They sought assurance that the Maoists would handle this mobilisation but were unsure whether the Maoists could achieve it on the agreed-upon date of 6 April 2006. I had to confirm at least three times from the Maoists that they were confident of doing so, and then convey this to Girija Babu through Shekhar and Sitaula. Mobilisation of more than a hundred thousand people on the agreed-upon date on Kathmandu's streets was possible primarily due to the Maoists' efforts. This mobilisation was sustained for nearly two weeks, during which the SPA also brought its cadre on the streets, to force the King to yield.

India's role was critical in opposing the King's autocratic moves and forcing him to accept the demands of the SPA and Maoists for democratisation. This role has been discussed and analysed elsewhere from different perspectives.[2] India strongly disapproved of the King's move to take direct control of power and continuously persuaded him to reverse his action. Prime Minister Dr Manmohan Singh, on three different occasions in one-on-one discussions, asked King Gyanendra to accommodate the mainstream parties and restore democratic functioning. The King would agree to do so every time, but would not act on this advice.

Frustrated by the King's obstinacy, India helped in the finalisation of the 12-Point Agreement. Foreign Secretary Shyam Saran and the then R&AW chief P.K. Hormis Tharakan helped soften India's attitude towards the mainstreaming of the Maoists and the conclusion of the 12-Point Agreement. Resistance to the accommodation of Maoists had come from M.K. Narayanan, who had succeeded J.N. Dixit as India's National Security Adviser, and Pranab Mukherjee, who assumed the charge of India's Defence Minister. In April 2006, the situation in Nepal became volatile with

---

2 For my take on this role, see, S.D. Muni, 'Bringing the Maoists Down from the Hills: India's Role' in Sebastian von Einsiedel, David M. Malone and Suman Pradhan (Eds), *Nepal in Transition: From People's War to Fragile Peace* (New Delhi: Cambridge University Press, 2012) pp. 313-331. Also see books by Prashant Jha, Sudhir Sharma, and Hisila Yami.

massive protest demonstrations against the King and refusal on his part to yield.

Fearing outbreak of massive violence, India directly intervened, sending its special envoy, Dr Karan Singh, assisted by Foreign Secretary Shyam Saran, to persuade the King to yield. India distanced itself from the King and compromised on its two-pillar policy primarily because the King was not executing his promises to India on restoring the parliamentary system and joining hands with the mainstream parties. He was insistent on his military approach to deal with the Maoists, which in India's assessment was a futile and undesirable attempt. For dealing militarily with the Maoists, the King was also collecting arms from China and Western sources which were a red herring to India.

Dr Karan Singh was chosen by India as a Special Envoy to persuade the King as a last attempt, in view of his close relationship with Nepal's Royal family. He had his one-on-one meeting with the King, while Shyam Saran had a separate one-on-one meeting with Nepal's then army chief, Gen. Pyar Jung Thapa. We learnt through different sources that Dr Singh, while persuading the King to give up direct rule and restore the dissolved Parliament, probably, gave assurances to the King that India will not support complete abolition of monarchy as demanded by the Maoists.

Later, I also learnt through Shyam Saran that he had a difficult time persuading Gen. Thapa to go and convince the King that military action against the 'Peoples' Movement' was not the solution and will not be allowed. It was only after this message that the King conceded what Dr Singh was asking for. He issued a half-hearted proclamation on 21 April 2006 to restore Parliament and for a new prime minister to be appointed by him. This was rejected by the SPA, which warned of stepping up their agitation and demonstration within three days if the King did not revise his position. The 'Peoples' Movement' had already resulted in some violence and more violence was feared if the agitation was to be prolonged and enhanced. This forced the King to issue another proclamation on 24 April, 2006 which restored the Parliament without any caveats and reinstated G.P. Koirala as the Prime Minister. All the political parties heartily praised the role played by India in the success of their movement.

I was also active, in different ways, in opposing the King's move and supporting the 'Peoples' Movement' led by the Maoists and the SPA. I spoke at several conferences and meetings, wrote opinion pieces in Indian newspapers and appeared on various TV news channels to speak in favour of the 'Peoples' Movement'. In ORF we organised a meeting which was participated by M.K. Rasgotra and Professor Lok Raj Baral (who was on a short visit to India) soon after the King's takeover in February 2005. Professor Baral was detained and harassed on his return to Nepal for his statement at the ORF meeting.

The Nepal Embassy in New Delhi was also active in propagating the legitimacy of the King's coup and securing public support for him. I participated in two conferences organised by them, one at the India International Centre (IIC) and another at the Constitution Club. In the IIC meeting, the King's Foreign Minister Ramesh Nath Pandey's son, Nishchal Nath Pandey, who was also the Director of Nepal's Foreign Service Institute, vigorously pleaded that the King would be able to finish the Maoist insurgency within six months with an enlarged and well-equipped RNA. I strongly rebutted his arguments by referring to the past record of RNA in dealing with the Maoists. In the Constitution Club meeting, I said that the best way for the King to resolve Nepal's political crisis was not through direct rule but abdication of his throne. If he wants to be politically relevant and active in the years to come, he should form his own political party, and contest elections. I was confident that he will win popular support as many old princely rulers had done in India.

The King had detained all the major political party leaders when he took direct control of the government. Girija Babu called me from his house arrest in Kathmandu asking me to do something in Delhi to get him released. I was in Mumbai for my periodic lecture at the Naval War College. I telephoned my contacts in MEA requesting them to extend whatever help they could. On my return from Mumbai, I was invited to a closed-door consultation meeting in MEA called by Foreign Minister Natwar Singh. Among other invitees were India's former Ambassadors to Nepal, M.K. Rasgotra, K.V. Rajan and Arvind Deo. Issue on the table was to continue or not the pipeline of arms supplies to the King after his takeover. While most of the other participants were in favour of continuing the supplies, I and Arvind Deo strongly opposed it. I submitted that the King will use these arms against his own people and for suppressing democratic movement. In support of my argument, I narrated the incident of the 1976 lunch of Mrs Gandhi for then Prince Gyanendra. I did that in the hope that Mrs Gandhi's reference, suspecting the King's democratic pretentions, may be found more persuasive by Natwar Singh. The decision taken a few days later by Government of India was to stop the supplies and force the King to make-up with the mainstream political parties.

During my studies on Nepal, I had hardly any contacts with the Royal Palace. I had known Kumar Khadga Bikram Shah, the son-in-law of the royal family, in his capacity as the Executive Director of the Centre for Nepal and Asian Studies (CNAS), Tribhuvan University. I participated in the international seminar on South Asian Security organised by the Centre in 1985. I met him every time I went to Kathmandu after that in his CNAS office but never discussed Nepali politics with him. Kumar Khadga Bikram Shah, unfortunately, got killed in the royal massacre of 2001.

In the pursuance of my Nepal studies, on a couple of occasions, I had interviewed the then personal secretary to King Birendra, Chiran

Shumshere Thapa. In June 2002, King Gyanendra visited India to garner support for his regime. The Nepal Embassy in New Delhi organised a reception for him. I met the King in that reception and asked him if he remembered my meeting him at Mrs Gandhi's lunch in 1976. He complained that I have not been meeting him during my Kathmandu visits. I promised to do so next time. I did call the palace secretariat on my next visit to Kathmandu and requested for an audience with the King, giving reference to the exchange of words with His Majesty in New Delhi. The office assured me that they will get back to me, but that never happened.

On another visit to Kathmandu after the King's direct rule, former foreign minister Ramesh Nath Pandey invited me for lunch at his residence. He described to me in detail how he succeeded in securing arms both from a reluctant India and a responsive China to help the King fight the Maoist insurgency. Details of his diplomatic efforts have been now recorded in his memoir, *Kootniti Ra Rajniti* (*Diplomacy and Politics*, Shangri La Books, Kathmandu, 2015). While leaving after lunch and discussions, he asked me for a favour saying, 'Please convey a message to Foreign Minister Natwar Singh that the King will happily accommodate all of India's economic and security concerns in return for support to his domestic political actions.' I personally conveyed this message as desired.

One Dr Asarfi Shah used to meet me both in Kathmandu and New Delhi to seek my support for the King. Once in Kathmandu, he organised a special worship (a*bhishek*) by me at the Lord Pashupatinath Temple. During a meeting in my IDSA office, Dr Shah once bragged that the Indian establishment, under the Narendra Modi regime, had assured the King that monarchy and Hinduism represent two faces of the same coin that India would support in Nepal. Questioning the need for additional support, I asked Dr Shah, 'If that is the case, then why does the King need support from someone like me?' It is, however, not in my DNA to support autocratic monarchy. I made this stance clear to Dr Shah on every occasion.

In 2017, a retired R&AW officer, whom I knew for many years because of our common Rajasthani origin, invited me for lunch at the Delhi Gymkhana Club. He conveyed that Uttar Pradesh Chief Minister Yogi Adityanath was keen to get monarchy restored in Nepal and suggested that I support these efforts. I firmly communicated that he had approached the wrong person for a wrong cause.

Writing a New Constitution

Nepal has had a difficult political evolution after the success of Jan Andolan II. The only thing that moved fast was the abolition of monarchy. The reinstated Parliament in its first major decision in May 2006, stripped the King of all his powers and made the prime minister as the executive head for all practical purposes. The King was turned into a figurehead.

In December 2007, the SPA and the Maoists decided to abolish monarchy completely when the first Constituent Assembly (CA) assumed office. Nepal had its first CA elected in May 2008. In its very first decision, the CA abolished monarchy and established a secular, inclusive, republican and democratic state in Nepal. I shifted to Singapore in January 2008 to join the Institute of South Asian Studies (ISAS), National University of Singapore. I accepted the offer to join ISAS as Senior Visiting Fellow for six months only, but continued there for the next six years as Visiting Research Professor, on the insistence of its Chairman Ambassador Gopinath Pillai.

My interest in Nepal remained active. While staying in Singapore as well as during my frequent visits to India and Nepal, I closely followed the political developments in Nepal. I also invited Dr Baburam Bhattarai to talk at the ISAS under a project related to left extremism in South Asia. Later he became Nepal's Prime Minister. I also met Girija Babu and Prachanda (for the treatment of his wife) in Singapore when they came for medical help. In the Singapore hospital, Girija Babu also asked me to help and support his daughter Sujata when he is gone.

Days before the declaration of the 2008 CA election results, I was in New Delhi. Nancy Powell, the US Ambassador in Nepal, was also visiting New Delhi, and she invited some of India's Nepal observers for dinner at Shangri-La hotel, presumably to gather insights into Indian perspectives on the Nepal elections. Among the invitees, besides myself, were seven or eight others, including Ambassador K.V. Rajan and Maj. Gen. Ashok Mehta.

She asked each of us about our assessment for the coming election results. Every response indicated that the Maoists would likely secure a poor third position, with the Nepali Congress expected to lead. I learnt through my friends both in New Delhi and Kathmandu that the Indian and US embassies in Kathmandu, relying on their intelligence surveys, shared this anticipation. The media in Nepal was also predicting a comfortable victory for the Nepali Congress. However, my analysis was very different. When Ambassador Powell enquired about my assessment after hearing from the others, I asserted that the Maoists would emerge as the leading party, followed by the Nepali Congress and the UML. Expressing surprise, Ambassador Powell remarked, 'How is that possible? Their violence and inhuman activities, including kidnappings, violent disruptions and ransoms have been fully exposed during the campaign. People are very angry with their acts and ideology.'

In response, I emphasised that the Maoists possessed a well-organized structure and superior human capacity to mobilise people. People's involvement in Jan Andolan II was primarily driven by grassroots efforts and this support played a significant role in favour of the Maoists. I highlighted that their strategy of kidnapping and seeking ransom from rich factory owners and managers, while unsettling the wealthy elite, had a different impact on the ordinary workers. Instead of alienating them, it tended to make the workers sympathetic towards the Maoists. I also pointed out that media reports and public perceptions of the erosion of Maoists' influence in urban areas in Nepal were often planted by various foreign intelligence agencies, resulting in highly exaggerated assessments. The estimates of Maoists' support were also downplayed. These agencies normally say what their immediate superiors in the embassies and respective governments want to hear. I emphasised that the people in Nepal were not enthusiastic about the old established political parties and might, at least temporarily, opt for the Maoists if they could deliver on their promises.

Despite Ambassador Powell dismissing this argument as my personal bias, the election results that came two-three days later validated my assessment. The Maoists secured 96 seats under the first-past-the-post system. Their rivals, the NC and the UML secured 35 and 32 seats, respectively. This gave the Maoists a further advantage in claiming more seats under the proportional representation system. In total, they had more seats than those of the NC, UML and the Terai-based parties put together. This CA was tasked with delivering a new Constitution within two years and also serve as an interim parliament.

Constitution-making posed a formidable challenge for the first CA. Sharp political differences surfaced among the signatories of the 12-Point Agreement, particularly regarding various post-Jan Andolan II issues. The first CA failed to deliver a new Constitution even after two extensions. The second CA was elected in January 2014, with a different political composition. The Nepali Congress was the dominant party in the second CA, followed by UML. Maoists were a poor third. Significant differences persisted among the mainstream parties, the Maoists and the Terai-based parties.

There were two key issues where the Indian establishment was directly involved, namely, (i) the accommodation of Madhesi's (Terai-based people) rights and (ii) the restoration of the Hindu character of the State. Soon after assuming power, Prime Minister Modi announced his 'Neighbourhood First' policy and paid a state visit to Nepal in August 2014. In his most impressive and well-applauded address to the CA, Modi pledged to support Nepal's development needs and urged the Nepalese to craft a Constitution resembling a bouquet of different flowers that accommodates the diverse aspirations of its people, referring to the status and rights of Terai-based Madhesi people.

There was strong resistance from the dominant Khas-Arya leaders of the mainstream parties on the Madhesi issue. India sought to mellow down this resistance. By inviting prominent Nepali leaders like Sher Bahadur Deuba of the Nepali Congress, Prachanda of the Maoist Centre and Madhav Nepal of CPN (UML), India aimed to persuade them to be more accommodating of the Madhesi demands. Informally, during their meetings with various ministers and senior BJP leaders, the visiting Nepali leaders were sounded for their views on the idea of a Hindu and monarchical state in Nepal.

I met Deuba in New Delhi during his visit. During Prachanda's visit, I happened to be in Sri Lanka. He reached out, and we had a lengthy conversation. Both leaders shared with me the gist of their discussions in New Delhi. They assured the Indian leaders that they would be sympathetic to Madhesi and Indian concerns. There was, however, no specific commitment on details of the demands. When they sought my advice on how to respond to the Indian leaders' inclination toward a Hindu state, I suggested, 'Ask them to establish a Hindu state in India first.'

Reluctance to concede all the Madhesi demands was widespread among the mainstream parties at various levels. I could feel that in my discussions with various political shades of the Nepali leaders, particularly the CPN (UML). I recall Prime Minister Modi's second visit to Nepal for the SAARC Summit in November 2014, where his statement asking for a consensus rather than a majoritarian Constitution was strongly and publicly opposed by the second tier of UML and NC leaders.

Once, I had a rather animated discussion lasting almost two hours with Bam Dev Gautam of the CPN (UML) in Kathmandu, where he vehemently opposed making any concessions to the Madhesis. The Constitution, adopted in September 2015, did not entirely meet the Madhesi demands. There was also steamrolling of some of the sensitive clauses by the ruling parties, by voting for them without any discussion whatsoever, on the basis of the party whip.

India refused to endorse the Constitution and intervened directly to get the Madhesi concerns accommodated in the Constitution. Prime Minister Modi sent his then Foreign Secretary Dr S. Jaishankar to Kathmandu as his Special Envoy. He was mandated to get the signing of the Constitution by the President delayed for some time so that a suitable amendment to meet the Madhesi demands could be incorporated. This was not acceptable to the Nepali leaders since the Constitution had already been adopted by the second CA. India reacted strongly.

After refusing to endorse the new Constitution, India decided to impose an undeclared economic blockade for nearly five months. As a result, partial demands of the Madhesi rights were incorporated and for the remaining demands, Madhes leaders were urged to find common ground with the mainstream parties.

The Madhes issue has lingered in Nepali politics for a long time. Even during King Mahendra's era, Gajendra Narayan Singh had championed the Madhesi rights through his Sadbhawana Party. The Madhes issue gained prominence in the context of the Maoist movement because the Maoists had mobilised both Madhesis and Janjatis (Tribal groups), and the Madhesis, in turn, lent support to the Maoists.

The Government of India had generally voiced a strategic and calculated support for the Madhes issue. Madhesi demands were legitimate and Madhes represented a strong pro-India constituency in Nepali politics. However, no government in New Delhi could afford to alienate the dominant Khas-Arya groups by excessively supporting Madhes. The Khas-Arya groups felt themselves as superior and treated Madhesi as the fifth columnists. India's support for the Madhesi cause certainly increased under the Modi regime, but it remained tactical rather than strategic. India was primarily concerned about the growing Maoist influence in Madhes, which was not in India's broader security interests. India also did not want Madhes to be completely alienated. In August 2010, India sent Shyam Saran as a special envoy to Kathmandu to prevent Madhes groups from supporting Prachanda for prime ministership for the second time. In my understanding, supporting the Madhesi cause was only one of the reasons behind India's interventionist and coercive diplomacy (blockade) towards Nepal.

There was another important reason which has often not been looked at by many analysts. The Nepali leadership personally offended the Indian leadership on two fronts. Firstly, during Prime Minister Modi's second visit to Nepal, he expressed a desire to address public meetings in the Terai region, which was turned down. Secondly, Nepal's new Constitution failed to remove the secular identity of the state.

During his second visit to Nepal in November 2014, Modi was eager to address public gatherings in Janakpur, Lumbini, and Muktinath. However, the Nepali side, citing 'security reasons,' did not allow this. The dominant Khas-Arya leaders did not want Modi to encourage Madhesi people in their demands for rights. Plans, including the distribution of cycles during the proposed public functions, had to be abandoned as a result. While Modi did not publicly express his displeasure, I am sure, it must have been communicated to the Nepali side through other channels.

On the second front, apart from the failure to accommodate Madhes aspirations in the Constitution, India's preference for the restoration of Hindu identity of the Nepali State in the Constitution was messed up by the Nepali leaders in working out a political compromise among themselves and their parties. In the final stages of Constitution-making, the top leaders of the three major parties—the NC, the Maoists and the UML—decided to maintain both 'Secular' and 'Sanatani' characters of the Nepali State in the new Constitution.

The UML, because of their proximity to the European Union, insisted on maintaining the 'secular' character in order to allow Christian missionaries from Europe, Korea, etc. to continue their religious 'conversion' campaigns. This stance, however, left the Hindu-oriented Indian establishment unhappy. The insertion of the 'Sanatani' character in the Article on the religious identity of Nepal was an attempt to accommodate Indian preferences, but it created an inherent contradiction for Indian leaders. The top leadership of the UML strongly resisted both Madhesi rights and the state's religious identity, causing the Indian leadership to feel more offended by the UML leadership than anyone else. In contrast, the NC and the Maoist leadership were perceived as more amenable to Indian concerns.

One strong indication of India's displeasure with the UML was evident in the prompting, persuading and supporting Sushil Koirala for prime ministership against K.P. Sharma Oli after the adoption of the Constitution. Despite a prior understanding between these two leaders on rotating the prime ministership, Sushil Koirala's attempt to contest against Oli violated that agreement. This not only created a rift between the UML and the NC, but also turned Oli, hitherto a long-time supporter of India, against India.

The sense of personal offence and clash of egos stemming from the denial of Modi's visit to Nepal Terai, indifference to Madhes demands, and a messy response to the religious identity of Nepali

State under the new Constitution created a very strong, imponderable and unexpressed context for India's stiff attitude towards Nepal. This was manifested in the form of economic coercion (blockade). Oli's strong push for political mobilisation of anti-Indian nationalism, and tilt towards China, on the lines resorted to by King Mahendra and King Birendra, may also be understood in the context of personal ego clashes. He succeeded in politically cashing it because the blockade affected Nepali people severely at all levels.

I clearly stated my disagreement with the blockade decision when informally sounded on it by India's strategic managers. I also explained the aspect of ego clashes to Arjun Karki, when he came to India in 2015 for lobbying as a part of Oli's back-channel effort to get the blockade eased. I told him to go back and ask Oli to massage hurt egos of Indian leaders and policymakers. Arjun Karki was Nepal's ambassador in the US appointed by Oli. We had known each other for a long time. We had discussions at the India International Centre over lunch. Arjun Karki must have approached many others also in pursuance of this mission. After his return to Kathmandu, Kamal Thapa, Nepal's deputy prime minister and home minister, came to India with a compromise proposal on the Constitution to partially accommodate Madhes demands.

It was this accommodation that finally led to some easing of the tensions between the two countries. A Madhesi delegation also visited India to ensure that all their demands be met in any proposed amendment to the new Constitution. This delegation, led by Mahanta Thakur, visited JNU for interaction with the students and faculty. I met them. They were to meet National Security Advisor Ajit Doval after their JNU meeting. They asked me for any suggestion for their talks with the NSA. I was very clear that Doval will ask them to compromise and accept only partial accommodation of their demands based on the formula brought by Kamal Thapa. There were four points in Kamal Thapa's proposal, namely: (i) constitutional amendment to change the provincial boundaries, (ii) accommodate Madhesi views in these boundary changes, (iii) boundary changes will be based on political consensus evolved within three months, and (iv) constitutional ambiguities regarding citizenship provisions to be addressed in the amendment. The Madhes leaders were not happy with this partial accommodation but had to accept it reluctantly in the hope that at some future junction, rest of their demands will be considered favourably.

Power-Sharing and Power Struggle

The broad national political consensus that mainstreamed the Maoists and abolished monarchy soon got fragmented. This gave place to a politics of conflicts and instability in a country that needed mutual cooperation and stability most. Nepal's political landscape has become so fragmented that at present, no party is without internal rivalries and no leader is fully acceptable to his party cadres.

The intensity of power struggle in Nepal has been so sharp and widespread as not to allow any power-sharing arrangements to last. Power struggle rages between, as well as within, all the political parties. I have closely experienced the lack of power-sharing between the NC and the Maoists and struggle for supremacy within the Maoists. Even when the King's excesses had forced the NC and the Maoist leadership to seek mutual accommodation with each other, a strong undercurrent of trust deficit remained between the two. It has been noted earlier that Girija Babu was not prepared to share the same public platform with Prachanda in the course of negotiating and finalising the 12-Point Agreement.

The roots of Girija Babu's distrust of the Communists and Maoists go back to the days of Jan Andolan I. In mobilising support against the Panchayat System, the NC troika of Ganesh Man Singh, K.P. Bhattarai and Girija Prasad Koirala played a crucial role. While Ganesh Man Singh and Bhattarai were in favour of joining hands with the Communists, Girija Babu had strong reservations. Sher Bahadur Deuba who rose in the NC with Girija Babu's support and encouragement, was more resilient and followed Ganesh Man Singh and Bhattarai's line. He has often been willing to work with anyone who could help him gain and retain power.

In addressing the Maoist People's War, Girija Babu fervently supported strong-arm measures. He ran into difficulties during his tenure as prime minister when differences arose with King Birendra regarding the use of RNA against the Maoists. King Birendra's reluctance to employ RNA prompted Girija Babu to establish the Special Armed Police Force for countering the Maoist insurgency. The disagreement over the use of RNA ultimately led to Girija Babu's resignation as prime minister in 2002.

The core alliance that drove the formulation of 12-Points and the Jan Andolan II was between the Maoists and the NC; between Girija Babu and Prachanda. This alliance started getting eroded and differences between them strengthened on many issues. Prominent among them were the questions of removing monarchy and establishing a Republic, management of Maoists' arms and security sector reforms, and elections proposed for November 2007 to be held on the basis of proportional representation.

Maoist threats in various forms and mediations by civil society groups and other stakeholders led Girija Babu and other parties to agree on declaration of a Republic in the very first session of the newly-elected CA. The Maoists also accepted arms management by agreeing to keep 3,000 weapons and 30,000 fighters in cantonments under the supervision of the UN. This paved the way for holding elections on the basis of proportional representation in 2008. The elections to the first CA delivered a shock to Girija Babu and his Nepali Congress besides many others in Nepal, India and the US. The Maoists had a clear lead over all other parties. This upset came to Girija Babu, who was confident of winning, like a lizard falling from nowhere onto his dinner plate.

He delayed handing over power to the Maoist leader Prachanda for more than three months. While the election results were declared in May 2008, Prachanda was elected as prime minister only on August 15, and he took the oath of office on 18 August 2008. In my two long discussions with Girija Babu on this delay, he cited the issues of the Maoists' violence and disruptions perpetrated by their youth wing (Young Communist League) and the Maoist fighters' (Peoples War soldiers) induction in RNA. At one juncture, he strongly snubbed me when I tried to explain the possible Maoist position on these issues, by saying: '*Aap ko kuch pata nahi hai Maoist yahan kya kya karte hain. Aap to Singapore aur Bharat mein ghoomtey rahtey hain. Hamein yahan Kathmandu mein unko bhugatana padta hai.*' (You do not know anything what Maoists keep doing here. You are roaming around in India and Singapore. We have to suffer them here in Kathmandu.) I could also sense that there was possible external pressure from India and the US behind the delayed power transfer to force the Maoists to concede on these points of disagreements before power could be transferred to them.

In my understanding, there was yet another important reason behind the clash between NC and the Maoists related to power-sharing and power struggle. It has been noted earlier that Girija Babu and his NC were never comfortable with the idea of sharing power with the Maoists. Despite the alliance between the SPA and the Maoists, it was as late as April 2007 that Maoists were inducted into the post-Jan Andolan II interim government of Nepal. Before doing that, the Maoists were forced to accept the process of their arms management.

It may be useful to keep in mind here that until the abolition of monarchy and its control of the armed forces, the Maoist arms management was not taken as a serious issue. Girija Babu viewed the presence of armed Maoist guerillas as a shield against the remote possibility of the King staging another coup with the help of the

RNA. Under the shock of the Maoists' electoral victory, the NC was keen on G.P. Koirala becoming president of the new republic. This was not acceptable to the Maoists under the fear that Koirala as president could be a serious constraint on their style of governance, in view of the pre-Jan Andolan II phase when as prime minister, Koirala had dealt strongly with the Maoists. The Maoists preferred a consensus based non-party president and proposed the name of Ram Raja Prasad Singh, a Madhesi and radical political activist. He had taught crude bomb-making to the Maoists during the Peoples' War. The NC and the other political parties were also adamant on not letting the Maoists have a president of their choice as that would concentrate all state powers in their hands.

I argued with Prachanda and Baburam to concede presidency to Girija Babu in the long-term interest of political stability and development in Nepal, but in vain. There was strong opposition to Girija Babu being made president within the rank and file of the Maoists. The breakdown of understanding between the NC and the Maoists was an important factor in ensuring political instability in Nepal. Girija Babu fought back to demonstrate his stronger grip over Nepali politics. He proposed Dr Ram Baran Yadav from the Nepali Congress for the presidential contest and secured his victory against the Maoist candidate. Prachanda later conceded, even publicly, that it was a serious mistake on his part not to accept G.P. Koirala as the President. I had very good personal relations with Ram Baran ji. He always hosted me for lunch or dinner during my Kathmandu visits and shared his unhappiness at the way the Maoists were conducting their politics and also at the internal rivalries and tensions within the Nepali Congress.

Another power struggle that I followed with interest was within the Maoists, between Prachanda and Baburam Bhattarai. I got an inkling of the conflict between the two for the first time when Ranjit Rae, Joint Secretary in charge of Nepal desk in the MEA, called me one afternoon, sometime in mid-2004, to ask if I knew Baburam's whereabouts.

I was told that there were serious differences between Baburam and Prachanda at the Phuntiwang meeting[3] of the Maoist Central Committee. This meeting decided to punish Baburam, his wife Hisila Yami and their associate Dina Nath Sharma for their anti-party activities and sabotage of the Peoples' War. All three leaders were arrested and there were rumours that they have either been killed or were to be killed soon. I had no idea about these developments. I seldom took initiative in reaching out to Baburam or Prachanda. I only responded whenever they called me. After Ranjit's message, I called Baburam but there was no response.

Throughout the Maoist movement and their 'Peoples' War', sharp ideological differences persisted between Mohan Baidya ('Kiran'), and Baburam ('Lal Dhwaj'). While Baidya stood for a military-based strategy for the success of their revolution, Baburam favoured collaboration with other political parties and India. Baidya and his supporters accused Baburam of being an Indian agent after some of his associates were arrested by the Indian police and handed over to King Gyanendra. I have discussed elsewhere that this arrest was possibly the result of a rivalry between India's intelligence agencies, namely R&AW and IB. Prachanda tactfully balanced between Baburam and Baidya, playing one against the other depending on the prevailing political context, thereby retaining his leadership through careful manoeuvres. Details of this ideologically oriented internal struggle for power from Baburam's point of view may be found in Hisila Yami's memoir cited here.

Weeks before Prachanda's first visit to India after assuming the office of prime minister in 2008, the National Security Council in India was preparing a profile of the visiting dignitary. Prachanda had

---

3 For details of Maoists' internal rivalries, see Hisila Yami, HISILA: From Revolutionary To First Lady (Gurugram: Penguin Books, 2021).

defied the long tradition of Nepali prime ministers undertaking their first foreign visit to India. He went to China first to participate in the concluding function of the Beijing Olympics. Ambassador Leela Ponappa, Deputy National Security Adviser, called me in Singapore to get my input on Prachanda's personality. I said: 'Prachanda is a highly motivated and ambitious power seeker. Beneath the ideological cover, he is a hardcore pragmatist and would cut a deal with anyone who will help him acquire and sustain power. He is very slippery also and may not stick to the deal until its full implementation if, at any point, he finds it going against his core interests.'

I was in Delhi to attend a family function when Prachanda's visit took place in September 2008. I visited him in Maurya ITDC Hotel on Sardar Patel Road. Briefing me on the course of his visit he said, one of the important sticking points in his talks with the Indian authorities was the integration of Peoples' War soldiers in the Nepal Army. I alerted him that he should agree on that specific figure for integration, and that specific process which he can honestly and efficiently implement. It did not happen. He agreed on a number, I think 4,000 plus, but did not carry out the process after his return to Kathmandu. This added to the trust deficit between Prachanda and the New Delhi establishment.

Prachanda lost his credibility in Nepal also on the question of the numbers of the 'Peoples' War' soldiers to be integrated in the Nepal Army. For quite some time, he had been playing with the numbers of the Maoist soldiers with the help and support from the UN Mission in Nepal (UNMIN), appointed by the UNSC in 2007 to help implement the Comprehensive Peace Agreement of 2006. However, once in 2009, while talking to his cadre, Prachanda had boasted that he succeeded in making others, including the UNMIN, accept 30,000 as the strength of the Maoist army while in reality he had only 8,000 soldiers. A video of this claim was leaked and became public causing considerable embarrassment to Prachanda. The UNMIN concluded its operations in 2011.

The issue of Maoist soldiers was eventually resolved in 2012, with Prachanda accepting the integration of around 1,500 of them into the Nepal Army. However, upon closer examination, I learnt that no more than 500 soldiers were ultimately integrated, as the majority opted for the financial compensation package. There was significant discontent among the ranks and file of the Maoists regarding Prachanda's handling of the integration issue.

The matter of security sector reforms landed Prachanda in a greater trouble. The army vehemently resisted the induction of Maoist soldiers, leading to retaliatory actions by Prachanda's Defence Minister Ram Bahadur Thapa, who blocked the promotion of senior army officers. The army also withdrew from the national games in protest against the participation of Maoists in those events.

The Maoist agenda for security sector reforms included a reduction in the strength of army. King Gyanendra, after taking over power in 2005, had doubled the strength of the army to counter the Maoist insurgency. The argument put forth was that, with the Maoists transitioning into mainstream democratic politics, the increased size of the army had become unnecessary. The conflict with the army over security sector reforms led Prachanda's government to make the decision to sack the then Army Chief General Rookmangud Katawal. However, with the support of other political parties, India and the US, President Ram Baran Yadav turned down this decision. In protest against the President's decision, Prachanda resigned as prime minister on 4 May 2009.

I was in Singapore. Prachanda called me and we discussed the issue. My opinion was that his decision was not proper. I said: 'You could have given the army chief a warning and left the issue at that, knowing well that rest of the country and other stakeholders are not in favour of such a drastic decision.' Nepal's entire political spectrum was pitted against the Maoists' demand of security sector reforms. His answer was: 'There is strong opposition within my cabinet and the party, including by Baburam Bhattarai, to let off the Army Chief's defiance lightly.' The Maoists were keen to appoint the next Chief, more acceptable to them in the vacancy to be created by Gen. Katawal's exit. Subsequently, months after his resignation, Prachanda conceded that it was a tactical mistake, but he could not change or oppose the mood in his party.

I tried later also to persuade Baburam and Prachanda to close their differences. In my view, both were complementary to each other; Baburam for his intellectual sharpness, broader vision and ideological resilience, and Prachanda for his organisational command and practical approach. If the Maoists were serious in building the 'New Nepal' of their vision then the country needed both of them to work together. I talked to both of them on this issue separately. This was one of the subjects of discussion whenever I met Baburam in conferences and met Prachanda in his house.

During Baburam's tenure as Prime Minister, I met both of them over a private dinner at the Prime Minister's residence in Baluwatar, Kathmandu. India's ambassador, Jayant Prasad, was also in attendance. During the dinner, I emphasised to both of them that it was crucial for them to collaborate closely for their personal benefit, the political well-being of the Maoists, and the national interest of Nepal. Despite their repeated assurances of commitment to working together, the reality was that they struggled to overcome their differences. This was primarily attributed to a significant clash of personalities and egos, combined with a deep-seated power struggle that originated with the establishment of the Maoist party in the early 1990s.

Baburam eventually left the Maoists and formed his own party called 'Naya Shakti Party' in 2016, which proved to be a futile effort. He has been moving from one grouping to another in search of a viable political constituency. He is primarily an ideologue without the political acumen needed for an organisational leader. Once I discussed this subject with Prachanda at Rashtrapati Bhavan when he was in India on a state visit in September 2016, during his second prime ministership. He assured me that his relations with Baburam have become very cordial and soon they would start working together. It is difficult to say with certainty if India contributed in any way to fuel the differences between Baburam and Prachanda to weaken and destroy the Maoists.

We noted earlier that within the Maoists, the section led by Mohan Baidya had the perception that Baburam was being favoured by India. I am however, aware that there were two views in the Indian establishment when Baburam emerged as the prime-ministerial candidate in 2011. While the PMO and the Indian Embassy in Kathmandu supported him, another senior Congress Party leader, Pranab Mukherjee was calling Nepal's President Dr Ram Baran Yadav not to let Baburam become Prime Minister. India's approach to Nepali politics has often been adhocist and personality oriented. During his term as Prime Minister, Baburam once complained that India was exercising undue pressure on him regarding bureaucratic decisions and delaying many of the developmental projects initiated by him. I conveyed this to Shivshankar Menon in Delhi who had taken over as India's National Security Adviser from M.K. Narayanan. The examples of India's interference in Nepal, however, are numerous and varied.[4]

Power struggles and ego clashes among Nepali leaders have made most of the power-sharing arrangements fragile, adversely affecting political stability in Nepal and souring its relations with India.

---

4 Siddharth Varadarajan, 'The danger in India's Nepal policy', *The Hindu*, 16 August 2010. Kanak Mani Dixit, 'India in Nepal: From Jawaharlal Nehru to Narendra Modi', *Nepali Times*, 20 April 2023. S.D. Muni, 'India's Nepal Policy' in David M. Malone, C. Raja Mohan, Srinath Raghavan (eds), *The Oxford Handbook of Indian Foreign Policy* (New Delhi: Oxford University Press, 2015) pp. 398-411.

This was the case when the then Prime Minister Oli, in May 2020, brought up the issue of a border dispute with India in the Lipulekh-Kalapani area. Internally, he was facing significant challenges within his party due to his failure to honour the power-sharing agreement with Prachanda.

He raised the border issue and whipped up anti-Indian nationalism to garner political support for his leadership, both within his party and within the country. When he found that the issue was becoming difficult to manage, he sought a resolution with India. His US ambassador Arjun Karki sent me a message from Washington, D.C., asking if I could help in this respect. I conveyed Oli's message, received through Arjun Karki, to External Affairs Minister Dr S. Jaishankar on 25 May 2020. Following this, India's Ambassador in Kathmandu also became actively involved in addressing the issue. A telephonic conversation was arranged between Oli and Modi. However, Oli did not respect the sanctity and confidentiality of this arrangement. Before talking to his Indian counterpart on the issue as agreed, he released an official map displaying the disputed area in Nepal. This resulted in a breakdown of communication at the highest political level, leading to Oli's move for a constitutional amendment to endorse the altered map. This helped him survive politically, but at the cost of vitiating relations with India for many years to come.

Oli seems to have borrowed the strategy from Nepali monarchs, using anti-India nationalism to safeguard his personal power. His approach has further complicated the border issue which still remains unresolved. Unless the current generation of Nepali leaders sets aside their egos and moderates their ambitions for power, Nepali politics may remain in turbulence with its unhappy spillover on relations with India.

4

Sri Lanka: A Friend as the President

URMILA JI INTRODUCED me to Sri Lanka academically. I had established a good personal rapport with her during my Sapru House days, and since then, she had always been very supportive and affectionate. In 1972, when I was in Jaipur, she invited me to collaborate with her on a paper to be published in *Economic and Political Weekly (EPW)*. The theme of the paper was the responses of Nepal and Sri Lanka on the emergence of Bangladesh as a sovereign, independent state in 1971. I was assigned to write on Nepal, and she on Sri Lanka. But since it was a joint paper, I delved into available literature on Sri Lanka's foreign policy. Later, in 1974, I wrote another paper on India's agreement to transfer Katchatheevu Island to Sri Lanka after years of dispute on its ownership. The earlier reading on Sri Lanka proved to be of great help in writing this article for *EPW*. I also engaged in discussions with Anuradha on Sri Lanka's politics and foreign policy as she was working for her PhD under Urmila ji's supervision.

After our marriage in 1972, Sri Lanka became a popular theme of discussion at our dining table between Anuradha and me. These discussions greatly enhanced my understanding and interest in Sri Lankan affairs. In 1973, we went to Sri Lanka, partly for research fieldwork and also as a honeymoon trip. Urmila ji introduced us to Niloo S. Bhatt (Niloo Bhai), an industrialist and businessman of Gujarati origin who had been naturalised as a Sri Lankan citizen. We stayed with him and travelled the length and breadth of the whole island with his nephews. Niloo Bhai introduced us to Arvind Dev, the second in-command at Sri Lanka's Indian Embassy, and Gopal, an intelligence officer posted in the embassy.

Niloo Bhai also facilitated our meetings with a large number of senior Sri Lankan politicians, journalists, intellectuals and social activists. A series of both formal and informal discussions with them provided Anuradha and me with a profound understanding of the nuances, complexities and insights into Sri Lanka's domestic politics, its relations with India, and Sri Lanka's foreign policy in general. During our visit, we also had interviews with the then Prime Minister Mrs Sirimavo Bandaranaike and her Deputy Prime Minister Maithripala Senanayake. At that time, Sri Lanka was in the process of regaining its confidence after the Janatha Vimukthi Peramuna (JVP) insurgency of 1971. The JVP was a radical Left-oriented Sinhala group suspected to have secured North Korean support. India had promptly and decisively helped Sri Lanka in countering the insurgency challenge. India also strongly and actively supported Mrs Bandaranaike's initiative in 1971 at the UN to declare the Indian Ocean as a Zone of Peace, free from great power rivalry.

This was a critical issue for India and Sri Lanka's security because the US was strengthening its Diego Garcia base and the former Soviet Union was trying to match the US military presence in the Indian Ocean. Our informal discussions in Colombo also suggested that Mrs Bandaranaike's presence in the United Nations was possibly also prompted by the need of securing herself from the consequences of the JVP revolt. Both Anuradha and I maintained regular contact with many of them for a long time, and we even received New Year greetings from Mrs Bandaranaike. I have carefully preserved a greeting card sent by the former Prime Minister to me in 1990. Lalith Athulathmudali, a young and dynamic leader of the Opposition party, the United National Party (UNP), also visited us at our residence in Safdarjung Enclave area of New Delhi. We lived there for a short while in a rented, small second-floor flat before moving to the JNU campus in late 1974. Many of these contacts have been immensely helpful in my numerous subsequent visits to Sri Lanka for studies and conferences.

Ethnic Conflict

The ethnic conflict between the minority Tamils and the dominant Sinhalese on the question of Tamil rights started getting sharpened by the beginning of 1980s. We in India were broadly sympathetic to the Tamil rights. The interest aroused in Sri Lankan affairs in India prompted me to write newspaper articles, including for the opinion page. My first meeting with the Sri Lankan Tamil leaders took place sometime in 1984. Mrs Gandhi had sent JNU's former Vice-Chancellor G. Parthasarathy to Sri Lanka to deal with the most violent eruption of ethnic conflict in July 1983, in which a large number of Tamils in Colombo were killed and their properties destroyed in retaliation to a Tamil militants' attack on Sri Lankan security forces. G. Parthasarathy might have suggested to the leaders of the Tamil United Liberation Front (TULF) to come to Delhi to meet decision-makers, experts and journalists to assess the public mood in India on the Tamil question.

The TULF leadership duo of A. Amrithalingam and V. Anandasangaree came to JNU to talk to all those interested in Sri

Lankan affairs. Urmila ji organised a meeting where I was also present. The TULF leaders' proposition was that why can India not intervene in Sri Lanka in support of Tamils and create an Eelam (independent Tamil State) as it had done in the case of Bangladesh. They explained that Tamils were being ethnically dominated and persecuted by the Sinhalese as the Bengalis had been exploited and suppressed in the erstwhile East Pakistan. The Tamil Eelam, proposed by the TULF in 1976, was to liberate Tamils from this persecution and it was to be a 'secular, socialist state based on right to self-determination'. Both Urmila ji and I explained to them why it was not possible and practical for India to intervene as in 1971. I have elaborated on some of the reasons, in my book *Pangs of Proximity: India and Sri Lanka's Ethnic Crisis* (Sage, 1993). It was not India's policy to have a separate sovereign Tamil State in close proximity to India's Tamil Nadu. Tamil nationalism had already erupted once in India during the late 1950s. The regional strategic context was also very different from what operated in 1971 for any drastic military action by India in the immediate neighbourhood. The TULF leaders went back disappointed from JNU but all of us made common friends and our contacts remained active thereafter, until Amrithalingam was unfortunately assassinated by the LTTE later.

The TULF leaders were patronising militant Tamil groups in order to increase pressure on the Sri Lankan government for the Tamil cause. There were seven or eight such militant groups; important among them were The Liberation Tigers of Tamil Eelam (LTTE), Eelam Peoples' Revolutionary Liberation Front (EPRLF), Eelam Peoples' Democratic Party (EPDP), Peoples' Liberation Organisation of Tamil Eelam (PLOTE), Eelam Revolutionary Organisation of Students (EROS), Tamil Eelam Liberation Organisation (TELO), etc. They all asked for a separate State for Tamils, but had deep differences on the nature, leadership and ideology of that state. The main dividing line was between the LTTE, which stood for military methods in achieving the goal of Eelam under their dominance, and the others who were open to a democratic structure for the Eelam and to negotiations and compromise to achieve the goals peacefully as far as possible.

I had close contacts with the EPRLF and EPDP. From EPRLF, Ketheeswaran Loganathan (popularly addressed as Ketheesh) came in contact with me first when he was lobbying for his cause in New Delhi. He introduced me to Shanthan Thambiah who was based in London and Varadaraja Perumal, another top-ranking leader of EPRLF. Both of them introduced me to their leader Comrade K. Pathmanabha, (popularly addressed as Com. Nabha), a suave, impressive and ideologically oriented personality. He disapproved of the LTTE's insistence on a political order that had no room for dissent and diverse opinions. Nabha's thrust was on having a polity that valued social justice and equality, not only among all the sections of the Tamil community but also in relation to the majority Sinhalese community. He had accepted the Indo-Sri Lanka accord of July 1987 as against LTTE's opposition to it. The LTTE could not stand his challenge to their ideological line. They assassinated him in June 1990 in Chennai where all Tamil leaders were scheduled to meet for mutual consultation and coordination.

Nabha visited me for dinner three days before his assassination where I witnessed his casual and overconfident approach to his personal security. He explained to me the approach of EPRLF to the struggle for Eelam under the situation created by the Indo-Sri Lankan Agreement. After dinner, when he was leaving, I cautioned him about his personal security in Chennai. I contributed to the Volume brought out by the EPRLF as a tribute to his memory.

Even after Nabha's assassination, I remained in close touch with the EPRLF activities through Ketheesh, Shanthan and Varadaraja Perumal. Ketheesh formally left EPRLF in 1994 and joined a Sri Lankan think tank working on peace. He has been the principal ideologue of the EPRLF after Nabha. Chandrika Kumaratunga who assumed Sri Lanka's presidency in 1994 (will discuss later) included Ketheesh in the Peace Council to work for the resolution of the Tamil question while she was still fighting the LTTE. Unfortunately, the LTTE also assassinated Ketheesh in cold blood in 2006. Varadaraja Perumal became Chief Minister of the Northeast Provincial Council in December 1988, established under the Indo-Sri Lanka Accord.

His government could not sustain for long, and on the issue of greater security control of the province, Perumal was dismissed by President Ranasinghe Premadasa in March 1990. He came to India with his family and settled here. He would visit us frequently in JNU and we remained in touch with him for a long time. He gave me the draft of his book on Sri Lankan economy for my observations. Shanthan's location in London did not allow us to remain in touch with each other regularly, but after a long gap we have re-established our contact.

EPDP leader Douglas Devananda demonstrated astuteness in managing his own security, navigating his political role, and ensuring the survival of his organisation, especially when compared to Nabha and Perumal. He also exhibited remarkable resilience in his political calculations and alliances. Douglas was one of the founding members of EPRLF and served as its military commander. Trained with the Palestine Liberation Organisation (PLO), he even fought alongside them at one point. However, ideological and organisational differences led to a fallout with his EPRLF colleagues, prompting him to establish EPDP. I was introduced to him by Ketheesh during his time with EPRLF.

Facing criminal cases in India, which he dismissed as fabricated and politically motivated, Douglas accepted the Indo-Sri Lankan Agreement of July 1987, and laid down his arms. In 1990, he chose to join the democratic mainstream by reconciling with the Sri Lankan government, then led by President Ranasinghe Premadasa, in exchange for security protection from the LTTE. Despite numerous attempts on his life by the LTTE, he thwarted their efforts.

In 1994, defying the LTTE's ban on participating in Presidential and Parliamentary elections, Douglas contested and won from Jaffna, along with seven EPDP members, albeit with very low votes. He pledged his political support to the newly elected President Chandrika Bandaranaike Kumaratunga (CBK). Knowing that I was friendly to her (to be discussed later), he requested my recommendation for a ministerial post to her. Informally, I discussed his case with CBK, and after her assessment, she appointed Douglas as the Minister of Refugees and Resettlement in the North in 2000. He carefully and assiduously used his parliamentary and ministerial positions to strengthen his organisation and constituency in Sri Lanka's Northern Province, Jaffna. Since then, Douglas has consistently been elected to Parliament and has served in successive governments of Sirisena, Gotabaya and Ranil Wickremasinghe. We have remained in touch. I have visited him in his highly protected underground den in Jaffna. While visiting other places in Jaffna, I also felt the strength of support and goodwill for him at the grassroots level. We often meet, whenever I visit Colombo, or he comes to New Delhi.

It was difficult for me to agree with the LTTE's line of safeguarding Tamil interests. They were not prepared to accept anything less than an independent sovereign state under their control. Despite the very limited territorial and human dimensions of such a state, they were overconfident in its viability, both financially and strategically. They were also dishonest and cruel in dealing with other Tamil militant leaders and organisations. The LTTE's reprehensible actions, including the killings of Nabha, Ketheesh, several other Tamil and Sinhalese leaders, and the brutal attack on CBK, reflected a disturbing disregard for human life. Particularly condemnable was the assassination of Rajiv Gandhi by the LTTE in May 1991 during an election campaign in Sriperumbudur, Tamil Nadu. Despite my disagreement with the LTTE's approach, I closely monitored their activities for academic purposes. I also had contacts with some of their leaders, such as Balasingham, Kittu and Mahattaya, and visited their offices in London and Oslo.

There was considerable financial help and political/social support for the LTTE and other Tamil militant groups from the Sri Lankan Tamil diaspora. I had seen money collected for them in Norway. This was also being done in other European countries and Australia. In the US in 1986, I watched a Congressional Committee Meeting on South Asia where Tamil lawyers and social activists strongly lobbied with the Committee members and witnesses in support of Tamil Eelam. Since my newspaper articles were critical of the LTTE's activities, I once received an anonymous letter warning me to desist from writing on Sri Lanka and criticising the LTTE. The best I could do was to ignore such warnings.

Ethnic politics in Sri Lanka took a sharp turn with the ascent of J.R. Jayewardene to power in 1978. The shift from a parliamentary to a Presidential system, as outlined in the new Constitution of 1982, and the ethnic conflict tore the Island Republic apart internally. India's support for Tamil rights had a profound and adverse impact on its relations with Sri Lanka. Despite these challenges, my visits to Sri Lanka for conferences and lectures continued and became more frequent in the aftermath of the Indo-Sri Lanka Agreement.

During this period, I met both President Jayewardene and his successor, President Ranasinghe Premadasa, alongside my academic colleagues Bhabani Sen Gupta and B.G. Verghese from the Centre of Policy Research, and Partha Ghosh from the ICSSR (Indian Council of Social Science Research). Our discussions with President Jayewardene focused on various dimensions of the implementation of the Indo-Sri Lanka Agreement, which had become a hot controversial issue both in Sri Lanka and India. We also raised concerns about the attack on Prime Minister Rajiv Gandhi, in the presence of President Jayewardene, during a Guard of Honour ceremony on 30 July 1987, after the signing of the Indo-Sri Lanka Accord. President Jayewardene expressed sincere regrets for the unfortunate incident and conveyed gratitude for Rajiv Gandhi's courageous assistance in managing LTTE violence. The President appeared confident in the successful implementation of the Agreement.

He was eager to grasp the intricacies of domestic political dynamics in India, especially when the Agreement and the deployment of the Indian Peace Keeping Force (IPKF) had come under strong criticism from various quarters. In a teasing manner, he remarked, 'It seems some of you are R&AW agents.' Clearly, his advisers and intelligence agencies had misled him about the background and academic credibility of our delegation. Anyone defending and explaining India's policy in the neighbourhood was being portrayed as an intelligence agent of India.

President Premadasa was a different class of politician, with a strong and rustic sense of nationalism. Emerging from a backward section of Sri Lankan society, his views differed from those leaders from the upper echelons. We met him in August 1989, shortly after he was elected to office. Our discussions were relaxed but intense and the subjects on the table were India-Sri Lanka relations as well as Sri Lanka's domestic politics with reference to the role of the LTTE and the JVP. President Premadasa expressed his displeasure with the continued presence of the IPKF in Sri Lanka and India's support for the North-East Provincial government headed by Varadaraja Perumal. We tried to explain to him that India had no bad intentions in Sri Lanka; the IPKF was there only at the request of the previous Sri Lankan government and would be withdrawn after it completes its mission. In response, he remarked, 'India was invited as a guest but it has overstayed, to the discomfort of the host.' When questioned about his approach to critical political issues, he likened it to a soccer player assessing a ball that needs to be put into the goal, showing little concern for other players or events on the field. Premadasa harboured such strong dislike for India that he did not hesitate in supporting the LTTE with arms supplies to confront the IPKF. After my return from this visit, I wrote an article titled 'Premadasa's View of India's Role' in the *Times of India* (10 August 1989) based on this interaction. I met Premadasa once again later after the IPKF had been withdrawn and he encountered conflicts with the LTTE. This was sometime in 1991.

His principal adviser, Bradman Weerakoon, had become a good friend of mine during my frequent visits to Sri Lanka. He arranged my appointment and organised transport for me on the day when Colombo had been put under curfew. This one-on-one meeting took place at President Premadasa's ancestral residence. Politely but firmly, I told him that Rajiv Gandhi has sacrificed his life for Sri Lanka, the IPKF was no longer in his country and his fears of Indian expansionism and intervention, expressed on my previous visit, had been proved baseless. I also emphasised that he had been misled by both the JVP and the LTTE in his approach to India and IPKF. Premadasa promised that he would make sincere efforts to befriend India, aiming to eliminate past misunderstandings between the two close neighbours permanently. I shared his commitment with Sri Lankan journalists who visited me in my hotel room soon after my meeting with the President. Dilip Mukherjee, the opinion page editor of the *Times of India*, also called from New Delhi to ask about my meeting with President Premadasa. He jokingly remarked, 'An academic and a news analyst have been transformed and elevated to become a newsmaker,' referring to the change in President Premadasa's attitude towards India, as conveyed to me, that became a headline in some Sri Lankan newspapers the next morning and was also reported in India.

President Chandrika Bandaranaike Kumaratunga

In 1990, I was invited by the Peace Research Institute Oslo (PRIO) on a short fellowship to write on India's role in Sri Lanka's ethnic crisis. The project was initiated by Dr Kumar Rupesinghe, Director of Project on Ethnic Conflicts at PRIO. He was a Sri Lankan national and a strong supporter of President Premadasa. The structure of the project was that Kumar would write from the Sri Lankan perspective and I would present the Indian approach. I completed my draft within the scholarship period but Kumar's other engagements did not allow him to do his part. I came to India and gave final touches to the draft. Since he was still unable to write his side of the story and I was uncomfortable with the undue delay in the publication of my effort, he agreed to get my report published without his contribution. The book *Pangs of Proximity: India and Sri Lanka's Ethnic Crisis* was published in 1993 under the PRIO banner by the Sage International Publishers. Kumar continued to involve me in his wider projects and even sent me to Chechnya to study the Russian role there. During my stay at PRIO, Kumar organised a two-day conference on 'Peace Process in Sri Lanka'. One of its participants was Chandrika Bandaranaike Kumaratunga (CBK). Kumar was also related to her. He was her former brother-in-law, who had married and later divorced her elder sister Sunethra. All three of them, and CBK's late husband Vijaya Kumaratunga had together, as young activists, faced the JVP insurgency of 1971.

Both Vijaya and Chandrika were known for their left-of-centre ideological orientation. They had strongly supported India's role in Sri Lanka in support of the Tamils, at very difficult times for India when its role was being widely criticised in Sri Lanka as well as in India. Fearing for her life after the assassination of her husband, Chandrika was living in Paris (the University of Paris was her alma mater) and London. She came to the conference from London where she was on a fellowship with the Institute of Commonwealth Studies. She impressed everyone in the conference by her clear analysis and articulate presentation. We became instant friends.

After Kumar's seminar, I remained in touch with CBK. From Sri Lanka she wrote to me in late 1992, to express her desire to visit India. I had taken over as Chairperson of the South Asia Studies Centre in 1991. I proposed that she be the guest of my centre for a week to deliver lectures at the SIS/JNU on Sri Lanka's ethnic conflict and Sri Lanka's foreign policy. She readily agreed. Her lectures were very well received by our School's (SIS) students and faculty. For the first time, they heard a Sri Lankan Sinhala leader talking so constructively and positively on the ethnic issue. She wanted to see the resolution of the issue in a peaceful manner giving respect and dignity to Tamil aspirations and rights. She also spoke very positively on the Indo-Sri Lanka relations. After completing the one-week period as a guest of JNU, she wanted to extend her stay in New Delhi. We had no provisions in the university to support her extension. I requested my friend Air Commodore Jasjit Singh, Director of the Institute for Defence and Strategic Analyses (IDSA) and he readily agreed to host her for another week. She then shifted to the India International Centre as IDSA guest.

Towards the end of her stay in New Delhi, she expressed the desire to meet Prime Minister P.V. Narasimha Rao. Securing this appointment proved challenging for us. I approached J.N. Dixit, then Foreign Secretary, for assistance, saying, 'Please suggest to the Prime Minister that he may be meeting Sri Lanka's future President.' Chandrika also personally requested Dixit as she had known him since his assignment as India's High Commissioner in Sri Lanka during 1985-89. With Dixit's efforts, the appointment came through. Chandrika had a productive meeting with the Prime Minister and went back to Sri Lanka happily.

Soon after her return to Sri Lanka, her party won the Western Provincial Council elections and she became the Chief Minister of this province on 21 May 1993. Her party also won the parliamentary elections held in August 1994 and she became Sri Lanka's Prime Minister on 16 August 1994. In November that year, she contested the presidential elections and won with an impressive majority of 62.28 per cent votes. In her officially released profile as President, her association with JNU and our centre as a 'guest faculty' was mentioned. We were all delighted to learn about this. Soon the MEA started calling our centre for details of CBK's visit, though they had hardly bothered about her presence in India as our guest earlier.

CBK had her first visit to India as President in March 1995. She was put up in Rashtrapati Bhavan. She invited me and Hardeep Singh Puri for a quiet lunch. Puri was a senior IFS (Indian Foreign Service) officer who served in Sri Lanka under Dixit. CBK had been interacting with him in Colombo and knew that he had closely watched the LTTE and interacted with them during his stay in Colombo. Puri was actively involved in assisting Dixit to persuade the LTTE to accept the 1987 Agreement and accordingly, cooperate in laying down arms and help in the establishment of an Interim Administrative Council for the Northern and Eastern Provinces. LTTE chief Velupillai Prabhakaran held many discussions with Dixit and agreed to cooperate. The agreement for laying down arms was signed on 28 September 1987. For signing the agreement, Prabhakaran personally backed out at the last moment and pushed his deputy to do this with the Indian High Commission. Explaining his refusal to sign the agreement, Prabhakaran said: 'Mahatma Gandhi never signed any agreement with the British government so why should I.' In reaction, Dixit also refused to sign the Agreement and deputed Puri to do so with the deputy of the LTTE leader,

K. Mahendra Raja.[1] This was disclosed to me by Dixit in one of our meetings and discussions in Colombo. I had known Puri since his posting in Sri Lanka and had many sittings with him discussing the Sri Lankan issues along with High Commissioner Dixit. Hardeep Singh Puri is presently the Union Minister for Housing and Urban Affairs and Minister for Petroleum and Natural Gas in the Narendra Modi government.

During the Rashtrapati Bhavan lunch, Chandrika told us very confidently that she would be able to strike a peace deal with the LTTE leader. She referred to the three months of ceasefire between the Sri Lankan Army and the LTTE since she assumed the presidency. She told us about the letters (seven in all, by then) exchanged between her and LTTE leader Prabhakaran. However, both Puri and I did not share her optimism and confidence. In our own ways, we tried to explain to her the deceptive nature of the LTTE's promises. I narrated to her the way in which the EPRLF and other Tamil leaders were assassinated by the LTTE. I also referred her to a PhD dissertation done under my supervision by Sudha Ramachandran on the LTTE, its character, strategy and behaviour. Puri shared his experiences in dealing with the LTTE, especially Prabhakaran. He recounted accompanying Prabhakaran to a face-to-face meeting with Rajiv Gandhi after the 1987 Indo-Sri Lanka Agreement. Puri had previously mentioned in one of our Colombo meetings that Prabhakaran looked very nervous during that encounter, with his shirt soaked in sweat.

We emphasised to CBK that it is a part of the LTTE strategy to make the adversary complacent and relaxed and then strike so

---

1 The text of this Agreement is available as Appendix V, in my *Pangs of Proximity* book (pp. 216-17). In the original, as a typological mistake, Hardeep Singh Puri's name was spelled as M.S. Puri, M for H.

as to take him by surprise. We cautioned her and requested her
not to take the LTTE words on face value and remain prepared
for any eventuality. It did not seem that she was convinced by our
explanations. Within a few weeks of her return to Sri Lanka, we
learnt that the LTTE in April 1995 had broken the ceasefire and
declared war. They had put four conditions to move forward on peace
initiative of Chandrika. They were: (i) withdrawal of restrictions
on the movement of essential goods to Jaffna, (ii) lifting of ban on
night fishing in the Palk Strait, (iii) removal of army camps from
Jaffna and (iv) free movement of LTTE cadres even with arms. The
Sri Lankan government was willing to accept the first two of them.
The third and the fourth ones were not acceptable in view of the
Tigers' unreliability in the past. Prabhakaran made this an excuse for
breaking the ceasefire and resuming conflict.

CBK prepared herself to fight the war as bravely as she was
pursuing peace. I used to visit Colombo frequently during her
presidency, sometimes on her invitation but often on my own for
conferences and lectures. In one of my visits in the thick of the war,
she explained to me in detail as to how she would sit with the senior
Generals in the War Room of the President's House, to understand
the strategy and tactics of war. She tried to boost the morale of the
army. The Sri Lankan army being quite in a defeatist mood when
she assumed office, was encouraged and well-equipped to go on the
offensive. This helped the army to take control of a good part of Jaffna
that was hitherto under the control of the LTTE. By the end of 1995,
the Tigers were pushed into the Vanni jungle and the Sri Lankan
army was in control of the rest of Jaffna. In May 1996, one night
I received her call asking me to send Sudha Ramachandran's PhD
dissertation to her through the Sri Lankan High Commissioner in
New Delhi as soon as possible. She wanted to understand the LTTE
better so as to keep them contained and force them to accept peace.
Next day, I got the dissertation photocopied and handed it over to

Sri Lanka's then High Commissioner Mangala Moonesinghe for sending it to Colombo. Within a few days, she acknowledged the receipt of the dissertation and expressed her confidence in providing relief to the Tamils affected by the conflict. In a letter dated 4 June, 1996, she said: 'We are delighted at our recent success in winning back the civilians…We are doing our maximum to re-establish civilian administration and to provide for the people.' (Copy of the letter is attached as Annexure 2.)

The Sri Lankan Army, however, could not sustain the military push and the war continued with ups and downs for them, even after CBK left her office in 2005. While fighting the war, she wanted India's help regarding sharing of satellite intelligence of higher resolutions on the LTTE's deployments and movements. During one of my visits to Colombo in August 1997, she asked me to convey this message to then Prime Minister Gujral. The matter being sensitive, I asked her to give me a small note authenticating that she herself was sending this message. She did accordingly. I dutifully passed on this note to Gujral and verbally explained to him the nature of the specific request. He said he will look into it and respond to her after consulting with others in the government. He asked me to go and brief Foreign Secretary Salman Haider on the overall condition in Sri Lanka and the state of the conflict. The PMO alerted the Foreign Secretary about my visit. I met Salman Haider and briefed him on Sri Lanka as directed by the Prime Minister. Haider was quite dismissive of what I said and quipped: 'Yes, yes, we know the situation as it is evolving in Sri Lanka. You need not bother much about it.' I knew nothing as to what was India's final response to Chandrika's request. Chandrika was also pursuing peace, through the involvement of extra-regional players like Norway as also through some private channels.

The Tamil Tigers had no respect for the language of peace. Seeking vengeance for their defeat on the battlefield, they altered their strategy and intensified suicide attacks on various government establishments, causing huge loss of innocent lives and national property. On the final day of her second presidential campaign in December 1999, they attacked CBK with a suicide bomber. Over 30 people were killed in the explosion. She narrowly escaped death, but lost her right eye in the explosion, and had some metal rods inserted in her body to save her life. The incident occurred in the presence of *NDTV (New Delhi Television)* reporter Maya Mirchandani, who later described it as horrific and ghastly. The LTTE also turned the scales of war against the Sri Lankan forces.

One day, in the year 2000, Chandrika called me and asked if I could help her in obtaining a leased MIG fighter from India to alleviate the pressure from the LTTE. I approached Brajesh Mishra, the Principal Secretary and NSA of the then Prime Minister, with her request. He asked me to share my assessment of the Sri Lankan situation. I explained that the Sri Lankan Army was losing previously gained ground and was now backed against the wall. He then called Foreign Secretary Lalit Mansingh to his office. In my presence, Mishra asked Mansingh if India could do something on Chandrika's request. After a pause, Mansingh responded, 'Sir, let us examine the possibility.' Obviously there was no immediate answer, and if there was any, the Foreign Secretary chose not to disclose it in my presence. I left and briefed Mangala Moonesinghe to convey the message to the President and follow up on the matter with the Foreign Secretary. Unfortunately, the MIG fighter was not leased to Sri Lanka, as India was against the policy of supplying lethal weapons to Sri Lanka to be used against Tamils. Such a move could have had serious domestic political implications for India, particularly in Tamil Nadu. It may be recalled that the Gujral government had fallen because the Congress withdrew support over the Sri Lankan Tamil issue. Intermittent ceasefires between the LTTE and the Sri Lankan army occurred in

2001 and 2002, but only for short durations. Sri Lanka's ethnic war persisted with varying intensity until 2009.

CBK took two other initiatives towards resolving the Tamil question that were unique in some respects. One was a proposal in August 2000, for a new Constitution that pledged devolution of power to Tamils and Muslims through federal institutions. It also proposed trimming of the Executive Presidency to create a more transparent and democratic political system. The constitutional proposal was being worked upon since her coming to power and had been subjected to informal feedback and suggestions from all stakeholders before its presentation as a Bill in Parliament. It had support from all coalition parties in her government, including the JVP, which generally did not favour devolving powers to Tamils through federalism. It was for the first time that a federal solution to the ethnic issue had been proposed and that too with the support of diehard Sinhala parties like the JVP. However, the proposal faced resistance from a faction of the Buddhist Sangha and the Opposition parties, spearheaded by Ranil Wickremesinghe of the UNP (United National Party). She could not succeed in changing the Constitution in the face of this opposition. I wrote an edit page piece for the *Times of India* describing her Constitutional proposal as 'Bold and Beautiful'.

The second initiative was concerning the composition of her government. In the parliamentary elections of 2004, her party emerged victorious defeating the UNP. She decided to appoint her very able Foreign Minister Lakshman Kadirgamar, a Tamil, as the Prime Minister to instil confidence of Tamils in her government. I heard about this from some of her party members in her official residence during one of my visits. Here again she could not succeed because of stiff opposition from the hardline Sinhalese and Sangha pressures from within and outside her party. She was forced to appoint Mahinda Rajapaksa as Prime Minister, who eventually became her *bete noire*, after she left the government.

Lakshman Kadirgamar was a brilliant international lawyer of repute when picked by CBK to serve as her foreign minister. He had no political background prior to that, but proved himself to be one of the most dynamic and successful foreign ministers of Sri Lanka. Chandrika trusted him most on issues of foreign policy and ethnic conflict. Having met him many times in the President's house and elsewhere, we became good friends. During my diplomatic assignment in Laos, I discovered the LTTE's links with the small Tamil community there; being used for money laundering and transporting Tamils to Australia. The LTTE was also accessing leftover arms of the Vietnam war period in Laos and of the Khmer Rouge period in Cambodia. I alerted the MEA and also Lakshman about these transactions. Lakshman undertook an official visit to Laos and Cambodia to manage these issues.

The MEA was not very happy with Lakshman. India's reservations about him were on two counts. One, that on his advice, CBK, on the eve of the 10th SAARC summit in July 1998 in Colombo, offered to help India and Pakistan resolve their differences so as to make SAARC a dynamic and productive organisation. India has always been sensitive about getting any third party involved in the India-Pakistan conflict. Secondly, Lakshman was also very active in keeping close relations between Sri Lanka and China and thus balancing India's presence in the Island Republic. But his balancing act was always sensitive and supportive of India's security interests. Lakshman and I kept on meeting each other whenever there was an opportunity. In December 2004, he was invited by the Chinese Institute of Foreign Affairs in Beijing where he spoke on 'The Peaceful Ascendency of China: A South Asian Perspective'. He came to India before undertaking that visit and discussed with me, the draft of the lecture he had prepared to deliver there. It was mostly about China-Sri Lanka relations. He happily incorporated some of my suggestions.[2] Unfortunately, Lakshman was assassinated by the LTTE in August 2005 in his own house in Colombo. In his memory, the Lakshman Kadirgamar Institute of International Relations and Strategic Studies was established in 2006, in Colombo.

Lakshman was also Chairman of the Board of Governors of the Bandaranaike Centre for International Studies (BCIS) in Colombo, which functioned under the overall umbrella of the Bandaranaike Memorial International Conference Hall (BMICH). I was asked to join Lakshman in transforming and upgrading the BCIS from a training centre to a full-fledged and serious think tank on Sri Lanka's foreign and strategic affairs. He also asked me to help BCIS start a policy journal. We constituted an Editorial Advisory Board of the journal with Lakshman as the Editor-in-Chief, and I as one of the members. I managed to persuade Sage India Publishers to undertake the publication of the journal with bi-annual periodicity. The journal was named as *International Relations in a Globalising World*, a rather longish and somewhat odd title, but it was so preferred by Lakshman. The first issue came out impressively in January 2005. I also contributed one article. Journals are not easy to sustain in terms of mobilising contributors and keeping the time schedule of publication. Lakshman died in August 2005 and after him the BCIS Director and supporting staff failed on both of these counts. In a year's time of the launch of the journal, Sage informed me that they cannot continue its publication.

During CBK's Presidency, Gujral as External Affairs Minister visited Colombo in January 1997, leading the Indian delegation

---

2 The text of the Lecture is available in Sir Adam Roberts (ed), *Democracy, Sovereignty And Terror: Lakshman Kadirgamar On The Foundations Of International Order* (New York, London: I.B. Tauris Publication, 2012) pp. 223-36. The book was a tribute to Lakshman's memory. His wife Suganthi Kadirgamar presented a copy to me.

for the Third Meeting of the Joint Commission between the two countries. Gujral included me in the delegation. From the MEA, IFS officers Santosh Kumar and Meera Shankar were also in the delegation. We flew to Colombo in a specially chartered official aircraft from New Delhi's air force base. Our first engagement in Colombo was to have lunch with the President in her official residence at Temple Trees. For the post-lunch coffee CBK, Gujral, Lakshman Kadirgamar and I were chatting informally about the agenda of the Commission's meeting the next day. Chandrika turned towards me and asked, 'What else we can do; any new idea?' I proposed that we should establish the S.W.R.D. Bandaranaike Foundation to promote academic and cultural exchanges between the two countries. This could be on the basis of the B.P. Koirala Foundation, already established between India and Nepal. Chandrika promptly interjected to say, 'It's an excellent idea, but not as Bandaranaike Foundation. I do not want my family members' names to be brought in, otherwise I may be accused of nepotism at the cost of the State. Let us call it, India-Sri Lanka Foundation.' Gujral, responded by saying, 'It's a good idea worth pursuing but from where will the funding come to support travels and other activities?' Lakshman also supported the idea but reiterated Gujral's concern on the question on funding. My answer to the funding question was that one-time equal contributions from both the sides could be raised as a fixed lumpsum corpus and the activities may be carried out from the interest earned on that corpus annually.

They all agreed and asked me to make a brief note for consideration by the Commission before the meeting started next day. I made a long paragraph 'Note' suggesting that an equivalent of Rs 2 crores be raised by each side for the corpus fund to support academic projects, travels, cultural performances, seminars and conferences. The funding and activities may be governed by an Independent Council with equal representation both from India and Sri Lanka. I passed on the 'Note' to Meera Shankar for the consideration of the Commission where it was adopted next day in principle. The decision was incorporated in the Joint Statement issued after the meeting on 22 January 1997. The Foundation was established in December 1998 after Gujral had left the government and Vajpayee had succeeded him. Both India and Sri Lanka agreed to contribute the equivalent of Indian Rs 2 crores (20 million) each for the corpus. There was one major change from what I had proposed. Its governance was left to the respective High Commissions of the two countries. Two Advisory Committees were also established to help the High Commissions in the operations of the Foundation. Governments are often shy in handing over control of institutions to independent bodies. I was happy to have been involved in the founding of the India-Sri Lanka Foundation, though as an unacknowledged contributor to the initiative. The Foundation has been working actively for many years, though for the past few years I have not heard much about its activities. I was somewhat puzzled when I saw a document prepared by the Sri Lankan High Commission in New Delhi in 2023 where the India-Sri Lanka Foundation was listed under political and strategic activities along with some other Indian private foundation. The India-Sri Lanka Foundation was tasked to promote cultural and academic exchanges between the two countries without getting involved in political and strategic issues.

The day we were to fly back home after the Joint Commission meeting, Chandrika asked me to join her for lunch. I hesitated since there could be a clash of timings for me to reach the airport for our flight back to India in the same aircraft that brought us. She assured me that I would reach the flight on time. We had a one-on-one lunch. She asked me to explain to her the thrust of the 'Gujral Doctrine' and how it was affecting India's engagements with its other neighbours. She also discussed the kind of opposition she was facing on her initiatives and explained to me about the progress in the ethnic war and the discouraging prospects of her peace with the Tigers. After lunch, she sent me to the airport in an army helicopter directly from the Sri Lankan army's base near the President's House. The flight was waiting for me at the Colombo airport.

As President, Chandrika facilitated and encouraged my involvement with Sri Lankan affairs in various ways. Months after her becoming President, I was asked to help with the proposal of establishing an Institute for strategic and security studies in Sri Lanka. I went to Colombo on official invitation for this purpose. I had the model of India's IDSA in my mind. With suitable modifications, I presented it to a group of ministers, including of Home and Defence, for discussion over dinner. They endorsed the basic structure with one caveat. IDSA functions as a society and is theoretically independent of the government. The Sri Lankan Ministers of Defence and Home Affairs in the discussion, preferred theirs to be a government-controlled Institution in view of Sri Lanka's serious security situation. I explained to them the reality of the IDSA situation, where despite it being registered as an independent society, it was dependent upon the government fully for funding. With minor exceptions, the IDSA was also governed under the overall supervision and guidance of the Ministry of Defence. I accepted the point that in Sri Lanka's case, the decision had to be of the government of Sri Lanka to suit their specific requirements.

The Sri Lankan government did establish in the year 2000, the Sri Lanka Institute of Strategic Studies, with support from the foreign ministry. In 2006, under the Rajapaksa regime, the institute was renamed as Lakshman Kadirgamar Institute of International Relations and Strategic Studies. Under the Sirisena regime, yet another institute of strategic affairs was established in 2017 called Institute of National Security Studies Sri Lanka, funded and controlled by the Defence Ministry. In my subsequent visits to

Sri Lanka, I have visited and lectured at both these institutes. The Institute of National Security Studies has also affiliated me as its Honorary Fellow since 2019.

On another occasion, when I was on a visit to Colombo for a Track 2.0 conference, Chandrika accepted my request for a visit to Jaffna. It was sometimes in 1996, when the Sri Lankan army had pushed the LTTE back and was in control of the northern peninsula. Chandrika asked the Sri Lanka Army to arrange for my visit and granted my request to take along one of my colleagues Professor V. Suryanarayan who had also come to Colombo for the conference from Tamil Nadu. Both of us travelled from Colombo to Jaffna in an army helicopter in the morning and returned the same evening. Signs of war and devastation were writ large on the town. In Jaffna, we went to the open vegetable market where Suryanarayan talked to shopkeepers and customers in Tamil about the conditions in the town. They all said it was peaceful and they were doing their daily chores unhindered. But there was still a sense of insecurity and fear of the Tigers striking any time. We walked in some of the streets but were cautioned by our army escorts that it was not advisable to go deep into the township. We also saw a bit of the main Jaffna Highway A-9 (which connects Kandy with Jaffna). There was scattered movement on the highway but travel appeared to be safe. Back in Colombo, I thanked the President for enabling us to have this unique learning exposure to the ground reality in Jaffna.

The term of the President in Sri Lanka is for six years and any President can have two terms and no more. Since CBK had announced elections for her second term a year earlier in 1999, she wanted her second term to be extended by one year, up to 2006. The Sri Lankan Supreme Court turned it down saying that no single term could exceed six years. She therefore left office in December 2005.

In November 2005, she conferred Sri Lanka's national honours. Nine foreigners were bestowed with the highest national honour of

'Sri Lanka Ratna meant to be given for 'exceptional and outstanding service to the nation'. Two of them were from India. N. Ram of *The Hindu* newspaper and myself. I had no prior information about this nor was I officially informed or invited for the ceremony. I read about Ram in *The Hindu* paper. I learnt about this honour for myself only after weeks, from the Sri Lankan High Commissioner, C.R. Jayasinghe, in New Delhi. He came home in JNU to hand me the citation and the gold medal (gold plated) studded with nine different precious stones found in Sri Lanka. By then, Chandrika had ceased to be President, but I wrote to her, thanking for this kind and unusually generous gesture.

Post-Presidency

Chandrika continued to encourage my interaction with Sri Lankan affairs even after her Presidency. She invited me on behalf of BCIS to restructure and rejuvenate the centre. She was the Chairperson of the BMICH Society under which the BCIS functioned. In Colombo, I had meetings with the new Director and the Board of Governors of the centre. They were all willing and enthusiastic about building the centre into a strong think tank on Sri Lanka's international affairs. The initiative for this had been taken by Lakshman Kadirgamar, as noted earlier, but that initiative could not be brought to its logical conclusion. The main constraint was of financial support and available talent. I had no doubt that the expertise could be developed from within Sri Lanka and if any gap was left, that could be bridged through visiting scholars and academics from abroad. But financially it was difficult to sustain intensive research activity just on the basis of earnings from training courses as the centre had been doing. With Rajapaksa in power, there was no hope of any substantial support from the government to BCIS. I put on the discussion table, the idea of raising funds from various international foundations like the Ford

Foundation, various German foundations, etc. These foundations could be involved for specific project related support at least. One needed a very dynamic director and a strong group of experts for this purpose. I also suggested that the centre could plan different and more innovative training courses, relevant to the emerging market for jobs at higher training fees to increase resources; but a good think tank needed large and sustained funding.

In 2015, Mahinda Rajapaksa was succeeded by Maithripala Sirisena. This had become possible with Chandrika's dynamic political initiative and intervention wherein Sirisena defected from Rajapaksa and joined hands with the hitherto rival UNP, led by Ranil Wickremesinghe. This government was also not forthcoming in investing to make BCIS a strong think tank. Chandrika invited me in March 2017 to address the Convocation of BCIS where the chief guest was President Sirisena. I had the rare opportunity to meet him and share the dais with him and Chandrika. I also shared the dais with Chandrika in Singapore while attending an ISAS panel discussion on Sri Lanka in June 2015. In Singapore, she explained the work that she was doing in rehabilitating the Tamils. I drew the attention of the conference to the internal cracks that had developed in the coalition built by Chandrika under President Sirisena.

On the sidelines of the ISAS conference, she explained to me the contradictions developed between President Sirisena and Prime Minister Wickremesinghe. She was more supportive of the Prime Minister and disappointed with the President. Her main grouse against Sirisena was that he did not allow prosecution of Gotabaya Rajapaksa despite hard evidence collected by the investigating agencies against his financial corruption when Gotabaya was Defence Minister in the previous Mahinda Rajapaksa regime. In her assessment, Sirisena had been won over by the Chinese. This assessment had been shared with me by the Indian High

Commissioner Yashvardhan Kumar Sinha in Colombo during one of my previous visits.

Besides the China factor, his own political calculations and growing tensions with Prime Minister Ranil Wickremesinghe made Sirisena soft to the Rajapaksas. He resisted Indian projects like the East Container Terminal at Colombo port. This project had the approval of Prime Minister Ranil Wickremesinghe. This was corroborated to me by another source, a former student of my friend, late Professor Shelton Kodikara, who was a senior foreign service officer of Sri Lanka. This officer was present to take notes on a discussion between Indian Prime Minister Modi and Sri Lankan President Sirisena in May 2020 when the latter was on an official visit to India. Sirisena refused to concede to Modi's pleas for the project to be given to an Indian infrastructure company headed by Adani.[3] This was in pursuance of a Memorandum of Understanding (MOU) signed in 2019 between the two countries for economic partnership. The East Container Terminal project was being discussed within the framework of this MOU. Sirisena's contention was that the project was of national significance and would be handled by Sri Lanka itself.[4] There also had been public protests against the project being given to India (in collaboration with Japan).

I have had opportunities to meet Chandrika's successor Mahinda Rajapaksa. On his first visit to India in 2006, the Sri Lankan High Commission organised a public reception. High Commissioner Jayasinghe invited me and took me to President Rajapaksa for a one-on-one meeting introducing me to him as 'former President's friend'.

---

3 Also see press reports on the subject. Sri Lanka's Electricity Board MMC Ferdinando publicly disclosed that Modi had put pressure on Sri Lanka for the grant of project to Adani. *The Indian Express*, 14 June 2022. Also see *Wire* reports of 12 and 23 June 2022 on the subject.

4 For background information on the issue see, *The Indian Express*, 4 February 2021.

President Rajapaksa, after exchanging pleasantries, said: 'Professor, please ask your friend to support and cooperate with me.' I submitted that 'Excellency, in Sri Lanka's interest, it is desirable that both of you worktogether.' Chandrika then was the President of Rajapaksa's party, the Sri Lanka Freedom Party (SLFP), and it may be recalled that she made him Prime Minister in 2004. President Mahinda Rajapaksa also visited Singapore in February 2012 where my Institute the ISAS, invited him for an interaction over breakfast. I was working with ISAS as Visiting Research Professor. President Rajapaksa made a very brief statement on the end of the LTTE terrorism in Sri Lanka. Some of us asked him about the final political resolution of the ethnic problem in Sri Lanka after the end of terrorism. Almost all the questions to him were answered by Professor G.L Peiris, his foreign minister who accompanied him. There was no satisfactory response to any of the questions.

After the elimination of the LTTE, this question of resolving Sri Lanka's ethnic problem was on all our minds. I debated this many times with one of my Sri Lankan colleagues at the ISAS, Dayan Jayatilleka. My contention was that Mahinda Rajapaksa will not be able to show the statesmanship needed to find a political solution. He has been a Sinhala politician and would remain so in the interest of consolidating his personal and family power. Dayan, being the son of a great journalist Mervyn de Silva, was a very sharp and influential media analyst. He disagreed with me and resolutely defended Rajapaksa. In the midst of our debate, Dayan was appointed as Sri Lanka's Ambassador to France by the Rajapaksa regime.

I met Gotabaya Rajapaksa during my tenure in the ISAS also. A Sri Lankan academic Rohan Gunaratna, who was heading the International Centre for Political Violence and Terrorism Research at the Rajaratnam School of International Studies (RSIS), Nanyang Technological University of Singapore, invited a small group of people to interact with Gotabaya on his visit to Singapore. In the interaction, Gotabaya was completely dismissive of any ethnic issue left to be resolved in Sri Lanka and also of any human rights violations during the anti-LTTE operations. He was only concerned about the possibility of the LTTE's re-emergence. I met him again in Colombo as part of a Kalinga Foundation delegation under the leadership of India's former foreign secretary Lalit Mansingh. We had gone to Sri Lanka on the invitation of The Pathfinder Foundation in September 2019. We met Gotabaya at his private residence. While shaking hands with him, I said, 'Am I meeting the future President of Sri Lanka?.' He responded with a smile, stating that it was 'all in the hands of his party'. He was sworn in as President in November 2019.

During our meeting, I also enquired about his approval, during the previous regime, for the Chinese nuclear submarine to dock in the Colombo port. He explained, 'That file was presented to me as the docking of a warship, and since we were allowing warships of other countries for refueling, etc., I also permitted that.' He went on to mention, 'The Indian High Commission raised the issue with me, and I assured them that we would not allow the submarine to dock on its return. However, it seems that the return docking permission had also been granted with the initial approval.' Unfortunately, his response did not completely satisfy us.

Gotabaya's presidency was short-lived as he struggled to manage Sri Lanka's economy. His perceived image as a dictatorial and corrupt ruler triggered a significant popular uprising against his regime. Consequently, he had to relinquish his office and flee the country in February 2022. In a virtual public address to Indian and South Asian audiences in May 2023, CBK described the Rajapaksa regimes as rife with corruption, nepotism, and inefficiency.

During my visit to Colombo with the Kalinga Foundation delegation, I attended a conference at the Lakshman Kadirgamar Institute on China's BRI and Sri Lanka. The general tone of the participants was positive towards the BRI (Belt and Road Initiative). The Western media analyses of the Chinese debt burden on Sri Lanka were not given any credence. I also met Douglas Devananda, other Tamil leaders, Radhika Coomaraswamy, Dayan Jayatilleka, Ravinatha Aryasinha, many other old Tamil and Sinhala contacts and India's High Commissioner in Colombo, Taranjit Singh Sandhu. The Kalinga Foundation delegation tried to meet Chandrika also but the appointment could not come through. These discussions underlined the uncertain status of the Tamil question and tensions in India-Sri Lanka relations, then triggered by Sirisena's allegations that Indian intelligence agents were involved in an attempt to assassinate him. Ambassador Sandhu, who has been my former student at the South Asian Studies in JNU, explained to me why India had not officially reacted to Sirisena's allegations.

From our discussions with The Pathfinder Foundation, I observed that whenever the topic shifts to India's relations with Sri Lanka, the conversation inevitably circles back to Indian intervention on behalf of the Tamils during the 1980s and early 1990s. Under the skin, every Sinhalese treats India as a friend of the Tamils. Furthermore, a substantial portion of Indian development cooperation is concentrated in Tamil regions. To overcome past impressions and stigmas, Indian diplomacy should actively work to foster Sinhalese goodwill while also maintaining a positive relationship with the Tamil constituency. Sinhalese friends, on the other hand, also need to leave behind their historical baggage on India to accept that their northern neighbour is emerging as an economic power, which must be engaged for mutual benefits. India's assistance of US$ 4 billion to Sri Lanka to save its economic meltdown during 2022-23 was a commendable initiative.

5

Laos: An Insider's Story

THE THREADS OF a diplomatic assignment for me, casually initiated by the late Shri Dinesh Singh during his last term as foreign minister, gained momentum under Prime Minister I.K. Gujral. The fall of the Deve Gowda-led United Front government resulted in the election of Gujral as his successor on 21 April 1997.[1] Gujral received congratulations from his friends and admirers at his Maharani Bagh residence in New Delhi. I went to congratulate him. The security guard outside his meeting room informed me that there was a long queue of well-wishers waiting to meet him, and I had to exit within two minutes. After presenting a bouquet of flowers and wishing him great success in his much-deserved political elevation, I was about to leave when he stopped me and made a surprising offer, 'I want you to take a break from the university and join the government.' I replied, 'Sir, I am content with my position at the

---

1 The details of inner party dynamics in the election of I.K. Gujral may be found in his biography, *Matters of Discretion: An Autobiography* (New Delhi: Hay House Publishers (India), 2011) pp. 391-401.

university, but I cannot disobey your order.' Gujral said, 'Think over it. I will call you in a few days.'

After about two weeks, I received a call from the Prime Minister's Office (PMO). I visited Gujral at his residence at the appointed time. After enquiring about my well-being, he stated, 'I want you to undertake a diplomatic assignment; I will let you know the country later.' I answered, 'Sir, I would be honoured to serve your government in Delhi, may be in MEA, in the policy planning division.' I had expressed the same preference to Shri Dinesh Singh earlier. Gujral smiled and said, 'You have no idea of how the policy planning division in MEA works. That is not where real policies are formulated. We shall discuss the details later.' I came home and discussed Gujral's proposal with my wife Anuradha. She insisted that I should accept Gujral's offer, graciously made to advance my career.

Within a few days, I was called again to discuss certain aspects of the Gujral Doctrine, particularly concerning our immediate neighbourhood, and potential advancements within SAARC. At that time, Gujral had just returned from the Male SAARC Summit held in May 1997. He shared his experiences at the summit and his discussions with Chandrika Kumaratunga and Nawaz Sharif. Chandrika had briefed him on Sri Lanka's internal affairs, particularly the ongoing ethnic conflict. While seeking my insights into the internal situation in Sri Lanka, Gujral enquired, 'I understand that you are a good friend of President Chandrika. How are her efforts in the ongoing war against the LTTE progressing?

While I was providing my assessment of the challenging situation faced by the Sri Lankan Army in the ongoing war, he interrupted, proposing, 'Would you consider becoming our High Commissioner to Colombo? The position will be available in a couple of months.' I promptly declined, surprising him with my refusal of such a pivotal assignment. When asked for an explanation, I stated, 'Sir, for two reasons: Firstly, I am concerned that personal friendship might hinder impartial responses to the evolving complex situation in Sri Lanka. Moreover, there is a high likelihood of the Opposition parties and media, both in Sri Lanka and India, accusing both Chandrika and me of compromising our respective national interests due to our personal friendship if we take actions they disagree with. This could subject you personally and your government to unwarranted pressures for appointing me.' I suggested that he consider appointing someone from South India who is not of Tamil origin.

A few weeks earlier, Santosh Kumar, a senior IFS officer who was with us on the Sri Lanka visit in January 1997, had visited me along with a common Sapru House friend Surendra Bhutani. I was asked to recommend Santosh Kumar's name to Gujral for the Sri Lanka vacancy. I told Gujral about this but said that my personal preference would be for Shivshankar Menon, with whom I had remained in touch since the 1994 Nepal election study. Gujral must have consulted many others and considered all relevant aspects of this sensitive and important appointment. Eventually, Menon joined as India's High Commissioner to Sri Lanka in August 1997.

On Pakistan, Gujral said he was deciding to restart bilateral dialogue. He narrated his one-on-one discussions with Nawaz Sharif on the sidelines of the Male Summit, quoting Nawaz Sharif saying in pure Punjabi, the common language of both the leaders:

Asi jande hein ki military nal asi Kashmir le nahin sakde. Asi aye bhi jande hein ki tusi sanu Kashmir nahi devoge. Pher bhi gal karan whitch ki aitraj he ga. (We know that we cannot take Kashmir militarily and we also know that you will not give Kashmir to us. Still, what is the objection in talking on Kashmir.)

Gujral started a 'Composite Dialogue' with Pakistan to resolve all outstanding issues between the two countries at the level of foreign secretaries. This included the Kashmir dispute and trade and transit problems. I wrote two opinion pieces in *The Times of*

India in May 1997 on the subject which was appreciated by the Prime Minister.

Appointed as Ambassador to Laos

By the end of May 1997, I was informed about my appointment as India's ambassador to Lao People's Democratic Republic (Lao PDR or Laos). Bhabani Sen Gupta, who was very close to Gujral, told me that I should not agree to go to Laos and request the Prime Minister for another country. I chose not to follow his advice, deeming it impertinent to seek a revision of the Prime Minister's decision, especially since he had already sounded me on a very important option of Sri Lanka. Further, some common friends, including Muchkund Dubey, confided to me that Gujral had two options for my appointment—either as an ambassador or as a member of the Union Public Service Commission, a Constitutional position lasting five years. Some of the common friends, who were consulted by Gujral regarding my appointment, suggested the latter position for a more extended government tenure, but Gujral ultimately rejected it, stating that given my professional background, a diplomatic assignment was more fitting.

I kept the decision to appoint me as India's ambassador to Laos confidential, sharing it only with my wife and immediate family members. I did not want to make it public until there was an official communication. Unfortunately, Mushahid Hussain, a friend and cabinet minister in Nawaz Sharif's government in Pakistan, disclosed this information. During his visit to India in late May, I had invited him to address the students and faculty in SIS/JNU. Before making his presentation, he congratulated me and informed the gathering that he had just attended an informal lunch with Prime Minister Gujral, where he learnt about my appointment as an ambassador. I found myself embarrassed by this premature disclosure.

I received the first communication from MEA offering me appointment as ambassador only in early July when a new Foreign Secretary, K. Raghunath, had assumed office. I accepted the offer and said that my 10 years' experience as a Professor in JNU must be taken into account while designating my status. I was subsequently informed that I would be ambassador in Category I, which is equivalent to that of a secretary in MEA. The post in Laos, a small country, was generally filled up by an officer of the rank of joint secretary. I went to the PM to thank him for the appointment. He explained to me that Laos had gained significance in India's Look East Policy, as it had become a member of ASEAN (Association of Southeast Asian Nations) and there was also defence cooperation now between India and Laos.

Years later, Ambassador A.N Ram, who was an additional secretary in the Southern Division (handling Southeast Asia and Australia) of MEA at the time when my appointment was being worked out, confided to me that Foreign Secretary Salman Haider had held onto my file for nearly two months, causing a delay in issuing the formal letter of appointment. Ambassador Ram developed a friendly association with me, particularly as I was contributing a paper for a volume on the 'Look East Policy', which he was editing. This revelation perplexed me because Haider was considered one of Gujral's favourites, and Gujral had even appointed him as next high commissioner to the UK after his retirement in July 1997. It raised questions about why Haider might resist a decision taken by Gujral and why did he not favour my appointment. In 2014, I shared a panel on India's foreign policy at a Banaras Hindu University seminar with Haider. While waiting at the Varanasi airport to board our return flight to Delhi after the seminar, I asked him about the delay in processing my appointment papers during his tenure as foreign secretary. He said: 'This happens sometimes.'

Political appointments made by Gujral had run into serious controversy soon after he assumed office. One such appointment was that of Bhabani Sen Gupta, a close friend of Gujral for many years, as Officer on Special Duty (OSD) in the PMO. This position would give Bhabani the advantage of overseeing all important file movements, a prospect that was not acceptable to the higher bureaucracy and Opposition parties. A serious debate on this appointment was raised in Parliament by Opposition leader Chandra Shekhar. Bhabani faced accusations of being overly pro-US at the expense of India's national interests, particularly regarding India's nuclear capabilities. Some of his past writings, opposing India's efforts to attain nuclear status, were brought to light. To avoid political controversy, Gujral had to request Bhabani's immediate resignation from the post.

Gujral also nominated several individuals to the Rajya Sabha, including some of his close friends and acquaintances such as eminent journalist Kuldeep Nayyar, M.J. Akbar, and film actor-social activist Shabana Azmi.[2] The media and bureaucracy criticised Gujral for these appointments and caricatured the persons involved as FOG(s), or Friends Of Gujral. The media also caricatured me as one of the FOGs. Many well-wishers, including K. Subrahmanyam, former IIC Director N.N. Vohra, C. Raja Mohan and many of my SIS/JNU colleagues, congratulated me on my appointment and praised Gujral for reviving the Nehruvian tradition of inducting outside talent into the government. Former Foreign Secretary J.N. Dixit generously hosted a dinner at his residence in Gurgaon to celebrate my appointment. Before the dinner, Dixit gave a tour of his impressive library, a place where he dedicated much of his time. My interactions with Dixit, affectionately known as Mani, date back to

---

2 Gujral has also discussed this in his autobiography. Ibid, pp. 399 and 404.

his tenure as the High Commissioner of Sri Lanka in the late 1980s, and I remained in regular touch with him. Dixit wrote several books on various aspects of India's foreign policy. I also had the opportunity to review his book on Sri Lanka.

There was, however, no dearth of friends and colleagues who advised me against accepting the appointment due to the controversy surrounding it and the perceived instability of the Gujral government. In July 1997, I attended the famous Wilton Park conference in England, on South Asian security. I arrived in London, and from there, I was chauffeured to the secluded Wilton Park palatial venue. Jaswant Singh, a prominent BJP leader, was also present at the conference. Both of us, being from Jodhpur, had known each other for a long time and gelled well together. We also met frequently in the IIC's Saturday Discussion Group. During a post-dinner stroll at Wilton Park, Jaswant remarked: 'I hear that Gujral has promised to send you out as an ambassador. Let us see if he is able to carry out his promise because he is in the habit of making impractical promises to his friends.' Jaswant later became the foreign minister in the government that succeeded Gujral. During my tenure as ambassador, I found him too occupied to respond to my requests for appointment on two separate visits to New Delhi from Vientiane.

I could not disrespect Gujral's decision. He had always been kind to me and gave an unprecedented break to my career. In SIS/ JNU, two other senior colleagues before me had been chosen for diplomatic assignments, Prof. Sisir Gupta to Vietnam and Spain, and Prof. Bimal Prasad to Nepal. This appointment made me an object of envy for some of my senior colleagues who went to Bhabani Sen Gupta to convey to the Prime Minister that people of higher seniority (more than me) like himself should not be ignored for diplomatic assignments. It also triggered the aspirations of other colleagues like Prof. Parimal Kumar Das and Prof. R.P. Kaushik, both of whom succeeded in securing such appointments later under Vajpayee and Dr Manmohan Singh's governments, respectively.

As a result of my appointment, I also gained insights into the profound and intense turf consciousness among IFS officers when individuals from outside their ranks entered their profession. Various signs, ranging from active resistance and mockery to benign indifference, greeted my entry into MEA. Foreign Secretary Salman Haider sitting on my appointment file has already been noted earlier. There is a customary practice in MEA to take newly appointed ambassadors on an all-India visit (called *Bharat Darshan)* to enhance their awareness of India's strengths and weaknesses so that they can represent India better in their assignments abroad.

I was told to get ready for the *Bharat Darshan*, at least to India's North Eastern Region due to its cultural proximity with Laos. Such a trip, however, never came through. I got no proper briefing for my assignment. Appointments for briefings were fixed with joint secretary concerned Nilima Mitra, additional secretary A.N. Ram, the official in-charge of security affairs in MEA, the Prime Minister and the President. When I reached Mitra's office, I was shown a bundle of files kept on a separate table and asked to browse through them for any information I deemed necessary. Ambassador Ram was very courteous and told me that 'a scholar like you does not need any briefing'. He gave me a cup of coffee and bid me farewell for my journey to Laos. The official in-charge of security affairs was polite and advised vigilance against terrorist and espionage activities, emphasising prompt reporting to the home office.

I found the cold and inadequate briefing disheartening, especially for someone unfamiliar with diplomatic protocol and MEA norms. Surprisingly, I was also not asked to sign any oath of secrecy and confidentiality. There was, however, no lapse on MEA's part in sanctioning funds for my official attire (*Sherwani* and *bandgala* jackets, etc.) and arranging for the selection of artifacts and carpets from the MEA store for my residence in Laos.

Initially, my departure was scheduled for October 1997, but at the last moment, the office of the joint secretary requested me to postpone my travel by a few more weeks. The reason was that D.R. Pahuja, an IFS (B) officer (one who does not clear the UPSC test but rises through internal promotions in-service), officiating as ambassador in Vientiane, was keen to lead an exhibition to Luang Prabang, an ancient city in northern Laos. The MEA officer said, 'Mr Pahuja has worked for the exhibition with considerable efforts. Let him have the satisfaction of leading it. If you go now, he would not be able to do so.' I readily agreed.

Finally, I took my flight to Vientiane, via Bangkok, on 25 November 1997. My mother was extremely pleased to know that I was going to represent India in a foreign country. All other members of the family were also happy. I missed my father's and grandparents' presence. Anuradha was to join me later as her college was working. Suresh Thapa, my domestic help, was thrilled to accompany me, as this was his first air travel and foreign visit.

The only useful tips that I got as briefing were from three persons, Prime Minister Gujral, my friend Shivshankar Menon and honorable President K.R. Narayanan. Gujral told me that though a small country, Laos' significance for India was increasing every day. Laos had become an ASEAN member and was seeking increasing development cooperation from India. In 1996, India's Foreign Minister Pranab Mukherjee paid a visit to Laos. We then discussed Laos' strategic significance in the context of China's rise. After the briefing session with the PM, I looked into the available literature on Laos' foreign policy and domestic politics. I also discussed the subject in the broader framework of the ASEAN region with my colleagues who were teaching Southeast Asia in my Centre.

As a landlocked country, Laos was encircled by China, Vietnam, Thailand and Cambodia. Throughout history, India has been a steadfast supporter of Laos, offering assistance in various challenges—from its struggle for independence against French domination to dealing with the spillover effect of the US war in Vietnam, and now addressing the digital divide within ASEAN. Strategically, Laos maintained close relations with Vietnam, and also sought space for its autonomy amongst its competing neighbours, particularly Thailand and China. It is in this context that Laos expressed a desire for enhanced relations with India. There was considerable goodwill for India in Laos, stemming from India's impartial and independent role in the UN Supervisory Commission for peace during the 1950s. Additionally, India had committed to supporting the development efforts of all new ASEAN members, in its extended neighbourhood, under the CLMV grouping (Cambodia, Laos, Myanmar and Vietnam).

I shared my frosty experience of MEA briefing with Menon when he was on a brief visit from Colombo. He said, 'Don't worry about such official briefings. They are, in any case, not of much use in the long run. Just use your common sense and be straightforward in communicating your assessment to the authorities concerned.'

I had known President Narayanan since February 1968 when he came to a conference on South Asian Foreign Policies organised by my Department of Political Science in Rajasthan University, Jaipur. I had discussed my PhD dissertation chapter on 'Nepal's Regional Non-Alignment' with him on the sidelines of that conference. Later, he was my Vice-Chancellor in JNU, from January 1979 to October 1980. He was very affectionate and reassuring. He expressed his unhappiness with the undue delay in my appointment. In his briefing on Laos, he underlined the cultural and political dynamics of the region comprising of Laos and its neighbouring countries because he had also served in Myanmar (then Burma) during his MEA years.

President Narayanan then cautioned me that the clouds of instability were hovering over the Gujral government. He wished that the government is not disturbed but, due to unpredictable politics of the country, if and when it falls, he asked me firmly, not to resign my position. He said, 'Diplomatic recall is not the tradition in India and the MEA seldom invokes it when governments change, unlike in the United States.'

In Vientiane

In Vientiane, I was received with all the necessary protocol formalities of the Lao PDR government. D.R. Pahuja, Head of Chancery (HOC), who was officiating as ambassador, greeted me at the airport. He was accompanied by about six to seven ambassadors of other friendly countries. It was a small airport with a modestly furnished VIP visitors' room. After exchanging pleasantries and introductions over tea, we drove from the airport directly to the embassy residence. On reaching there, I learnt that the car that drove me from the airport was not our embassy's vehicle; it had been borrowed from another friendly embassy. Our car, a recently acquired white Mercedes, was at Pahuja's residence, where his daughter, a child of 10-11 years, had misplaced the car keys for the past couple of days.

Pahuja said he had borrowed a car from another embassy until our keys were traced. I responded, 'No, we must arrange for our own alternative vehicle.' The embassy residence was an impressive French colonial building with five bed rooms on the first floor. A huge representational room was on the ground floor attached to a large kitchen and another side room. There were four staff quarters at the backside. The front and backside of the residence had spacious garden areas. There were fruit trees and space for a kitchen garden on the backside. The front side had a big lawn bordered with flower shrubs and tall trees. However, the residence was shabbily furnished.

The carpets and artifacts brought from the MEA store were to be unpacked and properly placed.

The next morning, I walked to the embassy office which was close by, around 200-300 metres distance. The office building was a two-floor structure. On the ground floor were office spaces for the visa and consular section, cypher room, receptionist and other administrative staff. There were also store rooms and an annexe on the ground floor. The first floor had offices for the ambassador, the HOC and their respective personal assistants. The office compound also had staff quarters for India-based supporting staff. They were: Lakshmi and Swaminathan, the husband-wife team as PAs for the ambassador and HOC, S. Mahesh as cypher assistant, Prashant Das, a consular and visa assistant, and Suresh, a security guard.

Pahuja had a separate residence, about two kilometres away from the embassy compound. He completed his term within a few months of my arrival and was replaced by a very competent IFS officer B. Nagabhushana Reddy, who proved to be a great asset to me throughout my stay in Vientiane. There were two defence officers of army captain's rank deputed to teach English, computer practice and basic tactics to the Laotian defence service officers. They had separate residences. Soon, they were replaced by upgraded officers, Major(s) Raju Chouhan and Ajai Malik. We neither had defence attaché nor an intelligence officer in the embassy. These officers based in Vietnam were also accredited to Laos. They paid periodic visits to look after our interests in these areas. In one of the visits in July 1999, Vietnam-based defence attaché, Col. P.K. Chakravorty tried to influence my confidential assessment of one of the defence officers. I reported his undesirable attempt to the Military Secretary in the Army Headquarters. My communication was taken proper note of.

In addition to the Indian staff, we also had five local employees: Khampai, a security guard at the ambassador's residence; Bupa, the ambassador's driver; Chintala, a gardener at the residence; Villay, the receptionist at the embassy; and a translator-cum-interpreter for local language at the embassy. They were all hardworking, polite and sincere people. On one occasion, as I was leaving my office after the day's work, I noticed our translator carrying a plastic bag with something moving inside. Curious, I asked him about it. He remained silent with a sense of guilt on his face. Other staff members said it was a large lizard he was taking home for dinner. This conversation revealed that the Laotians eat a variety of creatures that crawl, fly, or swim. No wonder, I saw no birds in our garden and no dogs on the streets.

Both the embassy residence and the embassy office needed a facelift, prompting me to convene a meeting with all Indian staff to introduce myself. I said that being unaware of diplomatic protocol and practices, I would need their help and support all the time, and called on them to work as a team, without much of a hierarchy consciousness. Stressing our shared commitment, I called for diligent efforts to elevate India's standing in Laos. During the meeting, specific tasks were delegated to each member to revamp both the embassy residence and the embassy office. Our approach involved acquiring new furniture and furnishings only when essential, while retaining functional old items. We aimed to economise within the approved budget, saving money while fulfilling essential needs. Additionally, the buildings required a fresh coat of paint, and old junk items stored over time were to be appropriately disposed of.

Not everyone was happy with my focus on economising, but they accepted the guidelines laid down. With great dedication and tireless efforts, the staff and officers worked sincerely to complete the assigned jobs. Within a month, both the embassy residence and the embassy building had respectable façades and interiors. The embassy staff informed me that we had to cross over to Nong Khai in Thailand almost every week to purchase our provisions and household necessities. I decided not to use the official car for my private travels and ordered a secondhand Toyota from Japan. The car came within two months. This helped me travel across to various places in Thailand, including Bangkok and Chiang Mai. I brought the car to New Delhi after the end of my term.

The Lao government was very kind in arranging my credentials presentation ceremony within a week of my arrival in Vientiane. It was completely a protocol-driven yet impressive ceremony, providing me with a thrilling and enlightening experience. Driving to the President's Residence with the national flag flying on the mast of my car (we got the keys of our car within a couple of days) was indeed a moment of honour and pride. Pahuja had accompanied me, and both he and the President's protocol officer briefed me on how to present my Letter of Credentials to the President, specifying the number of steps to take and the appropriate distance to maintain. I followed their instructions accordingly. After the exchange of pleasantries, in our formal brief addresses, Lao President Nouhak Phoumsavanh and I underlined the friendship and cordial relations between our two countries. We expressed confidence that these relations would be strengthened and expanded in the months and years to come. I emphasised that India has stood with Lao PDR in all its challenges and would continue to do so. I also assured the Lao government and people that India would be one of its crucial development partners, both through ASEAN and bilaterally.

The reception after the formal ceremony created a bit of difficulty for me, as red and white wines were being served liberally. As I do not consume alcohol, I had to hold a white wine glass and pretend to be drinking it. I had prepared for this scenario in my mind beforehand. After a while, I took a red wine glass, pretending to have consumed my earlier white wine. After the reception, we bid farewell to the President and left for our embassy.

A brief note was sent back home on the credentials presentation ceremony. The day after the ceremony I received a call from Dato Ajit

Singh, Secretary General of ASEAN, for a meeting. He had come to pay his farewell call on completing his term with ASEAN. He was a Malaysian diplomat of Indian origin. We met next day in a restaurant over coffee. After exchanging pleasantries, he talked about SAARC and India-Pakistan relations. He had read some of my writings on SAARC. He said he had been to Pakistan recently and the common people there were strongly in favour of normal relations with India. He accepted that Pakistan's army was the major obstacle. Knowing that Gujral and Nawaz Sharif had good personal equations, he hoped that cooperation under the SAARC umbrella would progress. He appreciated Gujral's initiative in starting bilateral dialogue between India and Pakistan. He also shared his experience of ASEAN and was happy that under his term as Secretary General, Vietnam, Laos and Myanmar could become its members and Cambodia was to follow soon. I filed my report to MEA on these discussions. Nilima Mitra, joint secretary concerned, called me to thank for this report sent so soon after my arrival in Laos.

For the next few days, I undertook courtesy calls to the prime minister and various other ministries. From India's perspective, the foreign, agriculture and defence ministries were important. The ministry of agriculture and mining played a crucial role in a principally agricultural country. For India, this ministry gained importance as we were exporting water pumps, which were supplied by the Kirloskar company. In defence matters, we had an agreement to service and repair Russian-supplied fighter planes for the Lao Air Force. We were also providing English language training to the Lao defence officers. There were four key officers in the Lao foreign ministry for our overall engagements and day-to-day issues. Foreign Minister Somsavat Lengsavad was assisted by two Vice-Ministers, Sobhan Siritirath and Phongsavat Boupha. Bounkeut Sangsomsak, the Permanent Secretary in the Ministry of Foreign Affairs (MoFA), joined a few months later. Lengsavad was considered closer to the Chinese in the Lao diplomatic community. However, I always found him courteous and helpful. I struck an instant rapport with Siritirath.

Within a few months of my arrival in Vientiane, President Nouhak Phoumsavanh retired. He was succeeded by General Khamtai Siphandon. Soon after this change, Siritirath shifted to the President's office as principal secretary to him. We arranged Siritirath's visit to India in November 1999 to deliver a lecture under the India-ASEAN Lecture Series. Vice-Minister Boupha also became very friendly. He was writing a book on Lao history, the outlay and content of which were discussed with me. He asked me to edit the draft of the book for its language as he was not very confident of his command over English. I readily agreed and read through all the chapters one by one in the months that followed. The book was published and he kindly presented a copy of the same to me. I arranged a visit to India for Boupha in March 1998, with the support of the Indian Council for Cultural Relations (ICCR).

Bounkeut and his family were very fond of Indian music and Bollywood songs. I gifted him several CDs of Bollywood songs and Indian music. He became one of our regular guests and helped me in my work in many ways, particularly in comprehending Lao history and its political landscape. I also struck an instant rapport with Agriculture Minister Dr Siene Saphangthong. We met regularly, benefitting from his cooperative and understanding approach towards mutual concerns. Dr Saphangthong also held the position of president of the Lao-India Friendship Association in Vientiane. His visit to India was organised in May 1999.

Issues of Interests

The agriculture ministry was very happy with their cooperation with India. India was supplying Kirloskar company's water pumps to

Laos for pumping water from riverbeds to uphill terraced farms. As a result, Laos had increased its paddy production. This transformed Laos from a food-deficient nation to one that was self-sufficient in food production. We successfully boosted the export of water pumps, benefitting both Laos and India. When I assumed my post in Laos in November 1997, Kirloskar Brothers Ltd had exported water pumps worth US$14 million. By the time of my departure for India in December 1999, the value of exported pumps had surpassed US$30 million. These figures did not reflect in our trade statistics, as the pumps were offloaded in Thailand and then transported to Laos by land route. I brought the matter to the attention of India's Ministry of Commerce, but the recording system was not corrected until my departure from Laos.

The Lao agriculture ministry and the Government of Lao PDR had an issue with Kirloskar company. While signing the contract, the company had agreed to set up a foundry, a manufacturing plant, in Laos for spare parts of these water pumps. During my predecessor's time, External Affairs Minister Pranab Mukherjee paid a visit to Laos in January 1996. During this visit, India proposed a Joint Venture to produce agricultural pumps in Laos and offered a soft loan of $US2 mn for the project. However, even after several years, the Kirloskars had not taken any action to set up the promised foundry for spare parts. The Lao agriculture ministry argued that a manufacturing plant would not only open up employment opportunities for the Laotians but also enable early and affordable supply of spare parts. This would help in quick repairs of pumps for reuse on farms.

I had long discussions with the representatives of Kirloskar in Laos. They contended that Laos lacked semi-skilled workers for the proposed manufacturing plant. Importing skilled workers from India would increase production costs and, consequently, the price of spare parts. However, I considered this argument invalid, as it contradicted a promised obligation. Despite my continuous persuasion, Kirloskar only established a showroom-cum-service centre in Vientiane in 1998. The Laotians perceived this as a half-hearted response to their genuine demand.

There were problems in Laos with India's other private companies as well. Consulting Engineering Services Pvt. Ltd. (CES), which was engaged in undertaking many projects globally, was involved in a road construction project before my arrival there. The Government of Laos found that the road had deteriorated rapidly. There were big creases on the road surface, making heavy transportation risky for trucks. The Laotian government felt that the coal tar spread on the road was less in thickness by half an inch or so than specified in the contract. This had caused creasing on the road. I communicated this to CES and MEA. CES's response was that the Laotian side was plying trucks carrying heavier loads than specified in the contract, which might have caused these waves on the road. CES also said that the Chinese contractor who built the road was at fault, and the Lao government was not questioning him while asking CES to pay all the compensation. We from the embassy made our best efforts to get the matter looked into as objectively as possible and finally got it resolved amicably.

India had also opened up defence cooperation with Laos. It has been noted earlier that two Indian Army officers of the rank of Major, were imparting English language, computer and basic tactics courses to Lao Army officers. In addition, India had entered into an agreement to service and repair fighter aircraft obtained from the Russian Federation. A Laotian defence delegation, led by the Head of the Technical Battalion of Fighter Planes, had visited India in November 1995 to look at India's capabilities and expertise in the field. The Laotian defence ministry was not initiating work in accordance with this agreement by releasing funds. I had a number of discussions with Minister Choummaly Sayasone, but the issue could not be resolved.

It appears that the initial agreement lapsed, and a new defence cooperation agreement was concluded between the two countries in 2008. Through my efforts, I gradually learnt that there were two reasons on the Laotian side for not implementing the original agreement. One was the international economic crisis of 1997 that hit the ASEAN region badly. Laos faced a serious crunch of foreign exchange. They were not in a position to pay for any services in dollars. There were indirect indications to offer timber as a commodity to cover the costs of servicing and repairing the planes. However, the Indian system was not set up to handle commodity payments effectively. The second reason could be that the Laotians were influenced by the Russians, who aimed to secure such contracts to boost their own dwindling economy. The Russians might have suggested to the Laotians that the fighter planes supplied by India had a limited lifespan of around 20 years and might not be safe to repair and fly beyond this period. If this was indeed the case, I wondered as to why India and Laos signed this agreement without assessing the life cycle of the planes. The Vietnam-based defence attaché accredited to Laos was not of much help to me in resolving this issue. There was not much that I could do on this issue after having discussed the matter with the defence minister.

The lesson to be learnt from all the three cases was that India's private and public sector companies have to do much homework and maintain professional integrity and credibility while undertaking international projects. The business and management styles of the public and private sectors are a critical factor in the conduct of India's foreign policy and diplomacy. There was also the need of having strict auditing by an independent mechanism by the Government of India to ensure that projects undertaken are properly executed.

The years of my ambassadorship, 1997-99, were full of challenges for Indian diplomacy throughout the world. We had to mobilise support for India's declaration of its nuclear status, following the

Pokhran-II tests in May 1998. We also needed the support of friendly countries for India's quest for permanent membership of the UN Security Council. And above all, we needed our friendly countries to support us in the war imposed on us by Pakistan in Kargil in May 1999.

Laotian friendship and understanding for India made these challenges far more manageable than I expected. I met Foreign Minister Lengsavad and Vice-Minister Boupha in the Ministry of Foreign Affairs soon after the Pokhran explosion of May 1998. They were both responsive and reassuring, telling me that we want India to be strong. It was, however, not possible for the Lao government to formally and publicly support India's position because Laos as a member of ASEAN could not go against the regional organisations' unanimous and well-known stand on non-proliferation and comprehensive test ban. India's declaration of its nuclear status had been strongly opposed by the West. The US had imposed sanctions and Japan and Australia reacted very sharply to denounce it. Strategically, Laos had mostly not supported the Western positions on critical issues of international significance. Both Vietnam and Laos had fought the war against France and the US for their independent existence. Laos therefore had unstated support and sympathy for India.

Closely related to this issue was the question of UN reforms, particularly the composition of the UN Security Council. India, along with Germany, Japan and Brazil, the Group of Four (G4) as they came to be identified, were seeking expansion of the UNSC and permanent seats for themselves. Laos as a developing Asian country was in support of India's stand. I tried to mobilise support in the ruling Lao People's Revolutionary Party both for India's nuclear power status and its permanent membership of the UNSC. Bounkeut, Permanent Secretary in the foreign ministry, was very helpful in this respect. The Laotian ruling party readily agreed as there was similar demand from the other three members, Japan, Germany and Brazil, as well.

The party adopted a resolution accordingly. Foreign Minister Lengsavad was authorised to publicly declare Laos' strong support in the forthcoming annual UN General Assembly meeting. When I got the confirmed information about the party's position, I promptly sent a telegram to MEA, requesting that the Laotian Foreign Minister be appropriately thanked for this when he delivers his statement in the UNGA. It seems that by the time my telegram reached MEA, Minister Jaswant Singh had already left Delhi for the UNGA meeting. I expected MEA to alert our UN Mission in this respect. This, it seemed, did not happen.

Lengsavad made a clear and categorical statement in support of the UNSC membership of G4. He was congratulated by Japanese, German and Brazilian representatives. But none from India was present in UNGA to listen to him or to congratulate him. This was told to me by Vice-Minister Boupha after the return of Lengsavad from the UN. What could I do except to apologise, feel embarrassed and write to MEA about this. MEA responded promptly and Minister Jaswant Singh wrote to his Laotian counterpart thanking him for the UNSC support.

On the Pakistani aggression in Kargil in May 1999, which was like a repeat of what Pakistan had done in Jammu & Kashmir in 1947, I briefed the Ministry of Foreign Affairs properly. I found that even in the MEA's briefings notes that were being sent to us regularly, Pakistan's consistent aggressive behaviour and our position and legitimacy of claims on Kashmir had not been made very clear and emphatic. I had written and taught much on India-Pakistan relations. So, I made detailed notes on the origins of the India-Pakistan problems in Kashmir, starting with Pakistan's intervention in Kashmir by violating its Standstill Agreement with the Maharaja of Kashmir in 1947. These notes were submitted and explained to the highest Lao officials and ministers. I got a call from the President's Office to brief him on the day-to-day developments on the war front through detailed notes. This was followed by my weekly briefings in person to the President. He showed keen interest in the developments on the war front.

By July 1999, when the tables were turned on Pakistan on the war front and India got the upper hand, many countries came out openly in support of India's position. The US, fearing escalation of war between the two nuclear armed neighbours, intervened directly by calling Pakistan's prime minister to the US and telling him in no uncertain words to respect the Line of Control with India. This was a clear acknowledgement that Pakistan was the aggressor. When I briefed the Lao President on these lines in one of the briefing sessions, he told me that this is the moment for India to resolve the Kashmir problem even militarily once and for all. I was happy to hear this as a clear and strong support for India, and reported the matter to MEA.

The Kargil War precipitated an unexpected concern for us; namely the possibility of a terrorist attack on the embassy. Suddenly, a R&AW officer from Delhi, Ajay Singh, came on a visit to alert our embassy that a Pakistani terrorist attack cannot be ruled out. After defeat in the Kargil War, Pakistan could mount such an attack on any of the vulnerable Indian Missions, which included ours in Vientiane. He gave me and the embassy staff basic tips of how to deal with such an unfortunate situation if it arose at all. We also met Lao foreign ministry officials and requested them that for such an unforeseen event, embassy security may be ensured.

There was another indirectly related security issue faced by us before the arrival of the R&AW officer. The Laotian government had detained a Tamil, who claimed to be an Indian citizen, for some visa and foreign exchange irregularities. We contacted the person through the Laotian security establishment and discovered that he had faked his identity and was actually a Sri Lankan Tamil on way to Australia. He had given money to the LTTE in Sri Lanka for his escape and they had fraudulently arranged for his travel via Vientiane under a faked Indian identity. For this purpose, the LTTE had networked with Indian Tamils running a hotel in Vientiane. I reported the matter to Delhi and also alerted my friend Sri Lankan Foreign Minister Lakshman Kadirgamar about the LTTE's contacts and activities in the region.

I was surprised when, just a couple of days after I communicated with Delhi about the matter, a member of the Indian Tamil community in Laos approached me to enquire about the incident. He failed to provide a satisfactory answer when questioned about his source of information on the matter. I also shared this information with the visiting R&AW officer. He suspected that the information leak might have occurred through our cypher assistant, who, being from Tamil Nadu, had close personal ties with the Tamil community in Laos. The R&AW officer promised to further investigate the matter. After my return to India, I learnt that the Vientiane-based cypher assistant was recalled before the end of his term.

An important event during my term in Vientiane was the visit of Mrs Vasundhara Raje Scindia, India's Minister of State (MoS) for External Affairs. She visited Laos for four days, from 17-20 January 1999, to lead the Indian delegation for the second meeting of India-Lao PDR Joint Commission. This visit was preceded by the visit of secretary in the MEA, Sudhir Devare, partly to inspect the work of the embassy and partly to prepare for the visit of MoS Scindia. He was accompanied by Gaddam Dharmendra, Director in the division dealing with SE Asia. He was my former student who completed his MPhil under my supervision in SIS/JNU before clearing the UPSC examination for foreign service. The MoS' visit was the first high-level political visit after three years. She was accompanied by secretary Sudhir Devare and joint secretary Nilima Mitra. One of the important subjects taken up during the meeting was India's grant of a Line of Credit (LOC) of $US2 mn. There was a small technical difficulty in finalising the agreement to that effect. Laos was expected to pay a small service charge in US dollars which it was unable to commit because of its foreign exchange difficulties.

India's Ministry of Finance had reservations due to established procedures. We informally discussed the Joint Commission meeting's agenda a day prior at Hotel Lao Plaza, where the Indian delegation was staying. I was of the opinion that India should waive this charge. I urged Minister Raje, who was chairing the meeting, to consider it. However, she expressed her inability, citing the finance ministry's last-minute withdrawal from the delegation. I was puzzled to see such small decisions constrained by bureaucratic formalities. Fortunately, during the meeting the next day, a resolution was reached, and the LOC agreement was signed. The meeting also concluded another bilateral agreement to continue and enhance cultural cooperation between the two countries.

During the delegation-level meeting, Minister Raje did not participate due to protocol norms. The Laotian delegation was led by Vice-Minister Boupha, whose status in the Indian protocol hierarchy was considered equivalent to that of a secretary in MEA. Our minister could not equate herself with a junior officer on the Laotian side. I was also out of the delegation-level meeting as I had to accompany the Minister on her sightseeing visit to a Laotian hydro-power project.

Laos has huge potential for generating hydro-power and selling it to its neighbours like Thailand. I admired this cooperation between a small and a big neighbour in contrast to the sad story of hydro-power non-cooperation between India and Nepal. While driving with Minister Raje through the picturesque countryside of Laos, I wondered if I had been excluded from the delegation-level talks for being a non-career diplomat. I had been encountering the turf consciousness of the IFS community ever since my appointment. I was, however, pleased to have the opportunity to spend time with the minister. She was very informal, engaging and courteous. Both of us hailed from Rajasthan, so also did our External Affairs Minister (EAM) Jaswant Singh. We talked about Rajasthan politics, and I sensed that she was not quite happy with the way the EAM had allocated responsibilities to her.

We also discussed Nepal and its politics, as Raje's sister was married to Pashupati Shumsher Jung Bahadur Rana, the grandson of Nepal's last Rana prime minister, Mohan Shumsher Jung Bahadur Rana. I had known Pashupati for many years; he was an intellectual political figure and had contributed a chapter to one of my books on Nepal (*Nepal: An Assertive Monarchy*, 1973).

After concluding the Vientiane meeting, the Indian delegation visited Luang Prabang, the cultural capital of Laos. It has impressive old temples with the *Ramayana* and *Mahabharata* carved on its walls. We also visited the famous Sun temple. In Luang Prabang, Raje took me along on her shopping spree, showcasing her keen interest in very old textiles and tapestry. She was also fascinated by the large number of Pajero SUV vehicles on Laotian roads, both in Vientiane and Luang Prabang.

It was a successful visit, with both sides expressing happiness and satisfaction with the outcome. The Laotian side was generous and meticulous in their warm hospitality. Our very competent HOC B.N. Reddy had taken care of all the arrangements for the delegation and handled protocol matters perfectly, ably assisted by the embassy staff.

A small sore aspect of the visit was brought to my attention a few days later. Vice-Minister Boupha conveyed his desire to meet me. I invited him for dinner. No one else was present. He began by expressing satisfaction with the visit of the MoS, stating they were very pleased with the results. He then mentioned that a few days before the visit, India's secretary and joint secretary had met

Lao PDR's Ambassador based in New Delhi in connection with the preparations for the visit. During those discussions, the Indian officers had expressed a preference for their accommodation to be reserved in a five-star hotel rather than the Lao State Guest House. 'Our ambassador in New Delhi informed us accordingly. Our guest house is well-equipped to cater to the comforts and conveniences of our esteemed guests. We cannot afford five-star expenses for our official visitors,' Boupha added. He expressed regret that the wish of the Indian officers could not be accommodated. This revelation made me very uncomfortable.

I recalled that the officer concerned had also discussed the accommodation matter with me over the phone a week before the visit. I apologised to Boupha for our delegation's demand for special accommodation, and assured him that we would exercise caution in the future. In my view, the Lao government had taken this matter seriously, otherwise why would such a senior foreign ministry official bring it to my notice. I promptly conveyed the gist of this conversation to MEA via telegram.

However, a couple of months after my return to India, I learnt from Mrs Raje, during a casual meeting at the Republic Day reception in Rashtrapati Bhavan, that my telegram had offended senior MEA officers officers. Ambassadors' telegrams, she explained, reach the highest levels, including the PMO, in the Indian system.

I responded by stating that, given the sensitivity and importance of the matter, I had a responsibility to report it back home. Raje mentioned that, according to MEA bureaucracy, telephone communication was the preferred mode for such personally sensitive matters. But then, how would I be aware of this distinction? No one had briefed me about the so-called desirable and avoidable modes of communication with the ministry in diplomatic assignments. And above all, why should attempts by senior officers to seek petty favours not be brought to light?

Public Outreach and Cultural Connect

In my role in Vientiane, I always adhered to the guidance provided by President Narayanan, PM Gujral and Menon. I concentrated on Lao's relationships with its neighbouring countries within the framework of its overall foreign policy and the cultural aspects of the India-Lao relations. Soon after my arrival in Vientiane, I realised that the domestic politics of Laos was not for me to follow. Laos was a one-party dominant state governed by the Lao People's Revolutionary Party (LPRP), the reincarnation of the Communist Party of Laos. This party had fought against domestic monarchical rule and external colonial dominance, first by the French and later by the Americans.

Laos shared a long history of relations with Vietnam, having joined forces with Vietnam against the French and the Americans. Laos was heavily bombed by the US during the Vietnam War. The American B-52 bombers that took off from Thailand to bomb Vietnam, dropped their unused payloads on Laos indiscriminately while flying back. Numerous American servicemen and writers have extensively documented this. The per capita bombs dropped on Laos was the highest in the world, and Laos had a full-fledged National Unexploded Ordnance Programme (UXO) to address the aftermath of such bombings. Accidental explosion of buried bombs resulted in the loss of limbs of many innocent Laotians. I explored the possibility of introducing the Jaipur Foot (prosthetic limb) in Laos to assist those affected. While the Lao government initially expressed interest in the proposal, it couldn't be advanced further.

Laos, Vietnam and Cambodia were not included as members of ASEAN initially because of their Communist legacy. Since its liberation from feudal rule, Laos had been closely coordinating its major foreign policy moves with Vietnam. It also had close relations with Cambodia. The leaders of the three countries exchanged frequent visits to each other. China was gradually expanding its influence through economic engagement. It was flooding the Laotian markets with cheap consumer goods and was encouraging private Chinese investors to build hotels and casinos in the border areas.

After completing my assignment in Laos, I was offered a short-term fellowship in 2001 by the Institute of Defence and Strategic Studies (IDSS, subsequently renamed as the Rajaratnam School of International Studies, RSIS) of Nanyang Technological University, Singapore. I completed a study on 'China's Strategic Engagement with the New ASEAN' under this fellowship. This was published by IDSS and sold by Kinokuniya, a Japanese chain of booksellers. Having observed the growing influence of China in Laos and the adjoining region, I suggested to New Delhi that we must work out some mechanism of close cooperation with all the three Indo-China countries. I did not get any response to my suggestion during my term, but was happy to note that a year after my leaving Vientiane, the Mekong-Ganga Cooperation Initiative was established between India and the five Mekong countries namely, Vietnam, Laos, Cambodia, Myanmar (India's CLMV group) and Thailand in November 2000. This excluded China.

I remember Rakesh Sood, a senior IFS officer, calling me from MEA in October for some discussion on this initiative. He told me that External Affairs Minister Jaswant Singh will lead the Indian delegation for the 'Mekong-Ganga Swarnabhoomi Cooperation Initiative'. I asked him to remove the words 'Swarnabhoomi' from the name because Thailand had appropriated this name and the rest of the Mekong countries, particularly Laos, were not happy with it. I understand that this was done only after the advanced party reached Vientiane.

I also wrote to New Delhi that it may help streamline our regional diplomacy if Indian Missions could be given freedom to interact with each other bilaterally and collectively, (without going through

New Delhi), on issues of mutual interest. There was considerable overlap in such issues of concern to Laos with Vietnam, Cambodia and Thailand having significance for India. Mutual coordination on such issues can give a sharper edge to Indian diplomacy in the region if consultations take place promptly and regularly. The regional Missions could finance such meetings from their own budgeted resources without putting extra burden on the MEA. The Foreign Secretary responded by underlining the priority of protocol. I was asked to concentrate on bilateral matters with Laos only. Regional issues must be left to the head office.

Public and Cultural Diplomacy

Laos has been a closed polity. My common sense prompted me that in a closed society, public diplomacy may be of some help. There were not many reliable public sources of authentic information and interaction. Public diplomacy may create some openings. I therefore, started outreach efforts. To begin with, I cultivated the editor of *Vientiane Times*, who had access to key political figures. This enabled us to have our activities find a place in his paper to reach the wider public. I also established contacts with academic institutions. During the Kargil War, in an interaction with the Lao Institute of Foreign Service, I explained our stand on Kashmir and Pakistan's aggressive behaviour since partition. The India-Lao Friendship Association was activated. A special lecture by the president of the Association, Dr Saphangthong, was organised on 24 June 1999. The theme of the lecture was 'Prospects of Growth in India-Lao Economic Cooperation particularly in the field of Agriculture'. The meeting was attended by some 200 persons.

The small Indian diaspora in Laos, comprising about 500 persons mostly located in Vientiane, played a significant role in our public outreach programmes. Predominantly Tamil Muslims with roots in Tamil Nadu, they also included individuals from various parts of India, including Goa. Engaged in diverse occupations such as jewellery and precious stones trading, hotels and restaurants, readymade garments, mining, plantation and agarwood, they were consistently our first invitees at all embassy functions. I always appreciated visiting them during personal and social occasions when invited. Lalita Miranda, along with her husband, who ran a business establishment of manufacturing readymade garments and exporting them to France, was always forthcoming to help the embassy when cultural events were organised. Similarly, Rahim, a senior and respected representative of the diaspora community, was the first person to visit me within the initial week of my arrival in Vientiane. He brought a tin full of homemade *murukku* (a South Indian popular snack) as a gesture of affection. Although not a fan of *murukkus*, I graciously accepted a few pieces and returned the rest, expressing my appreciation without diminishing his thoughtful gesture.

The embassy actively extended assistance to the diaspora community during times of need, and I initiated a group consisting of fellow ambassadors from friendly countries for informal exchanges of views during lunch or coffee. Ambassadors from Singapore, France, Bangladesh, Myanmar and Brunei, and representatives of international organisations engaged in informal interactions to share information and gain insights into day-to-day developments in Laos.

Our embassy commemorated the 50th anniversary of India's Independence throughout 1998, including organising a photo exhibition in Laos' southern provinces of Savannakhet and Champasak. In July (27-29), we organised a seminar in Vientiane on 'India and Laos: Areas of Understanding and Cooperation'. This event was attended by Laos' Buddhist monks, academics, and journalists. With the support of ICCR, we successfully engaged

Indian scholars to participate and present papers. However, during the search for Indian scholars on Laos, I realised the paucity of academic interest and expertise in India on the Indo-China region.

The ICCR sent a Bharatanatyam dance group, led by Ms Leela Samson, which delivered an impressive performance on 12 August. We hosted a public reception at Lao Plaza Hotel, where India's progress across various sectors was screened. In November 1998, we commemorated Maulana Abul Kalam Azad's birth anniversary by screening the Hindi feature film *Aasman Se Gira* (Fallen from the Sky) at a prominent theatre. Despite widespread love for Bollywood films in Laos and the entire Southeast Asian region, language posed a challenge. I suggested that, for popular films that couldn't be dubbed, subtitles in Lao language could be provided for wider screening. However, this was deemed as a costly endeavour. Additionally, the Lao government was also sensitive towards films depicting political violence and protests, preferring not to expose their population to such content.

Our embassy also organised an Indian food festival where all embassy households enthusiastically contributed dishes from various regions of India. The menu featured *dosas, idlis, parathas, chole-bhature, samosas,* vegetable and chicken curries, vegetable and chicken *biryanis,* and desserts such as *laddus, gulab jamuns* and *kheer.* The embassy ladies and staff efficiently managed these food stalls. A significant number of Laotians, including some ministers and senior officials, attended the festival and relished the diverse Indian dishes. Through the sale of food items, we collected approximately US$300 worth in local currency, and the entire amount was donated to a local charitable organisation.

Under capacity building programmes, very few Lao students and trainees were being sent to India when I joined my duties. We raised the number of ITEC (Indian Technical and Economic Cooperation Programme) and ICCR scholarships from two to 50 in the first year and further to 100 in the second year of my stay. Officials from Lao government, students and artisans were sent to India for training and higher education under various programmes supported by these scholarships. Senior scientists from India were also invited to help Laos in the field of agriculture.

There had been a strong cultural connection between India and Laos spanning centuries. Until the seventh century, Hinduism left a significant impact on the entire region. Subsequently, Buddhism gained prominence and gradually supplanted the influence of Hinduism. Many Hindu temples were turned into Buddhist temples, with Buddha statues replacing Hindu idols in the sanctum sanctorum. As mentioned earlier, inscriptions of the *Ramayana* and *Mahabharata* adorn the temple walls in Luang Prabang in northern Laos Similarly, in the southern provinces of Savannakhet and Champasak, Hindu temples underwent conversion into Buddhist establishments.

I visited the Wat Phou Temple and travelled to Linga Mountain (the summit of the hillock is shaped like a *Shiva linga*) during my visit to the southern provinces. In Pakse, Champasak, the local governor arranged for me to visit a huge hall where archaeological remains of old temples with Hindu idols had been dumped. The Governor asked for India's help in creating a museum to showcase these artifacts. Upon my return, I communicated this to New Delhi, emphasising that Champasak's strategic location at the crossroads of Laos, Thailand, Cambodia, and Vietnam would make it an ideal site for an Indian museum showcasing our civilizational impact, which could serve as a very good tourist attraction. The Archaeological Survey of India sent an expert to assess the feasibility of such a museum. I was assured that the proposal was very good and the expert report will initiate the process. No such report came until the end of my term despite a couple of reminders. I remain hopeful that the project has made progress in some form since then.

Laos, a predominantly Buddhist country, has a long tradition of performing the *Ramayana* in a dance drama form. We organised such a performance in Vientiane. Laotians call *Ramayana* as *Lamakyan* and have interesting and innovative variations on its themes from what we have in India. We also received a communication from the Ministry of Culture in India to collect Ramayana artifacts from Laos. The sources of such artifacts were identified, contacted, and preparations were outlined to send such artifacts. However, obtaining such artifacts required financial resources for compensation to be paid to the donors of such artifacts. The culture ministry had no funds to spare and there was no provision in our small embassy budget either. As a result, the project was dropped unaccomplished. Human Resource Development Minister Murli Manohar Joshi was kind to send me a watch as a token of appreciation for our efforts.

While touring the southern provinces, we discovered a large number of stone-carved *Shiva lingas* in various forms, excavated from the riverbed of the Mekong. Along the riverside, we found small Shiva-Parvati temples where local villagers worshiped these deities as symbols of fertility. To enhance the awareness of India's cultural heritage in the Mekong region among our embassy staff, we organised a day-long river cruise picnic on the great river.

The Lao government invited all the resident diplomats to participate in a big cultural event in Luang Prabang. Air flights from Vientiane to Luang Prabang were organised by the government. I, however, opted for a road trip to experience the countryside's natural beauty. After some hesitation, the government agreed to my travel by road. I learnt later that one of the factors behind the hesitation on the government's part was the presence of a small rebel group of Hmong tribals, loyal to the royalist regime ousted in 1975. They had reportedly received CIA support to fight the communists in the last phase of the revolution. They disturbed the road traffic to extract food, cigarettes and biscuits from the travellers passing through their pocket in the mountainous region covered by dense jungle. The Russian ambassador had also decided to go by road but I could not coordinate my travel plan with him.

For the journey, my wife Anuradha, my son Shantanu and I stacked our car with cigarettes and biscuits for the rebels. When they approached us, our driver, Bua, initially felt uneasy. However, he explained in Lao language who we were. The rebels, who collected the biscuits and cigarettes from us, warmly greeted us by bowing down on hearing that we represented India.

It was a long journey of about 10 hours. We made a night halt in between at a scenic place called Vang Vieng. I developed a spondylitis problem on the way. I visited the government hospital in Luang Prabang for some relief. The doctors were competent and helped me fight the painful condition, but the hospital was found to be short on facilities. While participating in the cultural festivities, I and Anuradha were asked to join the dance group with ministers, other diplomats and local dignitaries. About 50 people moved rhythmically in a circle with their hands raised up to their shoulders and both the palms moving left and right. It was a very simple but interesting Laotian dance form performed by us.

This visit was a learning experience with a good feel of the Laotian countryside. Observing the serene landscapes made me realise that, with advancements in transportation, communication, and hotel facilities, tourist dollars could significantly contribute to the region. I believe the situation has likely progressed since then. After returning to Vientiane, I asked Bua about his experience of driving to Luang Prabang. He said: 'Ambassador very good, madam very good, journey and driving also very good but not again.'

During my stay in Vientiane, I also travelled to Xiengkhouang province, renowned for its hot water springs and the Plain of Jars. Our journey took us through extensive fields of sunflowers and papayas, prompting the thought that if these could be processed and exported, Laos could generate valuable foreign exchange. Locals informed us that due to the abundance of papaya cultivation, a significant portion of the fruits was being fed to pigs, resulting in large stocks going to waste every year.

Upon reaching the Plain of Jars, we found tubular-shaped stone jars of various sizes and dimensions scattered across the landscape. Archaeologists are currently investigating their origin, suggesting they date back to at least 773-987 CE, i.e. 8th-10th century. The hot water spring site was modestly developed for tourists, and we spent the night there, enjoying a couple of bathing sessions. During our visit, the Governor of Xiangkhouang province hosted a dinner to welcome us. While the meal included sticky rice, vegetables, and several local non-vegetarian dishes, unfortunately, we, being incorrigible vegetarians, couldn't enjoy those particular offerings.

Back Home

Diplomatic posting of persons from outside the IFS cadre is for two years. In September 1999, I went to India on home leave and met NSA Brajesh Mishra. The question of India signing the Comprehensive Test Ban Treaty (CTBT) was being vigorously debated in the South Block and New Delhi's strategic community at that time. Brajesh asked my opinion about signing the treaty. I strongly opposed it. He was of the same view and was uneasy on the efforts of many others in the government, including EAM Jaswant Singh, who were lobbying for it. Then he asked me about my work in Vientiane. I happily shared with him the gist of activities that we were engaged in, as well as Laos' relations with its close neighbours, particularly China, Vietnam and Thailand. He asked me if I would like to continue to work there. I said, 'No, not at all in Laos, once my term comes to an end.' He mentioned that another posting could be a complicated matter. I clarified that I was not seeking one.

Back in Vientiane in October, as the end of my term was approaching, I wrote to MEA about my wish to go back to JNU. In mid-November, while on the Diplomatic Bag duty in Bangkok, I received a call from MEA instructing me to wind up my work in Vientiane at my earliest convenience, preferably within the next couple of months. I gladly acknowledged the directive, assuring them of my prompt action.

I would like to mention here that I had resigned in March 1998, immediately upon learning about the fall of the Gujral government. President Narayanan, as noted earlier, had urged me not to do so, but my conscience was uneasy. The resignation was addressed to the prime minister, with a copy marked to the foreign minister. Within a couple of days of faxing the resignation letter, Brajesh Mishra called me to say that there was no action on my resignation letter because Prime Minister Vajpayee was not accepting it. He said in Hindi: *'Atal ji keh rahe hein ki aap tab chodiye jab aap ko hum koi aisa kaam karne ko kahen jo aap ko manjoor nahi ho.'* (Atal ji is saying that you should resign if and when we ask you to do something which is not acceptable to you.) The topic of my resignation was also brought up in Parliament in response to a question.

At that time, the Vajpayee government was recalling at least two of Gujral's political appointees, Salman Haider from London and N.P. Jain from South Africa. Haider was deeply displeased about being recalled, asserting that he had received Vajpayee's approval for his appointment before joining in London. Rumours circulated in MEA that the personal chemistry between Haider and Brajesh was not very good. The intricacies of political decisions are often difficult to decipher.

After returning from Bangkok, I announced my departure date and started winding up my work. Numerous farewell calls, dinners, and lunches followed. On 24 November 1999, I received a letter from the Foreign Secretary, saying, 'I write to convey to you on behalf of the Government and specifically ministry of external affairs, our deep appreciation of your contribution to promoting our interests vis-à-vis Laos and in strengthening India-Laos friendship and cooperation'. (A copy of the letter is attached as Annexure 3.) I left Vientiane on 10 December 1999, two weeks later than the end of my term.

On my return to JNU, I resumed my teaching and research activities. The diplomatic assignment proved to be a valuable and enlightening experience. It taught me the real difference between textbook foreign policy principles and real-world diplomatic endeavours. I now had a better idea of how the Ministry of External Affairs worked and how imponderable aspects of human behaviour shape critical policy decisions. Over time, these experiences began to shape my approach to teaching and research.

Some of my senior colleagues and students started addressing me as 'Ambassador Muni', which I resisted stoutly. I maintained that my academic career spanned decades and should not be overshadowed or undermined by a two-year diplomatic assignment. I also disagreed with the notion that positions of power should be accorded more value than those of a teacher.

6

Special Envoy and Casual Contacts

Special Envoy For UNSC Reforms

AS PREVIOUSLY MENTIONED, I joined ORF in an honorary capacity in 2002 to oversee their research activities in the area of International Relations. I used to go to ORF only after concluding my classes in JNU, without adhering to any fixed hours. It was only after May 2006, having retired from JNU, that I joined ORF on a full-time basis as the Director of Research for International Relations. In late April 2005, while at ORF, I got a call from the UN Division of MEA, offering me the role of a 'Special Envoy' to SE Asian countries. The purpose of this assignment was to plead for UN reforms and India's permanent membership of the UNSC.

This came as a pleasant surprise. Not fully understanding the implications of this assignment, I sought guidance from M.K. Rasgotra, a former foreign secretary and a member of ORF's Governing Board. He advised me to immediately accept the MEA offer because the assignment carried the status of a Minister of State.

Following his suggestion, I accepted the offer, assuming that it was a recognition of my dedicated work in Laos, as I had no political or bureaucratic connections with the United Progressive Alliance (UPA) government that came to power in 2004. The assignment required me to travel to Laos and Cambodia to lobby for India's case for UNSC reforms and permanent membership. Vietnam was excluded from my assignment, as its support was deemed assured. I had been visiting Vietnam on different counts as we shall note later. Laos and Cambodia were vulnerable to Chinese influence and therefore, needed to be approached. China, despite its rhetorical support for UN reforms, was not inclined to back India's permanent UNSC membership.

Meera Shankar, a long-standing friend, who was an additional secretary in-charge of the United Nations and International Security in MEA, facilitated all the travel arrangements for June 2005 and also briefed me on India's decision to send Special Envoys for UNSC lobbying.

The issue of UNSC reforms had been pending for a long time. There was strong support for India in the UN and it was deemed necessary to earnestly pitch its case during the UN World Summit, scheduled for September 2005. India, along with Brazil, Germany and Japan, had formed a Group of Four (G-4) to press for UNSC reforms and permanent membership. The altered stance of the other three members to accept permanent membership even without veto rights, compelled India to reluctantly change its position on this matter. The other three members of G-4 had already sent their envoys for UNSC lobbying. In view of this, India felt that its case was getting weakened and there was the need to garner as much support as possible.[1]

---

1 For some details on the issue, see 'Veto-demand or G.4 muscle?' *The Times of India*, 1 May 2005. www.timesofindia.indiatimes.com; 'India at the UN: Growing Insecurity', *Hindustan Times*, 3 July 2005. www.

The MEA gave me briefing notes for Laos and Cambodia where India's bilateral cooperation and development assistance for these countries was highlighted. I was expected to incorporate these details into my talking points. MEA also gave me gifts to be presented to my interlocutors in Laos and Cambodia.

In preparation for this new and challenging assignment, I extensively studied available literature on the political dynamics of UNSC reforms and India's relations with the countries I was scheduled to visit. Though I had served in Laos, there was a need to update, as more than five years had elapsed since I completed my assignment. I had visited Laos and Cambodia in 2001 for a research project focusing on their relations with China. Collecting all these experiences, I developed four broad talking points as follows:

1. India's contribution to the UN, particularly in peacekeeping operations, conflict resolution and disarmament.
2. The need for expanding the UNSC to democratise decision-making at the UN. The current structure, established in the aftermath of World War II, had become dysfunctional due to the UN's expansion and the increasing complexity of global conflicts.
3. Highlighting the historical and civilizational bonds of India with Laos and Cambodia.
4. Articulating India's cooperation with Laos and Cambodia, both within the regional framework of ASEAN and bilaterally.

I shared these points with our ambassadors in Laos and Cambodia and incorporated their valuable suggestions. I also

hindustantimes.com. Also see, Ruchita Beri and Arpita Anant (Eds.) 'United Nations Security Council Reforms: Perspectives and Prospects', *IDSA Monograph* No. 38, June 2014.

recommended that they actively contribute to elaborating on any of these points, particularly concerning areas of bilateral cooperation, during our discussions with ministers and officials in these countries.

In Cambodia, Ambassador Aloke Sen had arranged my appointments with the foreign and home affairs ministers, along with a courtesy call on King HM Norodom Sihamoni. In these meetings, I conveyed India's long-standing commitment to the United Nations and its efforts towards world peace and development. Emphasising the post-World War II undemocratic structure of the UNSC, I underscored the urgency of UN reforms and India's legitimate claims, along with those of G-4 and Africa, for permanent membership of the UNSC. Cambodian Foreign Minister Hor Namhong, a seasoned and senior leader, reiterated support for India's position and assured me that as and when the matter arises at the UN World Summit, his country would extend its full support and vote for India's inclusion as a permanent member of the UNSC. We also discussed long-standing civilizational relations and strategic and developmental cooperation between India and Cambodia. It was agreed that the potential for development cooperation between our two countries was considerable and efforts should be made continuously to enhance this cooperation.

During discussions with the Cambodian home minister, reference was made to India's support against the Khmer Rouge regime. This prompted the home minister to draw my attention to the attempts made by Nepal Maoists and Sri Lankan Tamil Tigers to procure arms illegally stored by former Khmer Rouge guerrillas. After concluding this visit, I informed Sri Lankan Foreign Minister Lakshman Kadirgamar and MEA about this.

My meeting with King Sihamoni was formal yet courteous. The King enquired about the economic development in India and gave a beautiful return gift to me. I tried to meet Prime Minister Hun Sen through a former student of SIS/JNU, who was now one of his close aides. However, it did not materialise due to time constraints, as I had to leave Cambodia the next day for my onward visit to Laos.

In Laos, I met Foreign Minister Somsavat Lengsavad and had a good discussion with him on the issues involved. We both agreed that notwithstanding their rhetorical support for UNSC reforms, in their heart of hearts, the Permanent Five members of the UNSC (P5) were not willing to expand the UNSC, and certainly not in favour of granting veto power to new entrants.

Keeping in mind China's increasing presence in Laos, I also said that China was not publicly opposing UNSC reforms and its expansion, but it would be very hard for China to accept Japan and India, two other Asian powers, in the UNSC. I was aware of Laos' support for our claims for the UNSC since my time in Vientiane and also knew that Chinese influence was gradually growing there. Minister Lengsavad was sceptical if the matter would really come up for voting at the UN World Summit, but if it did, he assured me that Laos would vote for India. We also discussed various areas of cooperation between our two countries and I assured him on behalf of the Government of India that every effort would be made to enhance this cooperation. During my brief stay in Vientiane, I also met old friends and acquaintances, including Siritirath, Boupha, members of the Indian community and the embassy staff.

Our embassy had now shifted to a new place with an attractive location near the river bank and much larger space. I complimented Ambassador Tsewang Topden for the impressive changes brought in the embassy's profile and for making my visit successful and comfortable. The reports of these two visits were sent to MEA by the respective ambassadors. On my return, I also briefed additional secretary Meera Shankar about the assurances of support to our UNSC bid extended by Laos and Cambodia.

I again visited Cambodia in October 2006. This was to represent Minister of State for External Affairs, E. Ahamed, at the 15th anniversary of Cambodia's Paris Peace Accord. The ministry made all the arrangements for travel. Our ambassador in Phnom Penh looked after my stay and diplomatic engagements. Cambodia had been celebrating the anniversaries of its Paris Peace Accord since 1991. The celebration was attended by many other dignitaries and the ambience was very impressive. India was not a party to this Accord but had contributed towards it. India had also been strongly supporting the Cambodian fight against the Pol Pot-led brutal and most inhuman Khmer Rouge insurgency. India was one of the first countries to recognise Cambodia's Vietnam-supported Heng Samrin regime in 1980.

I had prepared a draft of my statement highlighting India's long and historical relations with Cambodia and emphasising that peace and stability were very critical conditions for Cambodia's development. I showed this draft to our ambassador in Phnom Penh who made a number of changes to moderate it. I was expected to make a short speech at the anniversary function. My presentation at the function went off smoothly. Back in India I reported the visit to MEA though a detailed report must have been sent by our ambassador in Phnom Penh.

Casual Contacts

During my academic visits, which involved research, fellowships, academic grants, and participation in conferences within and outside India, I seized the opportunity to engage in discussions on political and policy issues with heads of state or government, ministers and policymakers. While I have previously shared narratives of sustained interactions in the cases of Nepal and Sri Lanka, there were also casual and short-lived meetings in some other countries that left a lasting impression on me, and they are worth recollecting.

BHUTAN

After completing my PhD on Nepal, I started exploring India's security dimension in relation to the broader Himalayan region, comprising Bhutan, Sikkim and Tibet. In 1977, while I was still in the Division of Diplomatic Studies, I wrote a 'Staff Paper' titled 'India's Defence Diplomacy Towards the Himalayan States'. Despite receiving appreciation when presented at a faculty seminar, the paper faced rejection for publication in *International Studies*, the journal of SIS. One of the reviewers had commented that the paper was critical of the Government of India's policies. I refused to revise the paper to suit the reviewer's comments, as my arguments were based on facts from authentic sources. It seemed unusual for a premier university like JNU to block views critical of the Government of India. Maybe my unknown reviewer might have been working in the Himalayan region and did not want alternate views to be published. Though unpublished, I kept on sharing the paper with friends and interested students, who found it useful and objective.

Motivated to further my research in this area, I visited Sikkim and Bhutan. In Sikkim, which had become an integral part of the Indian Union in 1975, I met both the deposed Sikkim ruler, Chogyal Palden Thondup Namgyal, and its former Prime Minister and new Chief Minister, Lhendup Dorjee. The Chogyal (king) seemed to have reconciled with the change, realising that undue encouragement to his American wife Hope Cooke to project Sikkim's independent identity was counterproductive. Lhendup Dorjee was enthusiastic that as a part of democratic India, people of Sikkim will enjoy freedom and progress, and will modernise fast.

In the summer of 1978, I visited Bhutan. I travelled by road from Phuentsholing to Thimphu. This was an adventure in itself, travelling in a crowded bus, passing through sharp and high mountainous curves. Prior to the visit, I had established contacts with India's

Representative in Bhutan, Jagdish Hiremath. He graciously received me in Thimphu and hosted me as his personal guest. During his briefing on Bhutan's internal politics and relations with India, he proposed the idea of meeting His Majesty Jigme Singye Wangchuck, the Fourth King of Bhutan. I readily agreed. What could be a better start to my visit than meeting the ruler of the kingdom. Hiremath informed me that we would take a chance during the King's evening tennis game. When we went to the Royal tennis courts, fortune favoured us—the King was playing there with his cousin, who was the Chief Justice of Bhutan's Supreme Court. On seeing India's Representative there, the King concluded the game and joined us with his cousin. After exchanging greetings with the King, Hiremath introduced me to him.

On hearing my name, the King spoke something in Dzongkha (Bhutanese language) to his cousin, mentioning my name twice. After the informal exchange of pleasantries with the King, both Hiremath and I returned to India House a bit puzzled. We did not understand the King's comments in Dzongkha and could only speculate about what might have transpired between the King and his cousin. It was intriguing to know that the King knew my name, and we were left with questions about what he conveyed to his cousin and whether the reference to my name was positive or otherwise. These questions lingered with us through our dinner.

The next day, I had an appointment with Bhutan's foreign minister Dawa Tsering, whom I had known earlier and who had addressed my students in South Asian studies at SIS/JNU. When I reached his office, he was in a hurry for an unscheduled meeting with the King. He asked me to settle down in his office, have a cup of coffee, as he would soon be back after the meeting. Upon his return about half an hour later, Tsering said, 'So you have had an informal meeting with His Majesty, I learn. He would like to see you again tomorrow morning at 10.45 a.m.' I was delighted to hear this.

I discussed with Tsering about Bhutan's foreign policy and relations with India. According to Tsering, India-Bhutan relations were smooth and friendly, with minor issues of trade and hydropower purchases, which were being resolved at the appropriate ministerial levels. Returning to India House, I informed Hiremath of my upcoming appointment with the King. He was happy to know this, and asked me to find out as to what the King said about me the other day to his cousin at the tennis court.

The next day, I was on time for my appointment with His Majesty, waiting for about five minutes outside the Throne Room before being ushered in. I was told that I had 10-12 minutes with the King. The King greeted me warmly. Our conversation covered Bhutan's economic development, ethnic issues related to the persons of Nepali origin in Southern Bhutan, Bhutan's foreign policy and its relations with India.

As I prepared to leave after the allotted 10 minutes, the King signalled me to remain seated. He complimented me on my book on Nepal's Foreign Policy, stating that he had confirmed with his cousin at the tennis court whether I was the author. The King said that he had read the book with interest and particularly liked my chapter on 'Regional Non-Alignment'. He then made a proposal, 'We would like you to conduct a similar study on Bhutan's Foreign Policy. We will provide all necessary documents and open our libraries to you. During the study, you will be our guest in Thimphu. Will you please undertake this work?' I promptly accepted the gracious offer and assured him that upon returning to Delhi, I would prepare my schedule, inform his office and commence the work on a mutually agreed timetable.

When I shared this information with Hiremath, he complimented me for the confidence the King had expressed in me for this study. He also suggested that such a study would be helpful to MEA. I explained to Hiremath that the chapter liked by the King dealt with

Nepal's attempts to reduce its dependence on India and use China for balancing India's heavy presence. I wondered if the King was also thinking along these lines in the long run. Hiremath dismissed my speculation, stating that Bhutan was firmly with India and would not follow Nepal's example.

On my return to Delhi, I felt happy and excited about the proposal. I started thinking about the structure of the book, and thought it would be proper for me to consult the Northern Division (dealing with Nepal and Bhutan) of MEA before sending a firm reply to Thimphu. Around the same time, I got an offer of a six-month fellowship from the Australian National University to work on Disarmament and Development Linkages in World Politics. Feeling greedy, I was keen to avail of both the offers. Since the timeline of the Bhutan project was supposed to be at my discretion, I decided to go to Australia first, fearing the fellowship offer might slip away. I planned to undertake the Bhutan book project once the Australian assignment concluded.

While in Australia, I completed the monograph on 'Arms Build-up and Development: Linkages in the Third World' (Australian National University, 1980). This topic was being vigorously debated in International Relations narratives those days. Developing countries were spending more on arms at the cost of their development priorities. I also contributed a chapter on the South Asian conflict between India and Pakistan for a book edited by Mohammad Ayoob, my erstwhile colleague who, frustrated by delays in his promotion at SIS/JNU, had moved to the Australian National University.

On my return from Australia in 1979, I wrote again to Thimphu, expressing my readiness to take up the project proposed by the King. However, there was no response to this letter. A few months later, I discovered that Leo E. Rose, a California University Professor of South Asian studies (who was also my PhD examiner) had already published a book on Bhutan's political system and foreign policy. Maybe, that led the King to avoid duplicating the efforts. I then realised my mistake of delaying the work on the King's offer, regretting that the allure of Australia had caused me to falter on my commitment to the King. In the long run, the Bhutan project could have been far more valuable in my career trajectory and for India's foreign policy and diplomacy in the neighbourhood.

My next meeting with His Majesty Jigme Singye Wangchuck took place in 1988. Along with Bhabani Sen Gupta, an eminent scholar, and B.G. Verghese, a celebrated journalist, I secured an audience with the King through the Indian Embassy during a conference visit to Thimphu. We discussed ethnic relations between Drukpas, the native Bhutanese, and the migrant Nepalis, which had been strained since 1954 due to the agitation for democracy by the migrant Nepalis settled in the southern belt of Bhutan. We also discussed India-Bhutan relations and the Bhutanese demand for the revision of its 1949 Treaty with India. Under this Treaty, Bhutan was expected to seek Indian advice on foreign policy. Bhutan's interpretation of this clause was that the acceptance of the advice given by India was not mandatory, and Bhutan could amend or ignore this advice in pursuing its foreign policy. The issue of revising this Treaty became public in 1979 when Bhutan's sensitivities were ruffled at the Cuba Non-Alignment Summit by the inappropriate statements of India's then Foreign Minister S.N. Mishra. Eventually, the Treaty was revised in 2007. During this meeting, I apologised to the King for my failure to undertake the book-writing project proposed by him.

In my third and final meeting with King Jigme Singye Wangchuck in 2003, our discussions focused on two key issues: the King's decision to abdicate and usher in democracy in Bhutan, and Maoist insurgency in Nepal. I commended the King for his bold decision to embrace democracy in Bhutan, despite facing resistance from the nobility and the people at large. I enquired about the motivation behind this decision, and he responded in general terms, stating that public representation and governance accountability were crucial for progress. However, I found this to be a rhetorical response, concealing the true reasons for the King's democratic initiative, especially considering his long-standing absolute power. It is, however, possible to argue that the Fourth King was carrying forward the legacy of his father, the Third King, Jigme Dorji Wangchuck, who had initiated modernising and liberalising the polity in Bhutan.

During our discussion, I reminded the King that his father had granted Bhutan's National Assembly the authority to recall a King and scrutinise his policies and actions. The King, in turn, probed me on the role of Maoists in Nepali politics and asked me how stable was the Nepali Monarchy in the face of the Maoist challenge. He also sought information on India's approach to the developments in Nepal. I shared my perspective, stating that, based on my studies, the Maoists were not in a position to take power and retain it in Nepal through their 'Peoples' War'. Instead, they appeared willing and keen to integrate into the democratic national politics. India, therefore, should facilitate this transition. I highlighted that the Indian government had repeatedly urged the Nepal King to collaborate with the mainstream national parties, liberalise the political landscape, and address the Maoist challenge. 'King Gyanendra of Nepal is, however, obstinate and if he does not agree to share power with the democratic forces in Nepal, then he may be in great difficulty,' I said. The Bhutan King also expressed concern about the role of Maoists in Nepal's refugee camps, where Bhutanese of Nepali origin were seeking shelter since the early 1990s.

There was a sensitive issue in India-Bhutan relations regarding the sheltering of India's North East militants in Bhutan. India had conducted military operations to flush out the United Liberation Front of Assam (ULFA), National Democratic Front of Bodoland (NDFB) and the Kamtapur Liberation Organisation (KLO), militants, who had sought refuge in Bhutan's south-eastern belt. Some of these militants had married Bhutanese girls and established families. Despite India's requests, Bhutan neither permitted Indian forces to enter and clear the militants, nor did it take independent action to flush them out. Bhutan clarified that any unilateral action by Indian forces would be considered aggression. I was briefed on this issue by Prabhat Shukla, an IFS officer posted in the Gujral PMO. I asked the King as to why Bhutan was hesitant to respond to India's request regarding the North East extremists. The King's concise response emphasised Bhutan's commitment to resolving the problem through dialogue and persuasion. 'If this approach fails, we shall try other alternatives,' he added.

Following my discussions with the King, it became apparent that the decision to guide Bhutan towards democracy was influenced by the prevailing political situations in neighbouring countries such as Nepal and Myanmar. It may be recalled that the plight of thousands of Bhutanese of Nepali origin seeking refuge in Nepal had taken a serious dimension attracting international attention. Bhutan's stringent citizenship Acts in 1958 and 1985, coupled with a contentious 1988 population census, led to the declaration of many Bhutanese of Nepali origin as non-citizens, for want of authentic evidence and citizenship certificates. Many such Bhutanese were forced to leave Bhutan.

In 1989, the Bhutan government introduced a national cultural code called Driglam Namzha, mandating every Bhutanese to wear Drukpa dresses and adhere to cultural discipline. This exacerbated the exodus of Bhutanese of Nepali origin. Since Nepal and Bhutan do not share a direct territorial link, many of these Nepalese initially sought entry into India. However, India declined to accept them, leading them to seek shelter in Nepal. The Maoist leadership was active among these refugees, justifying the King's concern about the potential radicalisation of these refugees and the looming threat they could pose to Bhutan in the future. The King was farsighted in broadening and democratising the support base of his government to preempt challenges from such radicalised groups.

In 2007, a solution to the issue of Bhutanese refugees in Nepal was reached through the intervention of the UNHCR (UN High Commissioner for Refugees). According to this solution, the US, some European countries and Australia agreed to share the Bhutanese refugees living in camps in Nepal. While many refugees have been settled in these countries through this programme, some still remain in Nepal. Recently, numerous Nepali Ministers and highly placed officials were found guilty of huge corruption related to sending Nepalis as fake Bhutanese refugees to these Western countries.

Regarding the matter of India's North East militants seeking refuge in Bhutan, the example of IPKF in Sri Lanka made the Bhutanese authorities wary about allowing India to independently resolve this problem. Finally, in December 2003, India and Bhutan coordinated their security operations to clear the militants from their hideouts in Bhutan. In these operations, Crown Prince Jigme Khesar Namgyel Wangchuck, who succeeded his father in 2006, had led the Royal Bhutan Army. While the Royal Bhutan Army conducted operations within the Bhutanese territory, India took control of the fleeing militants within its own territory.

My links with Bhutan's royalty extended beyond my audiences with His Majesty. During my visits, I also took my family to Bhutan. We travelled to Siliguri (in northern West Bengal) by train from New Delhi. On the way, someone drugged us through tea at one of the railway stations in Bihar and stole two of our suitcases. We had to buy the necessary clothes for the children in Siliguri before embarking on a long road journey to Thimphu. When the information of my family's presence in Thimphu reached the Royal Palace, I received a gift for my daughter Pallavi (11 years) and my son Shantanu (nine years)— two albums featuring Bhutan's internationally recognised postal stamps. On my earlier visits, I had been gifted beautiful Tangkas (Buddhist paintings on cotton or silk applique) by the ministers of culture and home affairs in Thimphu.

In early 2003, Bhutanese Ambassador in India Maj. Gen. Vetsop Namgyel invited me for a cup of coffee. He requested me to provide tuition to one of the princes, Jigyel Ugyen Wangchuck (son from the first queen), to prepare him for the admission test in Oxford University. I coached him at the Bhutanese Embassy in New Delhi for about two weeks in Political Science and International Relations. He was admitted at St. Peter's College, Oxford, for History and Political Science studies in 2003, and graduated in 2007. Then again in August 2006, I was asked to coach another prince, Ugyen Jigme Wangchuck (born of the second Queen), for a similar admission test. For this, I went to Thimphu as a royal guest for two weeks. He studied at the exclusive Swiss boarding school, Institut Le Rosey. I was offered an honorarium for both the coaching, but I did not accept. After the second coaching, Her Majesty the Queen, Tshering Pem invited me to her residence to thank me for my efforts. On both the occasions, I was presented with beautiful souvenirs (gold and silver plated). I had no direct contact with Crown Prince Khesar Namgyel Wangchuck, who succeeded his father, the Fourth King Jigme Singye Wangchuck. He had completed a course at the National Defence College (NDC) in India, where I used to lecture almost annually.

In February 2013, while I was at the Institute of South Asian Studies, National University of Singapore, I received a mail from Bhutan's first elected Prime Minister Jigme Thinley. He expressed his intention to visit New Delhi and requested a meeting with me. As he was a St. Stephen's College graduate from Delhi and had previously interacted with my South Asian students at SIS/JNU, I travelled from Singapore to meet him and went to his hotel room at the appointed time. After exchanging pleasantries, he mentioned that one of the topics on the agenda of his visit was to secure India's approval for advancing border negotiations with China and open diplomatic relations with Beijing if possible. I had learnt in Bhutan earlier that the Chinese were pressuring Bhutan to settle the border issue through territorial swapping in both the eastern and central fronts, as well as to establish diplomatic relations. They were encroaching on Bhutan's territories for grazing and other purposes, putting Bhutan in a difficult position to engage with them on these issues on a day-to-day basis. However, swapping of territories could have security implications for India, both on the Sikkim and Assam fronts. Therefore, India's approval was necessary. I was not aware of India's response to Prime Minister Thinley's proposal but there was no indication of India's acceptance during our discussion.

I returned to Singapore after the meeting and shared the gist of my discussion with Shivshankar Menon, who was then India's NSA. I suggested to Menon that it would be in India's long-term interests if Bhutan's border dispute with China was peacefully settled. China's persisting plans to encroach into the strategic spaces of Bhutan and India precipitated the Doklam standoff in 2017. It now appears that India has given the nod to Bhutan's continuing negotiations with China and resolution of the border dispute without adversely affecting India's security interests.

PAKISTAN

In June 1988, an officially sponsored international conference on 'Regional Security in South Asia', was organised in Islamabad. I was accompanied by two other Indian colleagues, Air Commodore (Retd) Jasjit Singh, Director of IDSA, and Dr Mohammed Ayoob, formerly with SIS/JNU, but at that time, with the Australian National University. Among other well-known participants was Prof. Stephen Cohen of the University of Chicago, Urbana-Champaign, USA. Several eminent Pakistani scholars and policymakers also participated. Pakistan President General Zia-ul-Haq invited all the international participants for an exclusive dinner at the *Aiwan-e-Sadr* (President's Palace). The President was very cordial and courteous to all the guests. He joined the table where we three Indians were sitting. We started discussing India-Pakistan relations. President Zia-ul-Haq reminded us of his efforts to bring about peace and stability in bilateral relations with India and underlined the significance of resolving the Kashmir issue in that context. We drew his attention towards international media reports that Pakistan had acquired nuclear weapons capability. We asked him about Pakistan's nuclear policy, whether Pakistan had already developed a nuclear bomb, and what its nuclear doctrine would be, specifically, if it will use nuclear capabilities only as a deterrent or as a weapon of war. The President kept on smiling while we were shooting our questions. In response, he said, 'We in Pakistan have been saying that we do not have nuclear bombs, but since you people in India think that we have a nuclear bomb, then it's very fine. This serves our purpose of deterrence, and we are happy about it.'

President Zia-ul-Haq was known for his generous hospitality and smart public relations, as we personally experienced. While concluding discussions on India-Pakistan relations at the dinner table, he enquired about our plans for sightseeing after the seminar. Jasjit mentioned his interest in visiting the Panja Sahib Gurudwara (near Rawalpindi). I expressed my willingness to revisit Mohenjo-Daro to refresh my memories of the Indus Valley civilization. During the conversation, the President noticed a Band-Aid on Prof. Cohen's finger covering a small cut. By the time we returned to our hotel, a doctor sent by the President was already waiting for Prof. Cohen to treat him for his cut on the finger.

Early next morning, I and Jasjit received a message from the presidential secretariat that a car would be available at 9.30 am to take us to Mohenjo-Daro and Panja Sahib. We had a comfortable guided tour to the places of our interest. The President also presented to us his personally signed copies of a coffee table book titled *Journey Through Pakistan*. I think this was the same book that he had presented to Mrs Indira Gandhi in 1982, but she immediately returned it as it contained a map showing parts of Kashmir as belonging to Pakistan. Though we noticed the map, we did not return the book.

Gen Zia died in August 1988 in a plane blast. There are various theories about that incident, blaming both the internal and external conspirators. The one less popular and barely discussed theory disclosed by India's former R&AW chief A.K Verma was that Zia had accepted India's position on the Siachen Glacier and was willing to sign an accord to resolve the issue, but his core commanders and senior officers in the Pakistan Army and Air Force did not approve of it. To stop him from making this concession to India, he was eliminated. There are no other credible sources to support this theory.[2]

I had been visiting Pakistan for a long time. In one of the visits organised by South Asia Free Media Association (SAFMA) in 2006, we had an opportunity to interact with General Pervez Musharraf. Senior journalists Barkha Dutt, K.K. Katyal and Vinod Sharma, along with others, were also in our group. Musharraf's Four Point Proposal to resolve the India-Pakistan dispute in Kashmir was being widely speculated in media. There were also reports of a back-channel negotiation between the two countries to finalise a mutually acceptable draft.[3] During our interaction, I asked General Musharraf

---

2 This was disclosed by former R&AW chief A.K. Verma in a seminar in Jamia Milia Islamia University, New Delhi where I was present. He also mentioned this in one of his articles published in *Rediff.com*, 30 June 2006.

3 First information of such back channel talks was made public in an article in *The New Yorker* (February 2009), by Steve Coll, titled: 'The Back Channel: India and Pakistan's secret Kashmir talks'. Also see the memoirs of Satinder Kumar Lambah, who was India's negotiator at these back channel talks, *In Pursuit of Peace: India-Pakistan Relations Under Six Prime Ministers* (New Delhi: Penguin, 2023).

about this proposal, and he responded, 'We are working out a non-territorial resolution which will involve a gradual withdrawal of troops and freedom of movement across the Line of Control.' This statement was reported in many Pakistani and Indian newspapers the next day. My frequent visits to Pakistan since early 1980s had allowed me to build a good network of friends, including academics, media persons, social activists and government officials.

I have previously mentioned about Mushahid Hussain, who held cabinet rank positions in some of Pakistan's federal governments. In the course of a conference organised under the Indian Council for South Asian Cooperation (ICSAC), headed by former Minister of External Affairs Dinesh Singh, in 1989 in New Delhi, we were invited by Prime Minister Rajiv Gandhi for breakfast. Mushahid made Rajiv blush when he said to him, 'Sir, you are young and charming, and so is my Prime Minister Benazir Bhutto. Why cannot the two of you discard the baggage of history and make India-Pakistan relations as charming as you both are?'

I also shared a panel with Aitzaz Ahsan, who was a cabinet minister of Law, Justice and Interior, in Benazir's government in 1988. We were discussing the concept of South Asian Parliament at a SAFMA-organised conference in Pakistan's Murree in 2003. While I was positive about the idea of a regional parliament and proposed its broad structural design, Aitzaz termed this idea as premature. The Indian group at this conference also included Ashwini Kumar and Ravi Shankar Prasad, both of whom became cabinet ministers in the governments of Dr Manmohan Singh and Narendra Modi, respectively.

During my two earlier visits to Karachi, I was invited to dinner, once by India's Consul General Mani Shankar Aiyar (1978-82), and on another occasion by Prof. Sikander Mehdi, Head of the Department of International Relations at Karachi University. On the first dinner, a car with Pakistani surveillance officers followed me both ways. Within a couple of days of my visit, Prof. Mehdi was questioned about who I was and the purpose of my visit to his residence. Prof. Mehdi had known me since 1978 when he was doing his PhD at the Australian National University, Canberra, during my fellowship period. These incidents did not disturb me because I knew that in India also, the visits of Pakistani scholars and important persons were being monitored closely.

Prof. Mehdi had also visited my residence in JNU. He, in the course of our conversations, expressed the desire to visit his in-laws in Bihar. He asked me if I could help him because he did not have visa for going outside Delhi. Both India and Pakistan were issuing visas only for three cities to visitors coming from the other side. I suggested to Prof. Mehdi to just take a train ticket and quietly visit Bihar. No one would question him since he looked like any other Indian train commuter. He did so and was happy to tell me on his return to Delhi that he had a happy stay with his in-laws for three days without any difficulty.

THE UNITED STATES OF AMERICA

I have been visiting the United States of America since 1982 for academic purposes on various grants and projects, and for participating in conferences, and 1.5 and 2.0 Track meetings. During these visits, I was affiliated to various universities, including Johns Hopkins University, Chicago University, American University, The New School in New York, and California University. In 1986, I was also invited to lecture on Indo-US Relations at the US Army War College in the National Defense University in Washington, D.C. My lecture did not go very well with the US defense officials because I argued that, in straining Indo-US bilateral relations, the US was as much, if not more, responsible than India.

In the US, the general perception was that India was closer to the Soviet Union and was not interested in mutually beneficial relations with the US. I presented facts to show that strains in the relations were precipitated by the imperatives of the Cold War in the US' approach towards South Asia. The reference in the US narratives to India's relations with the Soviet Union, in my view, was not relevant. It was the US that found Pakistan more useful as a subservient ally.

Nehru's first state visit to the US in 1949, undertaken with high hopes and expectations, ended in deep disappointment. Despite India having no close relations with the Soviet Union between 1947 and 1955, there was no warmth in the US' approach towards India. The US military intervention to stop the emergence of an independent Bangladesh stood as the glaring example of distrust between India and the US. During my visits on later occasions, I had the opportunity to interact with senior officials in the Departments of State and Defense. The US' recognition of India's strategic significance in the Indian Ocean region and its urge for a partnership to balance the Chinese challenge is a phenomenon only of the past 25 years.

Two of my meetings with the highly placed policymakers in the State Department were significant. In August 1995, I was selected by the US Embassy in India to visit the US under their International Visitors Leadership Program. I informed Dinesh Singh, the then External Affairs Minister in Narasimha Rao's government, about this. Despite recovering from a paralytic stroke, he briefed me on the deteriorating relations between India and the US and said, 'The Americans seem to be hell bent on creating problems for us in Kashmir. The newly appointed Assistant Secretary of State, Ms Robin Raphel, is allegedly providing funds and organising Kashmir separatists against India. Can you meet her to find out what she is up to? I will inform our embassy in Washington to arrange an appointment with her.'

I agreed promptly, considering it an excellent opportunity to understand the US approach towards India and conduct research on India-Pakistan relations. In the US, I contacted Kanwal Sibal, who, as Deputy Chief of Mission, was officiating as ambassador. He had already received communication from MEA about my visit and readily agreed to arrange the appointment with Ms Raphel. I met her after completing my assignments under the 'Visitors Program'. Although I was initially informed that I had 15 minutes with her, our discussions ended up taking more than 40 minutes.

After exchanging pleasantries, I provocatively asked her, 'How will the US' national interests in relation to India be served by creating and funding the All Parties Hurriyat Conference in Kashmir?' She denied vehemently that the US was funding the Hurriyat Conference but admitted that the US' support for Hurriyat was to ensure the protection of human rights in Kashmir. In a lengthy narrative, she also cast aspersions on the validity of Kashmir's accession agreement, claiming that the Kashmiris had the right to freedom and autonomy. I explained to her the sequence of events, starting with Pakistan's violation of the Standstill Agreement with Kashmir, followed by military intervention and ruthless violence under the guise of tribal uprising. I also reminded her that the accession agreement was endorsed by the British who have been advising and guiding the US' policy towards Asia in general and South Asia in particular.

However, Ms Raphel found none of this acceptable. Our meeting concluded on a sour note, and I came back with the impression that American policy would not relent in its support for Kashmiri separatists. I briefed Sibal in Washington and Dinesh Singh in New Delhi about this meeting. Notably, Ms Raphel was known for her close association with Pakistan, continuing to advise the Clinton administration even after leaving her State Department position. She was bestowed with Pakistan's national honour years later. The

Clinton administration's support for Pakistan and its dislike for India was moderated only after the Kargil conflict in 1999.

In August 2002, I received an invitation from the East-West Center in Hawaii to participate in a Senior Policy Seminar. Having previously collaborated with Muthiah Alagappa of Malaysia on an E-W Center project on Asian security, where he was one of the organisers, I attended this 1.5 Track event featuring senior government officials and academics. James A. Kelly, Assistant Secretary of State for East Asia, along with serving and retired senior military officers, represented the US. Other participants included Surin Pitsuwan, former foreign minister from Thailand, and Husain Haqqani, former ambassador from Pakistan. Alok Prasad, Deputy Chief of Mission in the Indian Embassy, Washington, D.C., represented India, while participants from Singapore, Japan, Korea and Australia were also present. The seminar's theme was 'September 11: What Has Changed,' aiming to assess Asian opinions on the implications of the 9/11 terrorist attacks on the US. We were informed that the Americans were present solely to listen to the opinions from across Asia.

In my presentation, besides making other points, I highlighted that 9/11 was a 'terrorism plus' attack on the US. I argued that to comprehend it properly, we must look at the chosen targets. If the attackers aimed solely to terrorise the American people and government, they could have chosen the underground rail system in Washington or New York, and killed many more Americans. Instead, they selected three crucial icons of American power, namely the World Trade Centre, Pentagon and the White House. This suggested that 'it was a politically designed and strategically focused operation to challenge the US' global hegemony'. The death of thousands of American citizens was an unfortunate collateral damage. I concluded that this marked the beginning of an unequal war, a war by other means against the US, and the US would need to reassert itself.

My explanation of the 9/11 attacks did not go well with Secretary Kelly and some other participants. During lunch break, Secretary Kelly invited me to his table to continue with our discussions. He said, 'We will contain these terrorists very soon. If they have any illusion of waging a war on the US, they will soon realise the cost and will be forced to surrender.' A year later, in August 2003, another similar Senior Policy Seminar was organised by the East-West Center, where I participated. This time, the theme was 'US Policy in the Asia-Pacific'. The seminar discussed China's rise and its implications for the US presence in the region. Various aspects of emerging global terrorism and the US' response to them were explored, with Pakistani participant Samina Ahmed closely scrutinising the US' approaches toward Iraq and Afghanistan.

SAARC AND BANGLADESH

I have been studying South Asian regional cooperation since the initiative taken by Bangladesh President General Ziaur Rahman in 1980. I co-authored a book with my wife Anuradha titled *Regional Cooperation in South Asia* (National Publishing House, New Delhi, 1984), much before the establishment of the South Asian Association for Regional Cooperation (SAARC) as an institution in 1985. In anticipation of the summit, I was contemplating ways to raise funds to go to Dhaka when Nikhil Chakravartty, Editor of *Mainstream Weekly*, invited me to observe the SAARC summit on behalf of his magazine. I readily agreed and received Rs 25,000 in cash from him for my expenses, with more than half of it being spent on travel arrangements. I supplemented the remainder with my own savings and went to Dhaka for a week-long visit.

During my stay, I contacted Mizanur Rahman Shelly and C.M. Shafi Sami for assistance. Shelly, Director of the Centre for Development Research, Bangladesh, had become a friend through seminar circuits on South Asian regional cooperation. He was a former Pakistan Civil Service bureaucrat who resigned from the Bangladesh government in 1980 due to his intellectual inclinations. Known by the adopted name 'Shelly', he was also a writer and poet. He also served as the editor of a journal called *Asian Affairs*. He became a minister under General H.M. Ershad's regime in 1990. Sami, a Bangladesh Foreign Service officer, was known to me during his posting in India at the Bangladesh High Commission. At the time of the SAARC summit, he was serving as Bangladesh High Commissioner in Pakistan and had been called to coordinate the summit. Both of them facilitated my movements in Dhaka during the summit, with Shelly arranging my stay at Dhaka Club, and Sami helping me obtain a media card for observing the summit.

The roads leading to the summit venue were cleaned and adorned with decorations and welcoming posters in Bangla and English. Despite my pointing out a few spelling mistakes in the English posters to Sami, they remained uncorrected throughout the summit. I was happy to have listened to the speeches made by SAARC leaders and witnessed the signing of the Dhaka SAARC Declaration on 8 December 1985. After returning from Dhaka, I wrote two articles for *Mainstream Weekly* on the summit.

I had extended my stay in Dhaka for another four days. With Shelly's help, I secured an appointment with Bangladesh President General Hussain Muhammad Ershad. Gen. Ershad, in a bloodless coup, ousted President Abdus Sattar and imposed martial law on 24 March 1982. He declared himself President of Bangladesh in 1983. Rumours in political circles, both in India and Bangladesh, blamed India for supporting Gen. Ershad's coup. During our meeting, I presented my book on South Asian Regional Cooperation to him. We discussed India-Bangladesh relations, and Gen. Ershad expressed contentment with the state of bilateral relations with India and expressed optimism about further strengthening them.

He also informed me of his plans to hold democratic elections in Bangladesh soon.

I also met Begum Khaleda Zia, the widow of former Bangladesh President the late General Ziaur Rahman, who was considered as the driving force behind the coup that led to the assassination of Sheikh Mujibur Rahman and his entire family in 1975. General Ziaur Rahman had taken the initiative in 1980 to establish SAARC. Begum Zia was accompanied by her political secretary, Abul Harris Chowdhury, who did most of the talking to answer my questions on Bangladesh's domestic politics and its relations with India.

I had visited Bangladesh even before the SAARC summit to participate in the conferences organised by the Bangladesh Institute of International and Strategic Studies (BIISS). These conferences helped me establish contacts with academics at Dhaka University like Professor(s) Raunaq Jahan, Amina Ahmed, Imtiaz Ahmed, and Akmal Hussain, and academics from other institutions like Rehman Sobhan, Gowher Rizvi and Iftekharuzzaman. With the support from Ford Foundation, I collaborated with Stephen Cohen of the US, Shelton Kodikara of Sri Lanka, Lok Raj Baral of Nepal, Pervaiz Iqbal Cheema of Pakistan and Gowher Rizvi of Bangladesh to establish the Regional Centre for Strategic Studies (RCSS) for South Asia in Colombo in 1992. Iftekharuzzaman succeeded Prof. Shelton Kodikara as the second Executive Director of RCSS.

I've met Bangladesh Prime Minister Sheikh Hasina Wazed on three occasions. In two instances, she was the Opposition leader. On the third occasion in 2010, she addressed a conference in Sweden organised by the International IDEA (Institute for Democracy and Electoral Assistance). During her time as the Opposition leader, she visited India, during which I attended her talk at the Saturday Discussion Group at IIC, New Delhi. Furthermore, in 2003, I met her at a lunch hosted by Gujral at his residence. For over a decade, my friend Gowher Rizvi has been serving as an Adviser on International Affairs to her.

While in Singapore, I often found myself engaged in spirited discussions about Bangladesh with my Bangladeshi colleague, Iftekhar Chowdhury. He had previously served as the foreign minister of Bangladesh under the Bangladesh Nationalist Party (BNP) government led by Begum Khaleda Zia. I had been acquainted with Chowdhury since he was pursuing a PhD at the Australian National University in 1979-80, a period during which I was also present there on a fellowship. Throughout our interactions, Chowdhury consistently supported the US' preference for Khaleda Zia in Bangladesh, while I firmly believed Hasina Wazed was the right choice for the country's development. Notably, Chowdhury actively lobbied for the 2013 elections in Bangladesh to be conducted only under an interim government.

After the Dhaka SAARC summit, it was India's turn to organise the annual event. Bangalore was selected as the venue for the second summit to be held in November 1986. Muchkund Dubey, serving as secretary in MEA, was deputed to coordinate the preparations for the summit. He invited several academics and journalists to contribute ideas for India's agenda. I was also one of the invitees. I offered several suggestions. First, I recommended the establishment of SAARC Chairs and SAARC Fellowships, not limited to nationals of the host country but open to individuals from other SAARC member nations. These fellowships and chairs, I argued, should be administered independently. Additionally, I put forth the idea of a SAARC University and suggested exploring the possibility of establishing a SAARC Parliament in the future, modelled after the European Parliament.

The Bangalore SAARC summit endorsed the concept of SAARC Fellowships and Chairs, leaving their administration to respective University Grants Commissions of SAARC member countries. Prof. Shelton Kodikara was invited as a SAARC Chair at India's Delhi University. Unfortunately, the institution of SAARC Chairs and Fellowships did not thrive, as educational bureaucracies did not see value in sustaining them. In 2007, a SAARC ministerial Memorandum of Understanding was signed to establish a multinational South Asian University. Although the university started functioning in 2010, a lack of commitment from some member states posed challenges to its healthy growth and expansion. Over the years, I have served on the panel of experts for faculty selections in Social Sciences.

Bangladesh was scheduled to host the SAARC summit in December 1992, but it got postponed to April 1993 due to Indian Prime Minister Narasimha Rao's refusal to participate. This decision was influenced by the anti-Hindu riots in Pakistan and Bangladesh, which erupted in the aftermath of the Babri Masjid demolition on 6 December 1992. Hindu temples and business establishments were under attack. Additionally, black flag demonstrations were being organised against Rao in Dhaka. Rao's decision was in reaction to the unstable situation in Dhaka. H.K. Dua, editor of *Hindustan Times*, called me to write an edit page piece on India's decision. My article questioning Rao's decision created a bit of a stir in the MEA and the PMO. Later, I learned that a senior official in the ministry, while reviewing my article, commented in a file that the 'author of this anti-India article (i.e., me) had been prompted by the Bangladesh High Commission, which often entertained such people at cocktail parties and dinners'. I wish the mentioned senior MEA official knew that I do not consume alcohol. Indian academics maintain robust integrity and are not swayed by incentives like Scotch or any other inducement to critique their own prime minister, unless they objectively believe a certain policy needs scrutiny. My passion was to strengthen SAARC, and I strongly felt that Rao's decision was not appropriate.

VIETNAM AND SINGAPORE

Vietnam held a fascination for us at JNU in various ways. We closely monitored its fight against America and celebrated its victory. In 1975, when the US conceded defeat in the Vietnam War, JNU students and faculty organised a march on the streets surrounding JNU. We raised slogans such as:

> *'Tera nam mera nam Vietnam Vietnam'*
> (Your name, my name; Vietnam Vietnam)
> *Azadi ka ek hi jam Vietnam Vietnam*
> (Freedom has only one peg; Vietnam Vietnam)
> *Lal salam, Lal salam. Vietnam Vietnam*
> (Red salute, Red salute; Vietnam Vietnam)

'Red salute' was the slogan of the Left groups on the campus, but the celebration of Vietnam's victory was joined by everyone. My first visit to Vietnam was in 1996. I was in Singapore on a Duncan McNeill fellowship grant at the Institute of Southeast Asian Studies, writing a research paper on 'ASEAN's responses to India's "Look East" Policy'. The fellowship provided for fieldwork visits to three ASEAN countries. I chose to visit Vietnam, Myanmar and Malaysia.

In Vietnam, I met individuals in the foreign ministry, business establishments and academic institutions, only to discover that hardly anyone was aware that India had launched a Look East Policy to enhance its economic and strategic engagement with the ASEAN countries.

My next visit to Vietnam was in 1999, from Vientiane, where a direct road connection to Hanoi existed. Bangladesh's ambassador in Vietnam, Shamsher Mohammad Chowdhury, was also accredited to Laos and regularly travelled by car to Vientiane. Opting to fly to Hanoi, Anuradha and I primarily went for sightseeing, exploring Ha Long Bay and the countryside. My third visit to Vietnam occurred once again from Singapore, where I was involved in a project with the Institute of Defence and Strategic Studies (IDSS) of the Nanyang Technological University. I was writing a monograph on 'China's strategic engagement with the New ASEAN'. The countries clubbed as 'New ASEAN' were Vietnam, Laos, Cambodia and Myanmar, all of which were admitted in ASEAN in and after 1995. I interviewed a number of experts on China in Hanoi, including those at the Centre of Chinese Studies, Institute for International Relations, Ministry of Foreign Affairs, Defence Ministry and ambassadors of Russia, France, Japan, India and Singapore.

At the Vietnamese Defence Ministry, I also met senior officers engaged in border negotiations with China. Parts of territory had been conceded by Vietnam to China, and there were still spots where the sovereignty issue was left unresolved. I was told by the Vietnamese negotiators that this was done consciously to avoid leaving the points of friction for any unforeseen conflict in future with a large aggressive and expansionist neighbour.[4]

In the last week of September 2004, I was asked by MEA to participate in a conference in Hanoi being organised by the Indo-Vietnam Solidarity Committee to mark the 50th Anniversary of Nehru's visit to Hanoi in October 1954 to meet President Ho Chi Minh and congratulate him for Vietnam's freedom from French colonial rule. I was to prepare a paper for the conference. The Indian group for the conference was led by Foreign Minister Natwar Singh, who was also leading the Indian delegation for the 12th Indo-Vietnam Joint Commission meeting. He addressed the inaugural session of the conference along with the Vietnamese Foreign Minister Nguyen Dy Nien, in the Vietnamese Institute for International Relations on

---

4 For the details of my discussions in Vietnam and its resolution of the border issue with China, see my IDSS Monograph No.2, on 'China's Strategic Engagement with the New ASEAN', Booksmith, Singapore, 2002.

17 October 2004. I titled my paper 'The Spirit of An Affectionate Encounter' and opened it with a quotation from Nehru on his meeting with Comrade Ho Chi Minh on 17 October 1954. Nehru wrote in his diary: 'He came forward – almost leapt forward – and embraced and kissed me. Obvious that this was not a showpiece. He felt it and meant it. Fine, frank face, gentle and benign – not at all one's idea of a leader of a rebellion.'

Vietnam is considered a part of the Sinic civilization in the Indo-Pacific region, but it has strong footprints of Indian civilisation as well. This is linked to the Champa civilisation or My Son as known in Vietnam. The ruins of Indian civilisation are located in Da Nang. I had the opportunity of visiting the site in August 2018 while attending a conference on the Indian Ocean organised by India Foundation. This was a 1.5 Track conference attended by Sri Lankan Prime Minister Ranil Wickremesinghe, the deputy prime ministers of Vietnam and Nepal, foreign ministers of a number of Indian Ocean countries, including the late Smt. Sushma Swaraj of India, and a number of other high officials, along with academics and strategic experts from the countries of the region. The ruins were spread around in a large area punctuated by big craters in the ground caused by the ruthless American bombing.

Singapore is one country in Southeast Asia where I have lived longest. I spent three months on the Duncan McNeill fellowship with the Institute of Southeast Asian Studies (ISEAS) in 1996, followed by another six months with the IDSS of Nanyang Technological University on their fellowship in 2001. Subsequently, from 2008 to the end of 2013, I spent six years with the Institute of South Asian Studies (ISAS), National University of Singapore. During I.K. Gujral's tenure as India's foreign minister in 1996, he visited Singapore when I was associated with ISEAS. He also addressed the Institute and expressed India's willingness to enhance cooperation with the Institute. He suggested that any proposals to that effect, including those related to funding exchange of scholars and joint conferences, could be finalised with me and forwarded for implementation. Despite my several requests to the Director, Prof. Chia Siow Yue, she never pursued this matter. She was an economist and it seemed, had not much interest in India. I wished that the former Director, Prof. Chan Heng Chee, during whose term I had joined this fellowship, was there. She had a better and broader regional strategic perspective. She left the ISEAS after being appointed as Singapore's ambassador to the US.

The IDSS, now renamed as the Rajaratnam Institute of Strategic Studies (RISS), was established in July 1996 on the initiative of Mr S.R Nathan. Having just retired from Singapore's intelligence services, Nathan recognised the need to develop strategic studies in response to the evolving security dynamics in the Asia-Pacific region. During his visit to India, he discussed the potential structure of IDSS with scholars and experts at the IDSA and SIS/JNU, subsequently becoming its inaugural Director. However, in 1999, with the support of former Prime Minister Lee Kuan Yew, Nathan became the President of Singapore. Though he formally left IDSS, he continued to show interest in its activities.When I joined IDSS in 2001, I had the privilege of attending a dinner with President Nathan, where we engaged in a fruitful discussion on Singapore's approach to contemporary global issues and its relations with India. He also expressed interest in my project on China's role in the new ASEAN member countries. President Nathan had fond memories of his visits to India and enquired about my colleagues with whom he had discussed the idea of setting up IDSS.

President Nathan's interest extended to the Institute of South Asian Studies (ISAS), which I joined in 2008. Ambassador Pillai, the chairman of ISAS, shared a close relationship with President Nathan and frequently invited him to preside over and inaugurate many ISAS events. This provided me with the opportunity to renew my contact with President Nathan, and discuss matters of common academic interest. Ambassador Pillai, a highly respected figure in Singapore's power circles, engaged in lively discussions with me on contemporary South Asian issues.

At ISAS, I collaborated with another colleague Ambassador See Chuk Moon, whom I had known since his tenure as Singapore High Commissioner in India. With close links to the Ministry of Foreign Affairs (MoFA), which made substantial financial contribution for the running of ISAS, Ambassador Chuk Moon took me to lecture Singapore's newly recruited Foreign Service officers on India's foreign policy. In collaboration with ambassador Chuk Moon, I also wrote a paper on India-ASEAN relations for the Eminent Persons Group set up to suggest prospects for further developing these relations. A couple of times, I was also invited by MoFA for briefings on Sri Lanka and Bangladesh. I participated in two Track 1.5 and Track 2.0 dialogues between India and Singapore, and India and Pakistan, respectively. The latter, organised by Maj. Gen. Ashok Mehta from India, included me due to the Singapore venue, but unfortunately, nothing significant emerged from this dialogue.

The convenor of the Indian delegation for the Track 1.5 dialogue between India and Singapore was former Indian ambassador Satinder Lambah. This initiative was possibly supported by the Confederation of Indian Industry (CII) and comprised senior MEA serving officers, India's High Commissioner in Singapore S. Jaishankar, academics, besides former diplomats and business leaders. I was included in the Indian delegation. The Singapore delegation had, among others, ISAS members, Chairman Ambassador Pillai and Director Tan Tai Yong. The primary focus of this dialogue was on expanding and strengthening India-Singapore relations. Extensive discussions were also held on the perceptions of the two countries regarding the role of the US in the Asia-Pacific region. I contested an argument put forth by a senior member of the Indian delegation, who asserted that the US was genuinely committed to promoting democracy in the region. While it might have been diplomatically indiscreet and contrary to the protocol on my part to question the line of argument in the presence of third parties, my academic background impelled me to express my objective perspective.

During my stay at ISAS, I also had contact with Singapore's former foreign secretary Kishore Mahbubani and the Ambassador-at-Large, Tommy Koh. Both Kishore and Tommy Koh are the acknowledged thought leaders on Singapore's foreign policy and international affairs. Ambassador Tommy Koh was kind to offer comments for the blurb of my book (in collaboration with Rahul Mishra) on *India's Eastward Engagement: From Antiquity to Act East Policy*, published in 2019. I left ISAS much against Chairman Pillai's advice and persuasion, largely because in the absence of enough social contacts, Anuradha and I were feeling Delhi-sick. Ambassador Pillai organised a farewell dinner for me at his residence and invited the then Deputy Prime Minister of Singapore, Tharman Shanmugaratnam, to be the guest of honour and present a shawl to me. Excellency Shanmugaratnam was elected as Singapore's President in September 2023, garnering unprecedented popular support with an approval rating of over 70 per cent. Upon my departure from ISAS, I was offered continued association as an honorary fellow, which I initially declined. However, later, at the insistence of the new Director and my former colleague from SIS/ JNU, C. Raja Mohan, and chairman Pillai, I accepted the position of honorary fellow at the Institute. My years with ISAS proved to be both personally and professionally rewarding.

MALDIVES AND IRAN

Mr Ibrahim Hussain Zaki, a senior politician from the Maldives, was our colleague on the Governing Board of RCSS, Colombo. He was a former cabinet minister and also a former Secretary-General of SAARC. During our RCSS meetings, Zaki shared with me the details of how, in 1989, Rajiv Gandhi saved the regime of Maumoon Abdul Gayoom from a coup attempt. I have fond memories of my visits to the Maldives and Iran.

My first visit to the Maldives was in 2007. At IDSA's Annual Conference on South Asia in March 2007 in New Delhi, the foreign minister of the Maldives, Ahmed Shaheed, was invited as a panelist, and I was asked to moderate that panel. In his conference paper, Ahmed Shaheed quoted from my writings on South Asian Regional Cooperation. After the panel discussion, he warmly invited me to visit the Maldives and speak to the Foreign Service officers there. The formal invitation came after a couple of months, and I was delighted to speak at the Foreign Service Institute of Maldives on the theme 'South Asia in the changing global context'. After my lecture, I had the opportunity to meet President Maumoon Abdul Gayoom and his daughter, Dunya Maumoon, who later became foreign minister (2013-2016). My second visit to the Maldives was in 2019 to participate in the 4th Conference on the Indian Ocean, organised by the New Delhi-based India Foundation.

I also met Mohamed Nasheed in New Delhi during his lobbying for political change in the Maldives. After his election as President in 2008, I sent him congratulations. His removal at gunpoint in February 2012 prompted me to write a strong article against his ousting and criticise the Government of India for not supporting him. During discussions with NSA Shivshankar Menon in New Delhi, I learnt that Nasheed was being excessively guided by his British advisers. His 'hobnobbing' with the US and the UK regarding naval access to the Indian Ocean were not well received in New Delhi. I have been meeting Nasheed during his visits to Delhi. I chaired a meeting in JNU addressed by him. We also met in meetings at Brookings India and I joined a dinner with him and the entire

Maldives government headed by President Ibrahim Mohamed Solih in the Maldives during the Indian Ocean Conference.

My visit to Iran in April 2007 was sponsored by the Iranian Embassy in New Delhi. A group of about 10 academics and journalists from India were taken to Iran for a week-long visit. Besides two of my colleagues from JNU, the group had Seema Mustafa, a senior journalist, and M.K. Bhadrakumar, a former ambassador-turned-prolific columnist. In Iran, we were taken to Iran's heavy water production facility in the midst of international controversy that Iran was vigorously pursuing the course of acquiring nuclear capability. In my understanding, the visit of our group was being used by Iran to inform the world about Iran's nuclear programme. We also had an opportunity to have discussions with the foreign minister and the minister of science and technology of Iran on nuclear proliferation related issues and India-Iran relations in general. We also explored Isfahan, Iran's second-largest city and its civilisational-cultural centre. We were given a beautifully carved white metal souvenir as our farewell gift.

My second visit to Iran was in 2010 to attend an international conference on Nuclear Non-Proliferation. This conference was addressed by Iran's Supreme Leader Ali Hosseini Khamenei and President Mahmoud Ahmadinejad. Both of them strongly criticised the Western policies on nuclear control and domination. During this visit, I also met Pakistani participants, including Shireen Mazari, who later became the minister for human rights in Prime Minister Imran Khan's cabinet. On my return to ISAS Singapore after this conference, I briefed my colleagues about Iran's determination to acquire nuclear weapons' capability.

7

Lessons Learnt

I AM BEHOLDEN to my academic profession that enabled me to walk in the corridors of power and dabble in diplomatic ventures and domestic politics in the immediate and extended neighbourhood. I found this dabbling professionally enriching and personally educating. It gave me an opportunity to meet and discuss subjects of mutual interest with a number of heads of state and/or government in India and the countries of my academic interest in the neighbourhood. It made me observe and understand the dynamics of real politics in these countries from close quarters. Several lessons were learnt from the experiences accumulated from such interactions.

My engagement with the neighbouring countries has enriched me with a large network of well-wishers and sympathisers in these countries. I am fortunate to count lifelong friends among them, with whom I maintain regular contact. We share in each other's joys and sorrows, strengthening our personal bonds. It has also helped me expand my professional network and broaden my areas of learning, research and writing. However, frequent visits to the neighbouring countries and close interaction with politicians and the political processes there have also led to gross misperceptions about me and my work among some people whom I have not met or who may not have read my writings, particularly in countries like Nepal, Bangladesh, and Sri Lanka. One common accusation levelled against me was that I have been an 'Indian agent' who speaks for the Government of India. Yes, I have defended India's policies towards its neighbours in many of my writings and conference presentations. But this advocacy has always been done on the basis of facts and data collected in the course of my research. I have never taken any brief from the Indian government in my academic work, and on several occasions have criticised India's policies where I found them at fault. Even in my commissioned reports for government establishments, I have critically examined India's role and explored policy options without hesitation.

In spite of my close association with I.K. Gujral, I took exception to his statement in 1990, regarding IPKF's withdrawal from Sri Lanka, when he said that India would never send its forces to a neighbouring country. I found this stance unsustainable. While it might have been applicable to his government at that time (under V.P. Singh's leadership), it cannot be an absolute position for the future. Situations may arise, as they have in the past, where India has to intervene, either at the request of a neighbouring country or in defence of its critical national interests. I recall P.N. Haksar's insightful observation that India and its immediate neighbours are 'lodged in each other's intestines'. Intervention in each other's affairs, thus, becomes an organic and natural aspect of mutual engagement. India's smaller neighbours also intervene in India in many subtle and explicit ways in pursuance of their vital interests. This dynamic is not limited to Pakistan but extends to other smaller neighbours as well. While some interventions may be legitimate and desirable, others may be unnecessary and unwarranted. However,

Prime Minister Dr Manmohan Singh launches the Journal of the Association of Indian Diplomats in New Delhi in 2006.

With Nepal's Maoist leaders Baburam Bhattarai and Prachanda, and former Foreign Secretary M.K. Rasgotra (extreme right) at the Observer Research Foundation (ORF) in New Delhi in 2006.

(Above): With Maldives President Maumoon Abdul Gayoom at Male in 2007.

(Left): At Isfahan, in central Iran, known for its Persian architecture, in 2007.

Chairing a conference panel at IDSA in New Delhi on March 2007. Panellists include Foreign Minister of the Maldives Ahmed Shaheed.

Vice President Hamid Ansari launches the author's book, *India's Foreign Policy: The Democracy Dimension*, in New Delhi in 2009. Amb. Gopinath Pillai (ISAS chairman) is also seen.

Bhutan's first democratically elected Prime Minister Jigme Y. Thinley with Indian friends and journalists in New Delhi on 31 August 2009. The author can be seen second from the right.

With Singapore President S.R. Nathan (centre) and Professor Tan Tai Yong at an Institute of South Asian Studies (ISAS) book event in Singapore in 2010.

National Security Advisor Shivshankar Menon launches the author's book, *The Emerging Dimensions of SAARC*, in New Delhi in 2010. On the dais are Amb. Gopinath Pillai (ISAS chairman), H.K. Dua and Amb. Eric Gonsalves (Retd).

With Nepal Prime Minister Baburam Bhattarai during his visit to India, in New Delhi in October 2011.

With Chandrika Bandaranaike Kumaratunga, former President of Sri Lanka, at a panel discussion organised by ISAS in Singapore in June 2015.

With Nepal Prime Minister Pushpa Kamal Dahal (Prachanda) and Mrs Sita Dahal at the dinner hosted by Indian Prime Minister Narendra Modi at Hyderabad House, New Delhi in September 2016.

With Sri Lankan President Maithripala Sirisena and former Sri Lankan President Chandrika Bandaranaike Kumaratunga at the BCIS (Bandaranaike Centre for International Studies) Convocation in Colombo in 2017.

Dinner with Chandrika Bandaranaike Kumaratunga and friends in Colombo in 2017.

With Nepal Prime Minister K.P. Sharma Oli during the dinner hosted by Prime Minister Narendra Modi at Hyderabad House, New Delhi, in April 2018.

Meeting Gotabaya Rajapaksa before his election as Sri Lankan President, in Colombo in 2019.

India, being the bigger and comparatively more capable neighbour, must always exercise caution, care, and restraint. During critical and transformative moments in the evolving history of neighboring countries, India may find itself drawn into the situation. However, India must scrupulously avoid getting involved in micromanaging their affairs to secure pliable governments and impose its own priorities on them.

A close look at India's long-term approach to smaller neighbours suggests that it is not free from periodic inconsistencies, contradictions, knee-jerk reactions and serious reversals. These policy bumps may result from India's huge diversity and the dynamics of its vibrant democratic polity. In India, there are a multiple and mutually incompatible stakeholders in its policies, particularly when it comes to its immediate neighbours. But this is not a matter of comfort to the affected neighbours as they are not expected to absorb them ungrudgingly in respect to Indian democracy. There are several examples of such policy bumps.

Just to illustrate the point, recall Nepal's first popular uprising (Jan Andolan) in 1989-90. At the time in India, the succeeding government of V.P Singh had deviated from that of its predecessor Rajiv Gandhi's approach that supported the Jan Andolan. Rajiv Gandhi faced opposition from many stakeholders in India's Nepal policy. V.P. Singh's government was also at odds with all other political parties and the public mood that was in support of democracy in Nepal. There were tensions even due to the approach of the newly appointed Ambassador as it differed from the line taken by the Indian Embassy.[1] We have also noted similar tensions in India's policy portals during the mainstreaming of the Maoists and termination of Monarchy in Nepal during 2005-08. In the case of

---

1 See, *Four Crises: Test of Diplomacy* by G.S. Iyer, (New Delhi: Heritage Publishers, 2023), Part III, Chapters IV and V, pp. 197-216.

Sri Lanka, the Central government's approach was at variance with that of Tamil Nadu. Rajiv Gandhi's IPKF approach was at variance with that of Mrs Gandhi, and his successors dissociated themselves from his approach.

The roots of misperceptions and misunderstanding braved by me in the neighbouring countries lie in the domestic politics of those countries as also the tone and temper of India's engagement with them. In Nepal, for instance, when I supported its democratic struggle against autocratic monarchy, the royalists and feudal forces attacked me. I learnt through my media friends in Nepal that during the first Jan Andolan in 1990 against the Panchayat system, the palace secretariat prompted their pliant media to portray me as an agent of R&AW. I have never had any dealing with any of India's intelligence agencies. In fact, I have been critical of their activities in Nepal and other neighbouring countries.

Again, during the early years of this century, my involvement in the mainstreaming of the Maoists earned me the title of being a Maoist and a Maoist supporter from those in both India and Nepal, who politically disapproved of the Maoists' activities and agenda in one way or the other. Despite consistently criticising Maoist violence and extremism, I supported their vision of a 'New Nepal' and their decision to lay down arms to enter mainstream politics. What drove me in this respect, however, was a rational and objective assessment that mainstreaming of the Maoists was in the interest of both India and Nepal; of the governments and people in both the countries.

In Sri Lanka, during the height of the ethnic crisis, when I advocated for federal solutions and an accommodative approach towards the Tamils, my Sinhala friends disapproved of me. I was not a staunch critic of the IPKF. It was invited by the Sri Lankan government. Many of its tactics and strategies of fighting the LTTE were flawed and erroneous, but it was carrying out its mission under very difficult circumstances. This position, though supported by research, was naturally not palatable to those in India and Sri Lanka who had raised a political storm against the IPKF. In India, it was a tool for criticising Rajiv Gandhi, and in Sri Lanka, Sinhala nationalism was woven into it.

It was the extreme form of Sinhala nationalism that led to the attack on Prime Minister Rajiv Gandhi by a Sri Lankan naval cadet in the presence of President Jayewardene on 30 July 1987, the day after the signing of the Indo-Sri Lanka Agreement on resolving the ethnic crisis. Rajiv displayed remarkable bravery in pursuing his policy despite this attack. It was unfortunate that even Tamil extremists, the LTTE, did not appreciate his concern for peace and Tamil rights, as they assassinated him during his election campaign in May 1991.

Many, who were not happy with Chandrika's leadership and supported Opposition parties, found my writings and utterances on various Sri Lankan developments unacceptable. All this misperception and occasional criticism about me, however, was a small cost one had to pay for being an active and involved observer of the turbulent contemporary history of the neighbouring countries. I have taken it in my stride, with no regrets, whatever, for what I have done professionally and personally.

My experience has made me realise that the ground reality of political dynamics and diplomatic relations of any country is critically different from what we learn through textbooks and classroom teaching. In my classroom lectures to postgraduate students and my research scholars on diplomacy and South Asia's international relations, I used to explain that foreign policy decisions have three layers: (i) the things thought (origin and planning of policy), (ii) the things said (speeches, statements), and (iii) the things done (actions taken, treaties and agreements signed, visits exchanged, etc.). Students were then asked to rigorously study and scrutinise 'things said' and 'things done', for which information and evidence exists in the public domain, to make a fair assumption about the 'things thought', which may otherwise be buried deep in the confidential files of the foreign and other ministries.

My experience now tells me that this approach is not enough. There are variations from the 'things thought' to 'things said' and from 'things said' to 'things done'. There are several decisions that do not take the course explained by me. What intervenes in changing the course of decisions at different levels are two other very critical factors: the **context** in which the decisions evolve, from the thinking and planning stage to implementation and execution, and the role of the **human factor** involved. The context is not static. A variety of forces keep changing and redefining it. Moreover, the context has multiple dimensions. Inability to understand and manage the dynamics of the context transforms the evolution of the decisions, and derails and deviates the outcomes from the goals initially envisaged or expected. We know that a large number of US think tanks working on the former Soviet Union could not foresee the way in which it disintegrated during the early 1990s. Similarly, the US policymakers could not imagine during their honeymoon period with China that building China would eventually boomerang on the US' global and regional interests one day.

The human factor is far more complex and unpredictable. And much depends on this factor, on human capabilities and frailties, placement, stresses and attractions beyond the parameters of policy issues involved, aspirations and ambitions, and more, involving individuals at various levels of the decisional processes. This human factor serves as both a liability and an asset, influencing everyone from top leadership to the last foot soldier in the chain of command for decisions. Gaps, leaks, initiative, innovation, or value addition at any level within this chain can subtly or drastically impact policy decisions and their outcomes. These are the two critical factors that will not allow a science of foreign policy or international relations to emerge.

Policy studies will always remain in the domain of arts; an art of possibility, an art of unpredictability. I recall the studies that I have gone through and participated in, on electoral behaviour, and the attempts of Western scholars to index domestic politics with foreign policy. All such well-meaning and sincerely pursued efforts completely failed after years of investment. The number of variables identified and studied keep on changing, and in some cases, become unfathomable. Social sciences cannot be sciences in the true sense and will always lag behind in fully explaining policies and political developments. While acknowledging this reality, I am not at all asking for giving up on studies and their scientific methods. Instead, I emphasise rigorous and continuous efforts to improve methodologies, keeping in mind that we may not be perfect.

Much of a diplomat's success or failure depends upon the State and its institutions that govern him. In Vientiane, I had a clear understanding that Lao PDR held a relatively small position in India's foreign policy and strategic spectrum. This was so despite India's historical role in Laos' struggle for freedom from colonialism and the considerable goodwill towards India within Laos' ruling and social circles. India's low foreign policy priorities had in a way also affected the extent of academic interest in and expertise on Laos in Indian universities, including my own prestigious institution. I experienced this when a seminar was organised by the Indian Mission in Vientiane on India-Lao PDR Relations. It became a difficult exercise to identify the right Indian participants for the event. This was understandable. Every nation has its priorities and it is neither possible nor desirable to allocate equal attention and resources to all the countries where you have your varying interests and diverse priorities. India cannot be an exception in this respect.

India's role in Laos was also constrained due to inadequate connectivity. I starkly realised the significance of connectivity during my visit to Chiang Mai (in Thailand) and the Myanmar border from Vientiane. Establishing a road link through Myanmar, which is already on India's agenda, has the potential to significantly enhance communication, people-to-people contacts, and the flow of goods and services. The road that took me from Vientiane to Chiang Mai could also connect me to Imphal and Kolkata. Multiple issues, including stability and security in Myanmar, need to be addressed to expedite land connectivity between India and ASEAN. In addition, India's chronic delivery deficit in its foreign policy, i.e. the gap between its promises and performance, contributes to undue delays even in executing strategically significant projects. The government is well aware of this deficit and is making efforts to address it, but there is still a long distance to cover.

Diplomats assigned to countries of lower priority of the home state must contend with more pronounced institutional and resource constraints. They have to moderate their enthusiasm and initiatives to avoid overstepping institutional boundaries. In contrast, Indian diplomats belonging to the cadre service, and or posted in higher priority stations have greater freedom and fewer constraints. Unfortunately, individuals in less fortunate circumstances, like myself, often bear a heavier burden of institutional ethos and norms. While concepts like 'thinking out of the box' and 'being innovative' are commendable in theory, they prove challenging and even misleading in practical operations. Lesser fortunate diplomats like me frequently find themselves trapped in the pressure of bureaucratic processes. A specific instance, such as the omission of greetings to the Lao foreign minister at the United Nations while he was supporting India's permanent UNSC membership serves as an illustrative example. The diplomatic conduct of an Indian Mission abroad is influenced by the efficiency, integrity and performance of many non-governmental agencies and organisations. The role and conduct of business companies, including infrastructure developers, in both the private and public sectors, are crucial in developing countries. They are as much representatives of India as the Indian Missions are. I do not know if there has ever been an effective accountability check on such business establishments by the Government of India. Indian Diplomatic Missions, however, are answerable to the host government for any acts of omission and commission by such business houses. The political leadership and diplomatic assignees must, therefore, carefully evaluate the integrity and efficiency of business houses before recommending, promoting and protecting them in pursuance of foreign policy.

Laotians are peace-loving and friendly people who have smoothly imbibed the essence of both Hinduism and Buddhism emanating from India. In their language, dress, art and dance forms, the cultural ethos of Indic, not Sinic (despite the Chinese neighbourhood) civilisation are clearly visible. This creates a huge potential for India to deploy its soft power.

India may not match China in displaying its economic power in Laos, but in the cultural domain, China has very little ground to stand on. India's move on the Mekong-Ganga Initiative was a bold and imaginative gesture nearly a quarter century ago. It linked India to the lower riparian countries of the Mekong that suffer at the hands of upper riparian Chinese dominance. It is, however, unfortunate that the Mekong-Ganga grouping has not yet acquired the desired strategic buoyancy. In the field of soft power, there is large scope for India to expand its educational presence, particularly English language and computer application teaching, science and technology courses and skill development.

We also need to pitch in for the entertainment sector, using Bollywood, classical dance and music forms. There could be attempts to link up and find common ground between the Laotian and Indian *Ramayana* plays and *Mahabharat* narrations. Buddha relics have been donated to Lao Buddhist temples on a token basis. Much more can be done to bring the Buddhist Sangha in India and Laos together through exchange programmes. But all this needs resources which were not adequate during my time. The resource crunch was clearly felt while collecting Ramayana artefacts, constructing a museum for the ruins of Hindu temples, offering Bollywood films with Laotian subtitles, if not dubbing, and organising more Bharatanatyam and musical performances, fashion shows, exhibitions and food festivals. Very little linkages exist also in the educational fields of the two countries. We also face the challenge of reaching out to the wider sections of Laotian society owing to its closed and controlled polity.

As I completed my assignment of Special Envoy on UNSC reforms, I was very satisfied. I was proud of my country's democratic polity, despite all its limitations and infirmities, and also realised the strength and versatility of my academic profession. I could serve as a diplomat of my country under three politically different establishments. I was appointed by the United Front government headed by I.K. Gujral from the Janata Dal, asked to continue, despite my resignation, under the NDA government headed by BJP's Atal Bihari Vajpayee, and after five years, appointed as Special Envoy by the UPA government led by Dr Manmohan Singh of the Indian National Congress. I have not been a political activist and as an academic, many times took a critical view of the foreign policy issues of these governments.

I am concerned about the signs of that democratic spirit, of accommodating dissent and political diversity, becoming blurred and fragile. My only feeling of uneasiness in my experience was regarding the turf consciousness and attitude of career foreign service officers towards outsiders. This attitude, which I may call as one of benign indifference, was particularly visible towards academics. Those coming from other professions or sister services like journalists, businessmen and Indian Administrative Service (IAS) officers were still treated more leniently. This attitude of 'we' and 'others' in the IFS community was not universal. There were strong and many exceptions to this. J.N. Dixit's affectionate dinner for me on my appointment as ambassador may be recalled here.

Upon my return to academics after completing my assignment as Special Envoy, Ambassadors M. Hamid Ansari and Satinder Kumar Lambah invited me to join the Association of Indian Diplomats (AID), where they were the president and secretary, respectively. They requested me to start a journal for AID and serve as its founding editor. *The Indian Foreign Affairs Journal* was launched by Prime Minister Dr Manmohan Singh in February 2006. I introduced two special features to the journal: the opening 'Debate' section focused on controversial and contemporary issues in India's foreign policy, and the 'Oral History' section recorded interviews with retired foreign service officers, shedding light on aspects of their diplomatic experience not publicly known. Both these sections attracted the attention of MEA which decided to subsidise the journal by purchasing bulk copies for distribution in various Indian Diplomatic Missions abroad.

The 'we' and 'others' attitude prevalent in a large section of the IFS community, however, perplexed me because, in academics, we enthusiastically invited and welcomed foreign service officers. In my discipline of international relations and area studies at SIS/JNU, numerous senior diplomats, both in service and post-retirement, joined us as visiting professors. At one point, MEA even introduced the concept of 'Diplomats in Residence', funding IFS officers' placements in JNU. Notable examples of diplomat visiting professors included I.J. Bahadur Singh, T.N. Kaul, M.K. Rasgotra, A.K. Damodaran and M. Hamid Ansari. In my South Asia Centre, we took pride in appointing Muchkund Dubey as a professor through standard selection process shortly after his retirement as India's Foreign Secretary.

Inviting serving Indian and foreign diplomats for seminars and lectures is a standard and appreciated aspect of our academic initiatives. Diplomats bring valuable practical experience and insider knowledge of the government operations, which significantly contribute to our academic endeavours. Academic studies gain depth and richness through the invaluable feedback and insights provided by diplomats. We actively seek to learn from their experiences. Similarly, academics and professionals from diverse fields contribute their expertise and experiences to enhance and refine foreign policy and diplomacy. Academics, in particular, invest extensive time and effort in studying a country or region, often surpassing the tenure of an ambassador's appointment. Despite this, diplomats are commonly perceived as superior experts, particularly on the countries they have served, even within a single term of three years.

In one of the seminars at IIC, New Delhi, I had an intensive debate with a former senior diplomat who had just retired as the foreign secretary, while I had just returned from Vientiane after completing my assignment. He vehemently opposed the entry of outsiders into foreign service, even for one-time assignments. On the contrary, I supported limited outside induction, citing the very inception of independent India's foreign service when Nehru had inducted individuals from various walks of life.

In response to his query about the performance of outsiders, I acknowledged that political appointees were often chosen due to political patronage exercised by the prime ministers. Some may not have performed well due to their appointment without considering their competence for the assigned job. However, I argued that this wasn't universally true for all political appointees. Performance concerns were equally relevant for regular foreign service officers, who come from diverse educational and training backgrounds, with many falling short of expectations.

I emphasised the need for a sincere and objective effort to comparatively assess the performances of both outsiders and regular foreign service officers. Looking at this issue in a historical context, I highlighted Nehru's ambassadorial appointees like Vijaya Lakshmi Pandit, S. Radhakrishnan, K.M. Panikkar, and Prem Bhatia, who had made a significant impact on India's foreign policy. Indira Gandhi also followed in her father's footsteps to some extent, while Gujral was criticised for reviving and strengthening this trend. Vajpayee continued this trend by appointing individuals like Dr Laxmi Mall Singhvi and H.K. Dua. This trend, however, faced strong resistance under Dr Manmohan Singh's leadership.

In places like Washington, D.C., London and Kathmandu, political appointees were generally sent to head India's Diplomatic Missions. But this practice now seems to have come to an end. Regular service officers have largely replaced the political (i.e. non-career) appointees. At the same time, there is a gradually growing feeling in MEA that it needs domain expertise in many areas like climate change, energy, cyber security, science diplomacy, law and jurisprudence etc. which cannot be appropriately handled by regular UPSC cleared IFS officers. Such experts are now invited to join for specific diplomatic tasks. To overcome the constraints of its lean size, the foreign ministry is also recruiting young researchers as interns but they are kept on the periphery of hard diplomatic processes. With Prime Minister Modi's initiative on the lateral entry of experts in the bureaucracy, one can hope that the MEA will also gradually become more accommodative of outsiders at senior positions. It would be better if outside induction is institutionalised by numbers as well as qualifications to limit the space for personal patronage. This will also remove the 'we' and 'others' or 'outsiders' feeling and turf consciousness in the MEA.

Close and participatory experience with the political processes in India's neighbouring countries, particularly Nepal and Sri Lanka, reinforced the well-known proposition that domestic political dynamics are primarily driven by the relentless struggle for power rather than ideals, ideologies and national interests. The pursuit of capturing and retaining power takes precedence for the political class, leading to political instability and malgovernance.

For instance, in Nepal, politics has become deeply fragmented since the end of the Panchayat system, necessitating constant coalitions and alliances among parties to secure a share in power. However, these power-sharing arrangements are often short-lived as key players prioritise their power ambitions over the initially agreed-upon norms. In Nepal, numerous instances abound where both democratic and communist leaders have shamelessly compromised their ideological principles and personal integrity to secure positions of power. A striking example is the Maoists, a once-radical political group that sacrificed lives, both of others and its own cadres, in pursuit of a vision for a 'New Nepal.' However, in the relentless race for power, the Maoists disintegrated and succumbed to opportunism.

Sri Lanka witnessed Chandrika's courageous attempt to address Tamil rights, garnering support even from the traditionally Sinhala chauvinistic JVP for a federal arrangement. Yet, the Opposition parties, led by Ranil Wickremesinghe of the United National Party (UNP), thwarted the initiative due to their presidential aspirations.

Interacting closely with the political class in neighbouring countries also made me aware of the depth of these countries' expectations from India. While seeking various forms of support, including assistance in power struggles, they are reluctant to be officially recognised as India's allies or supporters. Every time a developmental cooperation move is initiated by India, they weigh it in terms of their dependence on India. They are all the time struggling to figure out as to *how close is not too close to India*.

In addition to the India-Pakistan hiatus, the diverse forms of reservations vis-à-vis India among other smaller neighbours are an important impediment behind SAARC's tardy progress. Even Bhutan, India's closest neighbour, expressed reservations about the Bangladesh, Bhutan, India and Nepal (BBIN) Motor Vehicle Agreement proposed by India in 2014. Genuine concerns about identity emerge, as their cultural and political identities risk being overshadowed by India's vastness, prompting them to maintain a distance to preserve their sovereign and independent profiles. The popular saying 'proximity breeds contempt' resonates, and neighbouring countries often explore the lucrative option of aligning with China to balance India's influence and extract more concessions, particularly in light of India's growing prominence in Asia.

India's diplomacy, characterised by unnecessary and excessive intervention, and the use of economic and political coercion, coupled with a tendency to be complacent and take neighbours for granted, has significantly fuelled a quest for greater independence among its immediate neighbours. India is often associated with anti-establishment sentiments in neighbouring countries. In Sri Lanka, India is perceived as a friend of the Tamils by the dominant Sinhala-Buddhist establishment. In Nepal, the dominant Khas-Arya establishment views India as a supporter and promotor of the Madhesis. The minority Hindus in Islam-dominated Bangladesh look to India for protection.

The communalisation of India's own polity, with a dominant Hindu identity in recent years, has added to the identity factor in its relations with neighbours. Except in Nepal, Hindus are in a minority in all other neighboring countries. The dominance of Buddhism and Islam makes it imperative for India to approach its neighbours with a secular mindset. The perception of India as a Hindu-dominant and assertive country has enhanced India's vulnerability to the politicisation of anti-India nationalism in these countries.

India is gradually learning from its past mistakes, and the complexities of political dynamics in its neighbouring countries, albeit at a slow and hesitant pace. There is a need to discard its complacency and the 'taken for granted' attitude towards smaller neighbours. It must transcend its 'fire-fighting' approach and 'adhocist responses to crises' when dealing with neighbours. Instead, India should allocate greater resources and engage in sustained homework.

Annexure 1

12-Point Understanding between the Seven Party Alliance and Communist Party of Nepal (Maoist)

THE STRUGGLE BETWEEN absolute monarchy and democracy running for a long time in Nepal has now been reached in a very grave and new turn. It has become the need of today to establish peace by resolving the 10-year-old armed conflict through a forward-looking political outlet. Therefore, it has become an inevitable need to implement the concept of full democracy through a forward-looking restructuring of the state to resolve the problems related to class, cast, gender, region and so on of all sectors including the political, economic, social and cultural, by bringing the autocratic monarchy to an end and establishing full democracy. We hereby disclose that in the existence of aforesaid context and reference in the country, the following understanding has been reached between the Seven Political Parties within the parliament and the CPN (Maoists) through holding talks in different manners. The points reached in the understanding are:

1. The democracy, peace, prosperity, social advancement and an independent, sovereign Nepal is the principal wish of all Nepali people in the country today. We are fully agreed that the autocratic monarchy is the main hurdle for this. We have a clear opinion that the peace, progress and prosperity in the country is not possible until full democracy is established by bringing the absolute monarchy to an end. Therefore, an understanding has been reached to establish full democracy by bringing the autocratic monarchy to an end through creating a storm of nationwide democratic movement of all the forces against autocratic monarchy by focusing their assault against the autocratic monarchy from their respective positions.

2. The agitating Seven Political Parties are fully committed to the fact that the existing conflict in the country can be resolved and the sovereignty and the state powers can completely be established in people only by establishing full democracy by restoring the parliament through the force of agitation and forming a powerful party Government by its decision, negotiating with the Maoists, and on the basis of agreement, holding the election of Constituent Assembly.

    The CPN (Maoists) has the view and commitment that the aforesaid goal can be achieved by holding a national political conference of the agitating democratic forces, and through its decision, forming an Interim Government and holding the election of constituent assembly. On the issue of this procedural agenda, an understanding has been made to continue dialogue and seek for a common agreement between the agitating Seven Political Parties and the CPN (Maoists). It has been agreed that the force of people's movement is the only alternative to achieve this goal.

3. The country, today, demands the establishment of a permanent peace along with a positive resolution of the armed conflict. We are, therefore, firmly committed to establish a permanent peace by bringing the existing armed conflict in the country to an end through a forward-looking political outlet of the establishment of the full democracy by ending the autocratic monarchy and holding an election of the Constituent Assembly that would come on the basis of aforesaid procedure. The CPN (Maoists) expresses its commitment to move forward in the new peaceful political stream through this process. In this very context, an understanding has been made to keep the Maoists armed force and the Royal Army under the United Nations or a reliable international supervision during the process of the election of Constituent Assembly after the end of the autocratic monarchy, to accomplish the election in a free and fair manner and to accept the result of the election. We also expect for the involvement of a reliable international community even in the process of negotiation.

4. Making public its commitment, institutional in a clear manner, towards the democratic norms and values like the competitive multiparty system of governance, civil liberties, fundamental rights, human tights, principle of rule of law etc., the CPN (Maoists) has expressed its commitment to move forward its activities accordingly.

5. The CPN (Maoists) has expressed its commitment to create an environment to allow the people and the leaders and workers of the political parties, who are displaced during the course of armed conflict, to return and stay with dignity in their respective places, to return their homes, land and property that was seized

in an unjust manner and to allow them to carry out the political activities without any hindrance.

6. Making a self-assessment and a self-criticism of the past mistakes and weaknesses, the CPN (Maoists) has expressed its commitment for not allowing the mistakes and weaknesses to be committed in future.

7. Making a self-assessment towards the mistakes and weaknesses committed while staying in the Government and parliament in the past, the seven political parties have expressed their commitment for not repeating such mistakes and weaknesses now onwards.

8. The commitment has been made to fully respect the norms and values of the human rights and to move forward on the basis of them, and to respect the press freedom in the context of moving the peace process ahead.

9. As the announcement of the election of municipality is pushed forward for an ill-motive of deluding the people and the international community and of giving continuity to the autocratic and illegitimate rule of the King, and the rumour of the election of the parliament are a crafty ploy, announcing to boycott it actively in our own respective way, the general public are appealed to make such elections a failure.

10. The people and their representative political parties are the real guardians of nationality. Therefore, we are firmly committed towards the protection of the independence, sovereignty and the geographical integrity and the national unity of the country. It is our common obligation to maintain friendly relations based on the principle of peaceful co-existence with all countries of the world and a good-neighbourhood relationship with neighbouring countries, especially with India and China. But we request all the patriotic peoples to remain cautious against

the false attempt of the King and the monarchists to create confusion in the patriotic people by projecting the illusory the fake ('Mandale') nationalism to prolong the autocratic and illegitimate rule of the King and to raise question mark over the patriotism of the political parties, and we appeal to the international powers and the communities to support the democratic movement against the autocratic monarchy in Nepal in every possible way.

11. We heartily invite the civil society, professional organizations, various wings of parties, people of all communities and regions, the press community, intellectuals all the Nepali people to make the Movement succeed by actively participating in the peaceful People's Movement launched on the basis of these understandings reached by keeping the democracy, peace, prosperity, forward-looking social transformation and the independence, sovereignty, and dignity of the country in centre.

12. Regarding the inappropriate conducts that took place among the parties in the past, a common commitment has been expressed to investigate the incidents raised objection and asked for the investigation by any party and take action over the guilty one if found and make informed publicly. An understanding has been made to resolve the problems if emerged among the parties now onwards through the dialogue by discussing in the concerned level or in the leadership level.

22 November 2005

(Source: Government of Nepal, Ministry of Peace and Reconstruction, Official website)[1]

---

1 Copied from: https://peacemaker.un.org/sites/peacemaker.un.org/files/NP_051122_12%20Point%20Understanding.pdf (Accessed on 10 September 2023).

Annexure 2

Prof. S.D. Muni
Jawaharlal Nehru University
61 Dakshinapuram
New Campus
New Delhi 110067
INDIA

4 June 1996

Dear Professor Muni,

Thank you for your letter of May 16th and the documents contained therein.

We are delighted at our recent success in winning back the civilians back to Jaffna. They are happy to be under the Central Government. They clearly ask us to ensure that the LTTE does not return. They even point out to our forces, LTTE'ers who pose off as civilians.

Winning back the confidence of the Tamil civilians of the North is the crowning glory of our policy.

2.

We are doing our maximum to re-establish civilian administration and to provide for the people. Development work will begin soon in the Jaffna peninsular. Shall keep in touch.

With warm regards to Arunadha and self.

Yours sincerely,

Chandrika Bandaranaike Kumaratunga.

Annexure 3

No. 13692/FS/99

November 24, 1999.

Dear *Professor Muni,*

  As you approach the end of your tenure of posting as Ambassador of India to Laos, I write to convey to you on behalf of the Government and specifically Ministry of External Affairs, our deep appreciation of your contribution to promoting our interests vis-à-vis Laos and in strengthening India-Laos friendship and cooperation. Government has noted with satisfaction the all-round development of bilateral Indo-Laos relations, including understanding of our concerns on important issues, as well as mutual good will, during your term as Ambassador. Also noteworthy is the steady growth of bilateral cooperation in the economic and other functional areas, and of our exchanges in culture, education and other areas. Your efforts have played a major role in bringing this about. We know of the experience and knowledge of the region that you have brought to bear on your work. I trust you will keep in touch with the Ministry, and that we will continue to benefit from your advice on the conduct of our relations with Laos and other matters.

  I also take this opportunity to extend to you our best wishes for your professional work in the future as well for your good health and personal well being, and that of your family.

With warm regards

Yours sincerely,

(K. Raghunath)

Prof. S.D. **Muni**
Ambassador
Embassy of India
Vientiane (Laos)

Index

www.ingramcontent.com/pod-product-compliance
Lightning Source LLC
Chambersburg PA
CBHW051249250726
48656CB00004B/1201